"One of the most successful and accessible explicators of the riches of Ignatian spirituality, Jim Manney is the perfect person to write this beautiful book. Let the wisdom of St. Ignatius guide you gently through your days with these lovely meditations."

— **James Martin**, SJ, author of *My Life with the Saints* and *The Jesuit Guide to (Almost) Everything*

"If you are looking for a book to help you put your faith into action, *What Matters Most and Why* is the book for you! Jim Manney offers thoughtful daily reflections rooted in Ignatian spirituality that encourage you to not only prayerfully ponder what matters each day, but to also live what matters each day. Each day holds a moment of reflection with an invitation for action. A book I will recommend again and again to those seeking to put their faith into practice!"

— **Becky Eldredge**, Ignatian-trained spiritual director and author of *Busy Lives & Restless Souls* and *The Inner Chapel*

"There's no doubt, Jim Manney knows his Ignatius of Loyola. But what matters to me most is the attention Manney pays to what's essentially human. This book is for our common path of love, work, compassion, relationships, and God."

— **Jon M. Sweeney**, author of *James Martin, SJ: In the Company of Jesus* and editor of *The Complete Francis of Assisi*

"In this accessible volume, Jim Manney distills decades of prayer, writing, editing, and encouraging others. Readers who are intimately familiar with this tradition, as well as those approaching it for the first time, will find here ample sources for contemplation and action."

— **Tim Muldoon**, author of
The Ignatian Workout and *Living Against the Grain*

WHAT
MATTERS
MOST
AND WHY

Also by Jim Manney

Charged with Grandeur: The Book of Ignatian Inspiration

*God Finds Us: An Experience of the Spiritual Exercises
of St. Ignatius Loyola*

An Ignatian Book of Days

Ignatian Spirituality A to Z

*A Simple, Life-Changing Prayer:
Discovering the Power of St. Ignatius Loyola's Examen*

*What Do You Really Want?: St. Ignatius Loyola
and the Art of Discernment*

*What's Your Decision?: How to Make Choices
with Confidence and Clarity:
An Ignatian Approach to Decision Making* (coauthor)

WHAT MATTERS MOST AND WHY

Living the Spirituality of
St. Ignatius of Loyola

365 DAILY REFLECTIONS

JIM MANNEY

Foreword by Chris Lowney

New World Library
Novato, California

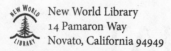

New World Library
14 Pamaron Way
Novato, California 94949

Copyright © 2022 by Jim Manney

Text design by Tona Pearce Myers

Library of Congress Cataloging-in-Publication data is available.

First printing, November 2022
ISBN 978-1-60868-776-3
Ebook ISBN 978-1-60868-777-0
Printed in Canada on 100% postconsumer-waste recycled paper

New World Library is proud to be a Gold Certified Environmentally Responsible Publisher. Publisher certification awarded by Green Press Initiative.

10   9   8   7   6   5   4   3   2

Contents

Contents

Foreword

L et me introduce you to some superb technology, ideal for navigating today's complex, volatile world. Surprisingly, this technology involves no software, uses no electricity, and costs nothing.

… And it's roughly five centuries old.

I'm referring to the prayer approaches, decision-making models, and self-awareness tools that were pioneered by Ignatius Loyola, founder of the Catholic religious order of priests and brothers that is popularly known as the "Jesuits."

Huh? Since when do "prayer approaches" qualify as "technology"?

Well, why not? Though we moderns associate technology with gadgets and software, the word's etymological roots have nothing to do with such things. Nor do many dictionary definitions of the word, like this one from Merriam-Webster: "the practical application of knowledge especially in a particular area."

Well, Ignatius and his Jesuit colleagues crafted "practical applications of knowledge" to the most fundamental life challenges we face: making difficult choices, relating to other people, keeping oneself recollected amid daily life's chaos. Above all, Ignatius's approach helps us figure out what a meaningful life entails.

Many of us would pay lots of money to download the app or acquire the gadget that could effectively deliver all the results enumerated above. And, surely, an "art of navigating life" app would be far more valuable to us than technologies that merely make it easier to book hotel rooms or order food deliveries.

Yet Ignatius's "spiritual technologies" are all available for free. What's needed is only a sincere, open heart and the commitment and discipline to learn and use the relevant tools and approaches.

My credentials for making such lofty claims about the benefits of what Ignatius offers are rooted in my own background story: I was once a Jesuit seminarian; my later life path involved service as a managing director of J. P. Morgan & Co. on three continents; and I currently chair the board of one of America's largest healthcare/hospital systems, CommonSpirit Health.

As a seminarian, I lived Jesuit spirituality firsthand; as an investment banker, I lived the chaos of modern life firsthand. I saw how Ignatius's insights and approaches can be relevant to challenges far removed from seminary life — and, let's face it, investment banking is about as far removed from seminary life as it gets.

Jesuit spirituality ultimately invites us to a way of living and leading characterized by heroism, self-awareness, love, and ingenuity. That's how I described its overarching vision in *Heroic Leadership: Best Practices from a 450-Year-Old Company That Changed the World*. My work tried to convey "here's what good leadership should look like"; Jim Manney's present work, *What Matters Most and Why*, is a daily guide to leading one's own life well in this spiritual tradition. To his great credit, Jim has taken the profound riches of the tradition and arrayed them in digestible, bite-size reflections.

Importantly, however, these are not just reflections to be read; they form an approach to life and a path to be taken. Enjoy the daily journey that follows!

— Chris Lowney, author of *Heroic Leadership:*
Best Practices from a 450-Year-Old Company
That Changed the World

Introduction

In the early decades of the sixteenth century, it was widely recognized that the conventional wisdom about how to live wasn't working anymore. In Europe, the feudal system was unraveling and the church was riven by controversy and division. New ideas about how to make money and how to worship God were floating around. The known world vastly expanded to include the Americas, Asia, and Africa. And because there are more ways for things to go wrong than to go right, there was much trouble, many mistakes, and considerable unhappiness. In other words, it was a time not unlike our own.

The man for this moment was Ignatius Loyola, the scion of a noble family in the Basque region of what is now northern Spain. Ignatius was a brilliant synthesizer of other people's ideas and a creative thinker in his own right. He brought a couple of special gifts to the table: He was a mystic, blessed with visions that gave him a profound understanding of spiritual truths, and he was a brilliant leader and organizer. He created the Jesuits, an order of Catholic priests that carried his ideas forward and developed them into the transformative outlook known as Ignatian spirituality.

Unless you went to a Jesuit high school or university, you probably haven't heard much about Ignatian spirituality, but we live in an Ignatian world. Cognitive behavioral therapy, the 12-step movement, the modern study of decision-making, and Christian humanism all have their roots in Ignatian thinking. Modern Stoicism, virtue ethics, and Ignatian spirituality share a concern with living a virtuous life.

The idea of "spirituality" as contrasted with "religion" can be traced to Ignatius, as can the idea that we can find God in everyday life. Ignatius's fingerprints are found in contemporary movements promoting social justice, cultural sensitivity, and ministries to the homeless and the oppressed, to prisoners and refugees. If you've ever gone on a retreat to recharge your spiritual batteries or consulted with a spiritual director, you've made use of methods of spiritual growth that Ignatius popularized five centuries ago. Ignatian spirituality is as fresh as our news feeds and Twitter streams.

What Matters Most

Ignatius and his friends focused on questions that preoccupy us today: How do I pursue the good? How can I think clearly? How can I pray? What can I do about my anger, my envy, my laziness? How can I have good relationships with others? Ignatian spirituality is intensely practical. It's concerned with living a better life.

Of particular concern to Ignatius was the challenge of making good decisions: How do I know what matters most? How can I distinguish between what's valuable and what's irrelevant? To say that Ignatius thought good decisions were important is an understatement. They were of *transcendent* importance, literally a matter of salvation. Ignatius believed that we come to know God and find the meaning of our lives in wise use of the "things of the world" — our work and relationships, the manifold opportunities for joy and growth we find in the world we live in. The choices we make about these things are just about the most important things we do.

Ignatius and his companions believed that God is

working *everywhere* in creation — in our sorrows and joys, in work and in prayer, in the world of nature and in the world that human beings have created. They were fervent Christians and faithful Catholics, but their spiritual outlook was not sectarian. It was curious and tolerant, comfortable with ambiguity, suspicious of rules and any urge to exclude. Today, the motto that expresses the heart of the Ignatian message is *God can be found in all things*.

Another of Ignatius's favorite sayings was that *Love is best expressed in deeds rather than words*. Ignatian spirituality is a spirituality of action. It is animated by a conviction that all of us share God's work to "repair the world." Everyone who hears a call to make the world a better place is an heir to the Ignatian vision of active, engaged Christianity.

A Journey, Good Friends, and a Book

The central figure in our story is Ignatius Loyola, born in 1491 to a noble family in the Basque region of northern Spain. The youngest of thirteen children, Ignatius made his way to the royal court of the kingdom of Castile, where he made a name for himself as an administrator, soldier, and man-about-town. In 1521 he was seriously injured in battle; during his recuperation he had a religious conversion where he discovered that his true desire was to serve others in imitation of Jesus Christ. He abandoned his sophisticated life at court, gave away his fine clothes, donned the tattered garb of a beggar, and hit the road seeking spiritual enlightenment.

It was a meandering journey. Over the next fifteen years, Ignatius traveled hundreds of miles on foot throughout Europe. He mixed with all kinds of people, prayed and reflected, had mystical visions, and received an elite education.

Other talented men were drawn to him, like Peter Faber and Francis Xavier, whose lives were transformed by Ignatius's talent for helping people understand what they most deeply wanted. In 1534, he and seven companions made a solemn promise to work together in whatever way God led them. This group became the Society of Jesus, or the Jesuits, the most acclaimed religious order in the Catholic Church. In Ignatius's lifetime, the Jesuits upended the old model of religious life, transformed the educational system in Europe, launched journeys of exploration in Asia and the Americas, and began a dazzling array of projects: schools, hospitals, missionary work, work with prostitutes and prisoners, street preaching, youth work, and evangelism. The Jesuits' work continues today.

Ignatius compiled his insights about the spiritual life into a small book that he called *The Spiritual Exercises*, which became one of the most influential spiritual books of all time. *The Spiritual Exercises* was not meant as a book of inspiring spiritual reading. Rather, Ignatius wrote it as a handbook for "spiritual directors," and these experienced guides — a combination of spiritual teacher and life coach — used the book to guide other people through a process of conversion and spiritual renewal. Millions of people have used the *Exercises* for this purpose over the centuries and its spiritual outlook has become known as Ignatian spirituality. *The Spiritual Exercises* is the heart of everything the Jesuits and their friends did — and continue to do.

A New Way to Pray, Live, and Love

To a world in upheaval, Ignatius introduced a new way of thinking about God. The old way held that God was mainly found in religious places and religious activities; Ignatius said that God was found in all things. The old thinking saw God as a stern lawgiver and judge; Ignatius saw him as an infinitely generous giver of gifts. The old idea saw God as elusive and remote; Ignatius said he was near at hand, energetically laboring in the world. What's more, Ignatius said, God invites each of us to share that work.

This attitude led to new ways of living a spiritual life. Before the Jesuits came along, the model of holy living was a quiet life of prayer in a monastery or convent. It was something that priests and nuns did, not ordinary people. The Jesuits changed all that. Ignatian spirituality was for ordinary people living busy lives. It saw God as present everywhere in the world: "Christ plays in ten thousand places, / Lovely in limbs, and lovely in eyes not his," as the Jesuit poet Gerard Manley Hopkins wrote. Christ beckons us to join him in his work; we come to know him as we do it with him.

The mentality that proceeds from this worldview is remarkably modern. The Ignatian mindset is reflective. Since God is present in all things, including — especially — our daily experience, it's vitally important that we notice him. This mindset is self-aware, alert to the ebb and flow of our inner life. It's keenly alert to our spiritual and psychological blind spots — the ways we fool ourselves and find reasons to do what we want to do. It's deeply suspicious of the conventional wisdom. It cherishes desires. In the Ignatian view, our deepest desires have been placed in our hearts by God. When we're in touch with our most authentic selves, when we know what we *really* want, we know what God wants.

All of this introspection is done for the sake of work and action. Today it's taken for granted that Christians should make the world a better place. It was not always so.

Ignatian spirituality insists that prayer is not an end in itself. God is at work to save and heal the world. We have a part in that work. We need to find it — and do it every day.

How This Book Is Organized

What Matters Most and Why is meant to foster daily reflection. Publishers call books like this "daily devotionals." I like to think of this book as a "daily actionable." It offers a reading and commentary for every day — something to think about and return to as you go about your daily activities — but the Ignatian view holds that reflection leads to action. As Ignatius said, love is expressed more in deeds than in words. I hope you find that this book's reflections have practical consequences in your everyday life.

Most of the daily readings are from books and writers in the Ignatian tradition, most of them Jesuits. But you will also find quotes from people like the Dalai Lama, Andy Warhol, and Nelson Mandela; Buddhist, Hindu, and Jewish texts; quotes from novelists, scientists, screenwriters, and journalists. This diversity of sources embodies the nonsectarian universality of the Ignatian tradition. It is a thoroughly Christian spirituality, but one which speaks to everyone and draws on wisdom wherever it can be found. Ignatian spirituality is not an exclusive possession of the Jesuits. (For brief biographies of everyone quoted, see "People Who Are Quoted," and for the published sources for quotes, see the Notes.)

I have organized the book according to a traditional Ignatian approach to learning and spiritual development, which has three components: experience, reflection, and action. A person *experiences* the physical, spiritual, and inner worlds; *reflects* on the meaning of this experience; and then *acts* according to this new understanding. In this book, the year is divided into three parts — "Experience," "Reflection," and "Action" — and each part includes four months. Further, each month has its own theme that links the days and relates to the larger part focus.

I have condensed some of the quotes that begin the daily readings. I have also modernized the language of some of the quotations from Ignatius's letters and the writings of his contemporaries. Finally, I've indicated Jesuit writers by putting the letters "SJ" after their names. These initials stand for "Society of Jesus," the Catholic religious order founded by Ignatius, and since then popularly known as the "Jesuits."

A Daily Practice of Reflection

My hope is that you will use this book as part of a daily practice of reflection. Heightened *awareness* of spiritual realities is the foundation of a rich spiritual life. Ignatius certainly thought so.

That said, many people use daily devotionals intermittently, as a way to add variety to their daily prayer. Feel free to use this book that way, or in any way you wish — but I'd like to make a pitch for making a habit of reading every day, at least for a while. Ignatian spirituality grows on you. It's more a way of thinking, an attitude, than anything else. Give it enough time to reveal itself.

There are other activities you can incorporate as well. Probably the most "Ignatian" of all Ignatian prayer practices is the Daily Examen, a step-by-step review of the preceding twenty-four hours with an eye toward noticing God's presence in one's life and responding to it. The Daily Examen was my entrée into Ignatian spirituality. A Jesuit spiritual director named George Aschenbrenner taught me how to pray the Examen while I was on a brief weekend retreat. This small suggestion had vast consequences; it helped me understand that *God is already here in my everyday life.* I could simply notice him and respond to him. God is *here*, not *out there.* That opened the door to everything else, including quite literally a new way of living and a writing career aimed at sharing Ignatian spirituality with others. I have included a brief description of how to pray the Daily Examen (see the next section), and I encourage you to add this to your daily practice.

These daily entries can also be used to start or strengthen the habit of writing in a journal as part of spiritual practice. Treat each day's reflection or topic as an open-ended prompt that you can explore further with your pen or keyboard.

I hope this book helps you find a better way of living. Ignatian spirituality did that for me. Only a few philosophies and ethical systems have the chops to do this. The bold claim of this book is that Ignatian spirituality is one of them. It has forever changed the way we think about God. It has already given hope and direction to millions of people. If you set your mind to it, and put your heart in it, Ignatian spirituality can do that for you, too.

The Daily Examen

The Daily Examen is a method of reviewing your day. It's a time set aside for thankful reflection on where God is in your everyday life. It has five steps, which most people take more or less in order.

The steps below are adapted from the article "Rummaging for God: Praying Backwards through Your Day" by Dennis Hamm (published in *America*, May 14, 1994). For more on the Daily Examen, see also my book *A Simple, Life-Changing Prayer: Discovering the Power of St. Ignatius Loyola's Examen*.

1. **Pray for light:** Ask for help to see and understand the events of your life.
2. **Give thanks:** Look at your day in a spirit of gratitude. Gratitude is the foundation of our whole relationship with God.
3. **Review the day:** Look back on all that occurred over the past twenty-four hours, and pay special attention to the feelings that surface.
4. **Choose one of those feelings and pray from it:** Choose the feeling that most caught your attention, whether you consider it positive or negative, and ask God what it means.
5. **Look toward the day to come:** What feelings surface? Turn them into prayer.

EXPERIENCE

January

AWARENESS

Wherever you turn your eyes the world can shine like transfiguration. You don't have to bring a thing to it except a little willingness to see.

— MARILYNNE ROBINSON, *GILEAD*

January 1

Eyes to See

The saints were attuned to an invisible reality: the fact that we are all connected in a web of love and that the universe is rooted and sustained in a reality that, if we had the eyes to see, would at once astonish and awaken us from the dream of separateness.

— ROBERT ELLSBERG

If you're looking for God, look around you. That's one of the core ideas of Ignatian spirituality: God can be found in our everyday world, in the mundane and routine, in the exciting and unexpected. Some spiritual traditions emphasize the otherness of God; Ignatian spirituality emphasizes his nearness. This attitude is summed up in the motto "finding God in all things."

In 1547, Ignatius was alarmed by reports that some young Jesuits in training in Portugal were spending long hours in church chanting the psalms and meditating in the chapel. He demanded they get outside: "They should practice the seeking of God's presence in all things, in their conversations, their walks, in all that they see, taste, hear, understand, and in all their actions," he told their superior. Enjoying nature, talking to each other, savoring our food, reading, studying, living our lives — *that's* where God is found.

January 2

Beginner's Mind

Thinking is really a pretty terrible way of encountering God. Words are even worse. I come around again and again to a deep intuition of Ignatius: sensing, savoring God is what we're after.

— TIM MULDOON

Though it's doubtful he ever heard the term, Ignatius would probably have liked the Buddhist idea of *shosin*, meaning "beginner's mind." It means coming to your subject or task with an attitude of openness, without preconceptions, as a beginner would. One Zen teacher notes, "In the beginner's mind there are many possibilities; in the expert's mind there are few."

There's some irony here. Ignatius was an expert: an intellectual with a graduate degree. The Jesuits, the religious order he founded, are renowned for their brainpower. Yet when it comes to knowing God, the Ignatian spiritual tradition prizes intuition and feeling more than thinking and talking. Words and thoughts are for *describing* your experience. As for *having* the experience, a beginner's mind is more helpful.

Try going through your day with a beginner's mind. Imagine you're seeing everything for the first time. Be one on whom nothing is lost.

January 3

In Tune with God

It's easier to see God in retrospect rather than in the moment.

— JAMES MARTIN, SJ

The Gospel of Luke tells the story of a couple of Jesus's friends walking to the village of Emmaus a few days after Jesus's crucifixion. A stranger joins them; they tell the stranger the sad story about the recent death of Jesus and mention the rumors that some had seen him alive after he was buried. The stranger listens, makes a few comments, talks about prophecies in the Hebrew scriptures. He shares a meal with them. Suddenly the disciples realize that the stranger is Jesus himself, but then Jesus vanishes.

A really interesting detail of this story is what happens next. The disciples *reflect* on the experience; they go over what Jesus said and consider what it means. *They weren't aware of Jesus when he was with them.* Now, in retrospect, they *are* aware of him.

Like Jesus's friends on the road to Emmaus, we seldom understand what's *really* happening when we're in the middle of it. Only later, when we look back, do we understand what our experience means. That's why memory is a powerful instrument of prayer.

January 4

Gratitude

Give thanks to God our Lord for the favors received.

— THE SPIRITUAL EXERCISES, 43

Gratitude is central to Ignatius's worldview. For him, everything begins with an infinitely generous God showering us with gifts, like the sun shining on the earth or a fountain perpetually flowing with life-giving water. To ignore this, to be a self-absorbed, dissatisfied, grasping complainer — to be *ungrateful* — is the worst of sins. We think of ingratitude as bad manners. He thought of it as willful blindness to the truth.

Gratitude is the foundation of Ignatian reflection. It gets our minds off ourselves. It directs our attention to God and to the ways he has blessed us.

January 5

It's about Others

There came to my mind the manifold afflictions of men: their diseases, their sins and their stubbornness, their moods of despair and their tears, disasters, famines, plagues, woes, and other trials. Then with a totally new awareness, I asked that I might at last be allowed to become the servant and the minister of Christ, who consoles, helps, delivers, heals, liberates, saves, enriches, and strengthens.

— PETER FABER, SJ

In the Ignatian scheme of things, heightened awareness is not an end in itself. Awareness of God should direct us to the needs of others. "Woe to us if we are only committed to bringing assistance to ourselves alone," said Jerome Nadal, Ignatius's chief lieutenant. Peter Faber, Ignatius's friend and a founder of the Jesuit order, describes an Ignatian awakening: Prayer leads to recognition of human afflictions, followed by an intense desire to serve others.

This vision of service includes every human affliction. Since God can be found in all things, God can be served in all things. Nothing is outside the grace of God. No one is unworthy of the attention of those who serve.

A Sign of Progress

If the work of our sanctification presents us with difficulties that appear insurmountable, it is because we do not look at it in the right way.

— JEAN-PIERRE DE CAUSSADE, SJ

"We don't know a millionth of one percent about anything," said Thomas Edison, who knew a lot about a lot of things. In Hollywood, "nobody knows anything," said William Goldman, the Oscar-winning screenwriter of *Butch Cassidy and the Sundance Kid* and thirty-two other movies. Ignatius wrote that as far as serving God was concerned, he was "nothing but an obstacle."

It seems that as we get better at what we do, things get harder, not easier. We realize how difficult it is to get really good. We face problems that we knew nothing about when we started. The bar gets higher, not lower.

So if you find yourself discouraged about your project of spiritual growth, take heart. Chances are it's a sign of progress.

Don't Forget the Why

The whole process of the Spiritual Exercises is geared to conscious-ness raising of the individual to be alert to one's own motivations and inclinations.

— MONIKA HELLWIG

Maria Konnikova is a social psychologist who studied the way poker players make decisions. She found that bad play-ers often make impulsive, gut decisions: *I have a hunch; this feels right.* Good players always know *why* they decide to fold, bluff, or raise. Because they know *why*, they can analyze their decisions and make better ones next time. Konnikova's first rule for success at poker is this: *Never do anything, no matter how small it may seem, without asking why you are doing it.*

It's a good rule for making any kind of decision. It's a principle of Ignatian decision-making. To choose wisely, you must know *why* you are acting. What are you after? To get rich, to impress others, to feel better? Or are you moti-vated to help someone else, or to become more like the per-son you want to be? When it comes time to choose among various possibilities, have reasons for the choices you make.

What Is This Thing Saying?

Reverence for Ignatius is not an artificial piety or a superstitious solicitude. Reverence means what one has been attentive to must now be accepted as it is, in its own terms.

— HOWARD GRAY, SJ

Malcolm Gladwell's book *Blink* is about our extraordinary ability to make split-second decisions about complicated situations and people. We size up situations, categorize people, perceive dangers immediately, unconsciously, in the blink of an eye. This skill often serves us well, but it also makes mistakes. It's often driven by prejudice and overlooks important data.

Ignatian reverence says: Stop, think, and listen to what the thing before us is saying. *What I'm reading is very disturbing.* Don't toss the book away; let it speak. *I feel terribly anxious.* Don't take a drink or turn on the TV; listen to the anxiety. *This teenager is angry and frightened.* Don't change the subject; listen and try to understand.

What is God saying in this meeting, this book, this round of errand-running?

Feelings Front and Center

Ignatius developed a practice of examining himself often in the course of a day in order to find the hand of God in ordinary experience. Jesuit spirituality is distinguished from other spiritualities by this personal attention to feelings, desires, dreams, hopes, and thoughts.

— WILLIAM A. BARRY, SJ, AND ROBERT G. DOHERTY, SJ

Usually, when we're engulfed in a powerful negative feeling like anger, we focus on the *object* of the feeling — the insolent teenager, the careless driver, the lying politician. We think about what they did, then think about it some more. We savor the offense. If we want to get angrier, this is the way to go.

Ignatian spirituality suggests a different strategy: Pay attention to the feeling itself. Ask: *Why am I angry at the careless mistake my coworker made?* Perhaps because it was stupid and dumb. *Lots of stupid things happen all the time. Why am I upset at this one?* Perhaps because now the mistake has to be fixed. *But fixing things is my job, I do it all day, so why am I upset this time?* Hmmm. Why, indeed? *Maybe because I enjoy it. My righteous anger means I'm right, and I like being right when others are wrong.*

By examining feelings, you might learn something useful or important about yourself. Through awareness, feelings become less intense and troublesome.

January 10

Everything Matters

We need to take seriously and prayerfully the meeting between the creatures we are and all else that God holds lovingly in existence. That "interface" is the felt experience of my day.

— DENNIS HAMM, SJ

"How you do anything is how you do everything" is a favorite saying of motivational speakers and management consultants. They usually invoke it to stress the importance of tending to seemingly small matters. If you frequently show up late for meetings, you may not take deadlines seriously. If you handle petty annoyances cheerfully, you'll be ready when a pandemic comes. Our mindset pervades everything we do.

In other words, everything matters. Our daily experience is the interface between the mysterious creatures that we are and God's glorious world. It's all meaningful — from the smallest to the grandest, the tedious and boring to the peak moments. The eighteenth-century Jesuit Jean-Pierre de Caussade said that the test lies in the small things — how well we "recognize God in the most trivial, the most grievous, and the most mortifying things that happen."

Turn Off the Chatter

Being silent is one of the best ways to listen to God, not because God is not speaking to you during your noisy day, but because silence makes it easier to listen to your heart.

— JAMES MARTIN, SJ

On farms in sixteenth-century England, sheep would bump into fences and hedges, leaving little bits of wool behind. Children and adults unfit for any other work were sent out to harvest these fragments. The job didn't require much brainpower, and it involved aimless wandering around the countryside. This practice is the origin of the idiom "wool-gathering," a term for idle daydreaming to no clear purpose.

But there's potential in woolgathering. Put the phone away and shut off the endless chatter in your head — or at least turn down the volume — and you can have moments of peace and tranquility that open other possibilities. Like the possibility of listening to your heart.

Monkey Mind

Show Christ your scattered mind and distracted heart.

— GERARD HUGHES, SJ

The Buddha said our minds are like a roomful of drunken monkeys, screeching, chattering, jumping around, clamoring for attention, never more insistently as when we settle down for some time of prayer and quiet reflection. Distractions are one of the great disruptors of prayer.

The literature on meditation is full of techniques for quieting the "monkey mind." Calm yourself with rhythmic breathing. Focus on a mantra. Incorporate distractions into your prayer. Let distractions come and go instead of obsessing about them. Shut them down by exercising self-control.

The Jesuit writer James Martin suggests talking to God about them. Prayer is a relationship, he points out; you're sitting down with a good friend. Tell God at the outset that you're distracted because you've got a lot on your mind today — work problems, errands, calls to make, emails to write, whatever — but you want to have a talk anyway. Of course God will understand. He'll invite you to stick around.

January 13

Noticing

Noticing helps you realize that your life is already suffused with the presence of God. Once you begin to look around and allow yourself to take a chance to believe in God, you will easily see God at work in your life.

— JAMES MARTIN, SJ

Cardinal Avery Dulles, SJ, a distinguished theologian, took an intellectual path to faith. His religious awakening was helped by his studies of Greek philosophy as an undergraduate at Harvard. But his spiritual epiphany happened one afternoon as he was strolling along the Charles River. He noticed the buds on a young tree, just opening in the spring. In his conversion memoir *A Testimonial to Grace*, Dulles writes, "While my eye rested on them the thought came to me suddenly, with all the strength and novelty of a revelation, that these little buds in their innocence and meekness followed a rule, a law of which I as yet knew nothing." The law came from God, Dulles realized.

The Ignatian way to God means noticing where God is already active in our lives. We find him in peak moments, but also in ordinary times, in walks along the river, too.

January 14

What Makes You Happy?

The aim is a developing alertness to what really motivates a person. For example, if one notes that all his or her choices are made primarily out of a desire to succeed, then questions confront that man or woman: What do I think a successful life really is? How do I imagine happiness, contentment, fulfillment?

— HOWARD GRAY, SJ

If you reflect on your life long enough and thoroughly enough, big questions will eventually surface for your inspection. For example, you might notice you have a strong desire to succeed. You are spending a great deal of time and energy positioning yourself for the next promotion. You're eager to make your mark. Well, what does success mean to you? What do you think will make you happy?

If you study Amazon product reviews for hours trying to find the best food processor or camping cookstove, why not spend some time scrutinizing your assumptions about the best way to live? Much of what you're thinking about today will be forgotten tomorrow. Don't lose sight of the really important questions. Are you living the way you want to live? Are your choices consistent with your values?

Overfitting

To escape the distress caused by regret for the past or fear about the future, this is the rule to follow: Leave the past to the infinite mercy of God, the future to his good providence, give the present wholly to his love.

— JEAN-PIERRE DE CAUSSADE, SJ

One of the biggest problems in data science is "overfitting" — having too much information to be useful. Machine learning systems are "trained" by loading them with sample problems. Just as math students learn new concepts by working their way through a series of examples, artificial intelligence systems learn when they can find patterns in the mass of data in a sample. The system then applies these patterns to new data. Overfitting happens when the system takes in too much information. It analyzes the data so thoroughly that it can't find any patterns, and thus it can't distinguish useful data from what's irrelevant.

That's what happens when we get bogged down in retrospective revision of the past and speculative brainstorming about the future. Like an overfit AI program, we get mired in detail. It's like dreaming while awake — or waking up from a dream and continuing the dream.

When you find yourself mired in the past and worrying about the future, get a grip on your mind. What demands your attention *now*?

The Bygones Principle

We ought to use the things of this world as though we used them not, and own them as though we owned them not — because the fashion of this world passes and in a moment is gone.

— Ignatius Loyola

One of the maxims of modern decision science is the "bygones principle." When you have to make a decision, forget about the past. Ignore the time and money and effort you've already invested in a project. All that matters is the future. Let bygones be bygones.

The bygones principle is widely ignored. People regularly continue failing projects and bad relationships because they've already invested so much in them. This is the "sunk-cost fallacy" — the mistaken belief that past investments justify further expenditures. Very smart and capable people succumb to it. The sunk-cost fallacy is why many CEOs lose their jobs. They can't make an objective decision because they've invested too much emotion in favorite projects.

The remedy is to do what Ignatius suggests and learn to hold things lightly. It helps, he says, to reflect on the transitory nature of things. The projects that consume you today will be gone soon, so "own them as though we owned them not." Own your work. Don't let your work own you.

What Will Become of Me If…?

We have to cultivate a sense of the presence of God in our daily lives to be able to live without being controlled by fear.

— WILLIAM A. BARRY, SJ

No doubt our inclination to worry is rooted in our evolutionary history. Human beings evolved in surroundings full of threats: A predator might come; that juicy plant might be poisonous; next winter might be hard; that stranger might be coming to take what we have. Natural selection favored creatures who took these possibilities into account. The result is *us* — people who lie awake at night fretting about climate change, viral infections, the stock market, and what our bosses, our neighbors, our government *might* do.

The Ignatian counsel is twofold: First, remember that most of our worries exist in our minds and not in reality; second, we should do what we can and leave the rest in God's loving hands. Nevertheless, some dangers are real, and in any case, our minds are designed for worry. So William Barry offers a third suggestion: Cultivate a sense of God's presence in your daily life. Love is at the center of all things; we can see if it we look for it.

January 18

Bells of Mindfulness

Only the present moment is real and available to us.

— THICH NHAT HANH

Bells are everywhere in Buddhist settings. Buddhist teachers call them "bells of mindfulness." They call our unruly minds back to the present moment. "The peace we desire is not in some distant future, but it is something we can realize in the present moment," says Thich Nhat Hanh.

The past and future have their place in our reflection and prayer, but the present moment is what's key. It's the only time God will come to us, and we don't want to miss it. "Keep watch," says Jesus. "You do not know on what day your Lord will come." This text refers to Christ's coming at the end of time, but it's also about this moment, *now*. The Spirit is working in your life right now. Look for it.

Thich Nhat Hanh makes a useful suggestion: Turn the annoyances of everyday life into bells of mindfulness. You're hungry. You forgot your password. Traffic is slow. Turn these irritations into bells of mindfulness that return you to the present moment.

January 19

Pay Attention to Where You Pay Attention

When we are feeling lonely — if we are brave enough to resist the urge to call someone up, or go shopping, or take a drug, or turn to music or TV or go to bed; if we are courageous enough to remain alone and instead of fleeing the pain, to go down into it — we will gradually notice another Presence there, silent, but benevolent and peaceful.

— KARL RAHNER, SJ

The human ability to pay attention is really quite extraordinary. Neuroscientists aren't sure how we do it. We're constantly bombarded with sounds and sights and smells, but we filter most of them out. We can have a conversation in a noisy restaurant; read a book in a chaotic airport; keep track of our child in a busy playground.

We get to choose how to use this powerful tool of attention. As the saying goes, "Attention is a limited resource, so pay attention to where you pay attention." Take Karl Rahner's advice the next time you have some downtime. Instead of using your amazing ability to focus on music or television or the internet, direct it to the Presence that is always there, "silent, but benevolent and peaceful."

January 20

Active Passivity

"Active passivity" captures the characteristic tone of Ignatian spirituality. It is a spirituality of attentiveness, of watching and waiting, of noticing the ebb and flow of our feelings and inner dispositions.

— DAVID L. FLEMING, SJ

"Active passivity" sounds like an oxymoron, like "organized chaos" or "sweet misery." But it captures something of the paradox of Ignatian awareness. It's contemplation that's essentially active. It's an attitude that is always alert, on the lookout for the movement of the Spirit in our lives. It's awareness directed to the world of our experience. "Our response to God is a *response*," says the Jesuit spiritual director David Fleming. "God initiates; we answer." This is the essence of Ignatian awareness.

Try it. In the morning, remind yourself that you are awakening into a world alive with God's presence. Pause in the middle of the day to ask what life is asking of you today. At the end of the workday, spend a few moments in watchful gratitude for the gifts of the day.

Stop Comparing

Shut your mouth; open your eyes and ears. Take in what is there and give no thought to what might have been there or what is somewhere else.

— C. S. LEWIS

The young C. S. Lewis loved to take walks in the country-side. One day he found himself wondering which was more beautiful — the landscape near his home in County Down, Ireland, or the vistas of County Surry in England, where he went to school. He realized such comparisons were ridiculous. The landscapes are very different: "Even a fool could not force them into competition. This cured me once and for all of the pernicious tendency to compare and prefer."

Notice; don't analyze. You walk past a thousand miracles every day. Birds are extraordinary creatures. Flowers are astonishing. Think of the skill and ingenuity needed to make a computer or a car. Imagine the fathomless mystery of the lives of the people who walk with you through the day.

The Lord on My Mind

I just sat there and thought of our Lord, and his visit to us all those centuries ago, and I said to myself that my great luck was to have had him on my mind for so long in my life!

— DOROTHY DAY

Toward the end of her life, the Catholic activist Dorothy Day sat down to write a memoir. She wrote the words "a life remembered," and what came to mind was the thing that was most important to her — that she had been aware of God's presence and goodness for so many years. She never wrote the memoir. Gratitude for knowing God was enough.

Dorothy Day experienced a kind of *satori*, a Japanese Buddhist term for "awakening." *Satori* is what Ignatius is getting at in his encouragement to notice, to listen, to pay attention to our lives and the people and events that fill them. He asks, "Did you see that? Did you notice what you were feeling at that moment? Can you experience God in all of this?"

Real Religion

The maxim of illusory religion runs: "Fear not; trust in God and he will see that none of the things you fear will happen to you"; that of real religion, on the contrary, is "Fear not; the things that you are afraid of are quite likely to happen to you, but they are nothing to be afraid of."

— JOHN MACMURRAY

The gospels tell two versions of a story about Jesus in a boat in a storm at sea. In one, Jesus is asleep in the boat when a fierce storm arises. The frightened disciples wake him up and he calms the storm with a word. In the second story, Jesus is nowhere to be found when the storm comes. The disciples see a figure walking toward them across the water. They think it is a ghost; they are absolutely terrified. The figure turns out to be Jesus, who says, "Take heart, it is I; do not be afraid."

Being Jesus's close friends didn't shield the disciples from suffering. Plenty of bad things happened to them — storms, ostracism, weariness and hunger, persecution, early death. But these were nothing to be afraid of as long as Jesus was with them. Awareness of God's presence was the basis of their faith.

As the Jesuit William Barry says, "Trust in God's presence will not keep us from being mugged on city streets, from contracting cancer, from experiencing bereavement and death." But Jesus stands with us in suffering. His presence is enough to assure us that the bad things that happen are nothing to be afraid of.

January 24

Hidden in Plain Sight

The duties of each moment are the shadows beneath which hides the divine operation.

— JEAN-PIERRE DE CAUSSADE, SJ

Konstantin Levin, a character in Tolstoy's great novel *Anna Karenina*, is an intellectual and nonbeliever who thinks himself into a state of philosophical nihilism. He stays away from ropes and guns lest they tempt him to suicide. His thinking tells him that his life is meaningless. But things look different when Levin examines the life he is actually living. He has a happy marriage and family; he's engaged in productive work; people admire and depend on him; he's a leader in the community. He's struck by the contrast: His mind says that life is a pointless struggle for survival, while in his work and living he pursues an ideal of the good. Levin decides that "his life was good, but his thinking was bad."

Levin uncovered "the divine operation" hidden in the shadows of everyday life.

If You Can Talk, You Can Pray

Prayer is conversation. If we can talk, we can pray. The essential activity of prayer springs naturally from our humanity. It is a matter of conversing with a very good friend.

— DAVID L. FLEMING, SJ

What makes good music? Duke Ellington's answer: "If it sounds good, it *is* good." Ignatius had a similar answer to the question: What's the best way to pray? Answer: The best prayer is the one that works for you.

Ignatius thought prayer should be simple. The styles of prayer in the Ignatian tradition all flow from basic human abilities and desires: memory, imagination, petition, reverence, conversation.

The prototype is the Lord's Prayer. It's a prayer that comes from the heart of a relationship. We are personally familiar with God ("*our* Father"). We reverence him ("who art in heaven," "hallowed be thy name"). We share God's desires ("thy kingdom come," "thy will be done"). We ask for what we need ("give us this day thy daily bread"). We beg our Father's protection ("deliver us from evil").

This is conversation with a friend: sharing experience, saying thank you, asking for help, crying out in pain, begging forgiveness, expressing love, just spending time together.

January 26

What We're Not *Aware Of*

You're making every day count, more than you think, in the impacts you're having.

— Chris Lowney

Chris Lowney, a writer and former investment banker with an Ignatian point of view, loves a story that his friend Bob told him.

Bob was walking down a street in Manhattan shortly after he had retired from a career in a big accounting firm. He was stopped by a younger man who said, "Bob, I can't believe it's you. I want to thank you for something." Years ago, the guy had been a junior accountant in a firm where Bob was one of the partners. He had been in a client meeting with Bob, he said, and the client, a very important client, wanted Bob to sign off on an accounting maneuver that bordered on the unethical. It was a tense moment; a lot was at stake. Bob patiently explained why the firm couldn't do what the client wanted. "Ever since that day I've tried to model my work on you," the guy said. He thanked Bob and went on his way.

Bob didn't remember the young accountant, didn't remember holding his ethical ground under pressure, didn't remember the meeting at all.

We're not aware of much of the good we've done — the ways we have encouraged others, inspired them, calmed them, stood by them, influenced them for the better. We've forgotten it or never knew about it in the first place.

The World as It Is

By attention Ignatius means allowing the reality of the other to be present to you in all its integrity.

— HOWARD GRAY, SJ

Saul Alinsky's *Rules for Radicals* is a classic guide for people who want to change the world. One of his most important rules is to "start from where the world is, as it is, not as I would like it to be." Look at what is really there. Let it be itself. Once you understand it, you can think about changing it.

The Delphic maxim "know thyself" makes a similar point. You can't improve yourself until you know who you are. The Buddha meant something like that when he told his disciple Ananda, "Dwell as a lamp unto yourself." He meant that happiness comes from illuminating your greatest virtues, making visible your true purpose.

Looking at things as they are means getting rid of biases and opinions. We lay a thick layer of opinion on top of the world: The weather is nasty; this food could be better; "things would be better if only..." We wonder what other people are thinking. We have opinions about other people's opinions, and opinions about opinions about opinions. Set all this aside and simply pay attention to the world as it is.

A Little Learning Is a Dangerous Thing

Self-knowledge invariably brings awareness of how ill-prepared we have been for some of life's challenges.

— CHRIS LOWNEY

One of the most pernicious cognitive biases is the Dunning-Kruger effect: We exaggerate our competence. People who know a little bit about something think they are experts. Someone watches a couple of YouTube videos and thinks they can replace the transmission in their car. Someone reads about Steve Jobs tinkering in his garage and thinks they can start their own business, too. In fact, the more incompetent someone is, the less aware they are of their incompetence. The Dunning-Kruger effect is the scientific proof of the maxim "a little learning is a dangerous thing."

The remedy is more learning — especially self-knowledge. Psychologists call it *metacognition*: thinking about thinking. Remind yourself that you're aware of only *some* of what's happening, and that what you know can blind you to what you *don't* know. It's what the early Jesuit Peter Faber meant when he said, "Reflect on how you comported yourself." A regular practice of reflection and self-scrutiny is a good way to achieve this precious self-knowledge.

January 29

Spirituality from the Inside Out

Attention is the beginning of devotion.

— MARY OLIVER

Spirituality from the outside-in features lists of things to avoid: Beware of those ideas; break those habits; shun those people; avert your eyes there; take refuge here. The classic tale of outside-in religion is *Pilgrim's Progress*. Little Christian trudges the path of righteousness through a multitude of threats and dangers.

The Ignatian approach is spirituality from the inside out. It looks to the inner movements of the spirit, not outside threats. It prizes awareness. What's happening in your spirit? How are you responding to the people in your life? Can you find God's presence in your everyday activities? What do you want?

The poet Mary Oliver said, "To pay attention, this is our endless and proper work."

January 30

Look at Yourself with Gratitude

Look at the world with gratitude and awe, but look at yourself with the very same attitude. We are more talented, gifted, and resourceful than we ever take time to consider.

— CHRIS LOWNEY

"Be grateful" is the Ignatian mantra. Be grateful for your friends, your family, your work, for the beauty of creation, for God's many blessings. But don't forget to look at yourself with gratitude, too. Ignatius suggests that we bask gratefully in the sheer wonder of our being by considering "how God dwells also in myself, giving me existence, life, sensation, and intelligence."

Be grateful that you're caught up in a great divine project to repair the world. Be grateful for the talents and skills you have to do your part of this great work. Ignatius wants you to know this deeply, in the core of your being. He said, "in order that, stirred to profound gratitude, we may become able to love and serve."

January 31

Trust in the Slow Work of God

Above all, trust in the slow work of God. Your ideas mature gradually — let them grow, let them shape themselves, without undue haste. Don't try to force them on, as though you could be today what time will make of you tomorrow.

— Pierre Teilhard de Chardin, SJ

We want things to happen quickly, but change takes time. In fact, you could say that time is the vehicle for God's grace. A good illustration is the career of the scientist and mystic Teilhard de Chardin. He's celebrated today as an original thinker; Popes Benedict and Francis have both praised his ideas. But during his lifetime he was hounded by church authorities, forbidden to teach, his books banned. The authorities disliked Teilhard's efforts to merge Christian theology and evolutionary science. It was an idea ahead of its time, and Teilhard suffered in silence for many years.

God's work is slow because a lot of it — practically all of it, in fact — must unfold in lived experience. We need reflection, study, the counsel of others, and trial and error to give ourselves over to what God is doing in our lives.

Slow time, the plodding pace of everyday life — all the more reason to cultivate a practice of awareness.

February

GOD

There is another world, but it is in this one.

— W. B. YEATS, *THE SECRET ROSE*

February 1

Knowing God

Knowing God is more important than knowing about God.

— KARL RAHNER, SJ

The Jesuit theologian Karl Rahner once startled a group of academic colleagues by blurting out, "You're really dealing with Jesus only when you throw your arms around him."

Rahner knew plenty about God; he was arguably the greatest of twentieth-century theologians. But he prized knowing God above knowing *about* God. He echoes Thomas Aquinas, who said that his experience of God made "all that I have written seem like straw."

Rahner was a Jesuit, and Ignatian spirituality is all about knowing God. Ignatius's core conviction was that God can be known personally, friend to friend, person to person. Ignatian prayer is about experiencing God personally, imaginatively, in the heart. It's about finding God in everyday experience, in work, in the inner movements of your spirit. It's about throwing your arms around Jesus instead of wrapping your mind around him.

February 2

A Rescue Mission

It was for this world that Christ had died: The more evil you saw and heard about you, the greater glory lay around the death; it was too easy to die for what was good or beautiful, for home or children or a civilization — it needed a God to die for the half-hearted and the corrupt.

— GRAHAM GREENE, *THE POWER AND THE GLORY*

The familiar sweet and gentle stories of Christ's coming — the manger, the shepherds and angels, the three kings and the star, the virgin visited by an angel — don't seem to take the ugliness of the world seriously. Ignatius tells a harsher story: Humanity is a mess. Christ's coming is a last-ditch rescue mission into the heart of darkness, not a Hallmark special at Christmastime. He imagines God deciding what to do about people he loves who are going to ruin in a world of violence and fear. The answer: God will go right into the middle of it.

Christianity's understanding of God is *incarnational* — that is, God entered the world in the person of Jesus Christ, took on human flesh, and lived a human life. It's an astounding claim. Whatever else you might say about it, it's not naïve. No rose-colored glasses here. It takes the misery of the human condition seriously. It means that God is present in the realities of everyday life — the good, the bad, and the ugly.

The Christian Story

*Job has a legitimate question for God: Do you have the slightest no-
tion how it feels to be bereft of everything — possessions, children,
wife, respect, health, meaning, even sleep?... Jesus changed all that.
While remaining fully God, Jesus was also fully human. Jesus erased
all distance between God and Job. In Jesus, God became suffering.*

— WILLIAM J. O'MALLEY, SJ

An incarnate god who suffers, dies, and rises again. A hero
on a great quest fails, suffers terribly, is redeemed in the end.
A person is laid low by a tragic flaw, repents, accepts responsibility, and is healed. It's an archetypal human story. The
ancient Greeks and Romans told it. So did Shakespeare, the
Buddha, and Dostoyevsky.

The Jesus story fits right in. Some see this as an argument against the truth of Christianity; the Jesus story is just
an oft-told myth representing wishful thinking. But maybe
the argument goes the other way: The Jesus story makes
sense because it springs from the deepest recesses of the
human heart. Every human heart is prepared to hear the
gospel. The story of Jesus *feels* true. If God were going to do
something about our predicament, this is the way he'd go
about it.

February 4

Come as You Are

God can meet you at any time, no matter how crazy things may seem. Your spiritual house does not need to be tidy for God to enter.

— JAMES MARTIN, SJ

Take a look at some of the characters who have dealings with Jesus in the New Testament: a grieving father, a woman ground down by chronic illness, frustrated fishermen, jealous disciples, a corrupt public official, an adulterous woman about to be stoned, desperate beggars, sinners, outcasts. People displayed all manner of bad behavior in his presence. If Jesus shows us what God is like, then God has a liking for people who are being themselves, warts and all.

So why do we so often try to become someone else when we approach God — someone who is kinder, nicer, more loving, "holier" than the person we actually are? We imagine that God doesn't want to hang out with the likes of us. But, clearly, he does.

February 5

"He Is at the Tip of My Pen"

God is not altogether apart from the world we see, touch, hear, smell, and taste around us. Rather he awaits us every instant in our action, in the work of the moment. There is a sense in which he is at the tip of my pen, my spade, my brush, my needle — of my heart and my thought.

— PIERRE TEILHARD DE CHARDIN, SJ

Teilhard de Chardin was an extraordinary character: a medic in the trenches in World War I, a world-class paleontologist, theologian, and mystic. His books gave a cosmic, evolutionary spin on the Ignatian vision of God as present in all things. He's known for the maxim that God "is at the tip of my pen, my spade, my brush, my needle."

Pen, spade, needle — Teilhard's technology is so *yesterday*. Let's update it: "There is a sense in which God is at the click of my mouse, my laser pointer, my snowplow, my steering wheel, the IV line I give my patient." God is *here* — in the everyday events of our lives.

"There is not a moment in which God does not present himself under the cover of some pain to be endured, of some consolation to be enjoyed, or of some duty to be performed," wrote Jean-Pierre de Caussade.

February 6

Simple Things

We frequently saw [Ignatius] taking the occasion of little things to lift his mind to God, who even in the smallest things is great. From seeing a plant, foliage, a leaf, a flower, any kind of fruit; from the consideration of a little worm or any other animal, he raised himself above the heavens.

— Pedro de Ribadeneira, SJ

We find an amusing story about pride and simplicity in the second book of Kings in the Hebrew scriptures. A very important Syrian named Naaman, a powerful general no less, goes in search of a healing for his leprosy. He comes to Israel because he's heard that the prophet Elisha has the magic touch. Naaman is a big shot; he's expecting a big healing show — lots of prayers, impressive ritual, a cast of thousands. But nothing goes as expected. Instead, Elisha tells him to simply wash in the River Jordan seven times. No fuss, no drama — just swim in the river. Naaman is irate, but he eventually does what Elisha asks and, sure enough, he's healed of leprosy.

Our search for God doesn't require a big drama, but often it does require an attitude adjustment.

February 7

Images of God

If our experience has taught us to think of God as a policemanlike figure, whose predominant interest is in our faults, and if our encounters with him have been mostly in cold churches where we were bored out of our minds with barely audible services and sermons presenting God as God who disapproves of most of the things we like, then we are not likely to want to turn to God.

— GERARD W. HUGHES, SJ

One Christmas season, the economist Arthur Brooks was driving into Manhattan and noticed a billboard at the entrance to the Lincoln Tunnel. It showed a silhouette of the Magi on their way to Bethlehem, with the words: "You KNOW it's a Myth. This Season, Celebrate REASON!" Brooks noted how this message was the opposite of an appeal to reason. It naïvely reduced faith to a children's story and then rejected the children's story because it was not literal history. It rejected a childish caricature of faith, not a faith that adults profess.

"Our first impressions of faith tend to be made as children," Brooks says, "and those impressions can haunt us as we mature. People often dismiss religion as a mishmash of myths and childish nonsense that well-adjusted adults should logically leave behind."

Ignatius's spiritual breakthrough came when his image of God changed. He met a God who was personal, generous, loving, and close by — something he knew in his heart as well as his mind. He wants us to meet this God, too.

February 8

God the Gift-Giver

God's love shines down upon me like the light rays from the sun, or God's love is poured forth lavishly like a fountain spilling forth its waters into an unending stream.

— THE SPIRITUAL EXERCISES, 237

"What does it matter? All is grace."

These are the dying words of the lonely, forgotten, anonymous priest in Georges Bernanos's novel *The Diary of a Country Priest* (also a terrific movie). They echo the last words of St. Thérèse of Lisieux: "Grace is everywhere." Thérèse and Bernanos both evoke Ignatius's image of God as a superabundant giver whose gifts are as ubiquitous as sunshine.

The image of God as the sun is hardly unique to Ignatius; ancient peoples thought about God this way, too. Does this image of God seem right to you? Does it "fit"? Is the human heart primed to see God as the source of endless blessing?

"How can I respond to such a generous giver?" Ignatius asked. This is a relationship. What are *you* going to do about this God who knows you so well and has given you so much?

February 9

God in All Things

*I will consider how God dwells in creatures; in the elements giv-
ing them existence; in the plants giving them life; in the animals
giving them sensation; in human beings giving them intelligence;
and finally, how in this way he dwells also in myself, giving me life,
sensation, and intelligence.*

— *The Spiritual Exercises*, 235

If you're looking for the beating heart of Ignatian spirituality, here it is: God can be found in all things — in
the elements, in plants and animals, in human beings. The
seventeenth-century Jesuit theologian Robert Bellarmine
went even further: "What various powers lie hidden in
plants! What strange powers are found in stones," he said.
God is *here* — not *up there*. "Finding God in all things" is the
motto of Ignatian spirituality.

One implication of this idea: *Everything is part of the
spiritual life*. Divisions between sacred and profane, spiritual
and secular, holy and worldly are fictions. Another implication: A spiritual life can be had at *any time and in any place*,
not just in special places like church.

We meet God everywhere — in frustration and sorrow
as well as peace and joy.

February 10

There's More

The world is charged with the grandeur of God.
— GERARD MANLEY HOPKINS, SJ

In Gerard Manley Hopkins's sonnet "Hurrahing the Harvest," the poet describes the autumn countryside in images of extravagant beauty. "Silk-sack clouds" are "melted across skies"; "azurous hung hills" stand "majestic as a stallion stalwart." The poet then reflects: "These things, these things were here and but the beholder Wanting." This glorious beauty has been here for a long time. All that's been lacking is someone to see it.

That's the job of poetry and of spiritual practice — to create beholders, people who see. It's a profoundly Ignatian idea. Hopkins's response to the beauty he sees in the countryside is a cry from deep in his Ignatian heart: "I walk, I lift up, I lift up heart, eyes, / Down all that glory in the heavens to glean our Saviour."

There's always more to God. Just when you think you've got it figured out, something new will come along to surprise you.

February 11

God Is a Worker

I will consider how God labors and works for me in all creatures on the face of the earth, that is, he acts in the manner of one who is laboring.

— *THE SPIRITUAL EXERCISES, 236*

Another image of God: God is a worker. He's *busy*. He's healing what is sick and repairing what is broken.

God brings order out of disorder. In the beginning, the Bible says, there was "a formless void and darkness covered the face of the deep." From this, God brought forth the sun, the moon, and the stars; day and night; the land teeming with plants and animals; and eventually us. God's creative work continues. Out of the chaos of our world — a seething mass of passion, energy, conflict, and desire — God's spirit brings order and light.

A challenging idea, to say the least. Sometimes it seems plausible and sometimes it doesn't. What are we to make of God the worker when we look at a world wracked with disease, hatred, and suffering? Ignatius says that God is here to heal it, and that we all have a part to play in this divine activity.

God Is Human

The Christian tradition does not say human beings are of such immense dignity that God really loves them. No, the Christian tradition says something far more radical: human beings are of such dignity that God has chosen to be one. God does not think being God is anything to be grasped; God empties himself and becomes human like all other human beings.

— MICHAEL HIMES

The theologian Michael Himes says that a couple of verses in Paul's letter to the Philippians may be the oldest expression of Christian faith: "Although Christ was in the form of God, he did not think being equivalent to God was anything to be held onto, so he emptied himself, taking on the form of a servant and becoming like all other human beings."

It's an extraordinary claim. It's hard to believe that human beings are as important as Christians say they are. One implication is that whatever makes us more human makes us more like God. Whatever engages our minds, our energy, our creativity; whatever makes us wiser, more generous, more grateful; whatever broadens our spirits and gives space for our talents — all of this makes us more like God. This is how we meet God in the incarnational tradition: "Not 'out there' somewhere, but *here*, being human along with us," Himes says.

God Who Is Poor

God is not only the God of the poor. God is God who is poor.

— PEDRO ARRUPE, SJ

Yet another facet to the Ignatian image of God: God is poor. In Jesus Christ, God came into the world as a laborer in a low-status, blue-collar family in a politically oppressed nation. He liked poor people. Many of his friends were people on the margins: working men and women, social outcasts, public sinners, the sick and disabled. "Our Lord so preferred the poor to the rich that he chose the entire college of his apostles from among the poor," Ignatius writes.

Like the Buddha and other masters of the spirit, Ignatius saw material poverty as the route to spiritual poverty — detachment, surrender, and dependence on God. It's the starting point on the path to virtue: first poverty, then indifference to the world's accolades, finally humility.

There's paradox and tension in this notion of poverty. Destitution, hunger, homelessness — the abject poverty that afflicts millions — is an evil to be resisted. But spiritual poverty that recognizes our dependence on God is to be welcomed and sought.

February 14

God Gets Us Moving

The God of the Bible is almost always encountered in a command. Everywhere he says: "Go, Come, Do, Come follow me." We rarely find anyone encountering God by squatting and contemplating; God appears and gets us moving.

— Anthony de Mello, SJ

Yet another image of God: God the Mobilizer, the get-off-your-couch God. There are some exceptions: The prophet Elijah encounters God in a "still small voice." A couple of times Jesus tells us to go off and pray. Most often he tells us to *do* something: Love our enemies, turn the other cheek, wash our brother's feet, follow me.

In one of his meditations in *The Spiritual Exercises*, Ignatius has us imagine Christ as a king issuing a call to action: "My will is to conquer the whole world," he says. "Whoever wishes to come with me must labor with me." Doing this work with Christ is the purpose of our lives.

God Wants to Be Your Friend

What does God want in creating us? My stand is that what God wants is friendship. God — out of the abundance of divine relational life, not any need for us — desires humans into existence for the sake of friendship.

— WILLIAM A. BARRY, SJ

God wants to be our friend — that notion doesn't come up very often in the long history of human reflection on the Divine. The mainstream tradition is summed up in the psalmist's invocation of "fear of the Lord" — solemn reverence with more than a touch of apprehension for the majestic (and unpredictable) deity. If you had a religious upbringing, there's a good chance you were taught to think about God this way.

Another tradition stresses God's mercy. "The Lord is merciful and gracious, slow to anger and abounding in steadfast love," says the psalmist. Several times a day Muslims pray the Bismillah: "I begin with the name of Allah, the Most Gracious, the Most Merciful."

But God as our *friend*? The Ignatian tradition is to hold God close. The habit of thinking about God as a friend dates back to Ignatius himself: "Talk with Jesus like a friend," he says, "as one friend to another, making known his affairs to him and seeking advice in them."

February 16

God Loves Us the Way We Are

Even though God is always calling us to constant conversion and growth, and even though we are imperfect and sometimes sinful people, God loves us as we are now.

— JAMES MARTIN, SJ

The story goes that the Hasidic rebbe Zusya decided he did not fear God enough. He prayed, "Lord, let me stand in awe of you like the angels do." God answered his prayer; Zusya felt the angels' awe — so intensely that he shook with fear. He crawled under his bed like a little dog, terrified, overwhelmed with awe. Finally he prayed, "Lord, let me love you like Zusya again." God answered that prayer, too, and Zusya once again loved God the way Zusya loved God.

God loves you the way you are. Love God in your own way, not in someone else's.

February 17

God Is Trying to Catch Your Attention

Whether we are aware of it or not, at every moment of our existence we are encountering God, Father, Son, and Holy Spirit, who is trying to catch our attention, trying to draw us into a reciprocal conscious relationship.

— WILLIAM A. BARRY, SJ

You are on vacation, riding on a highway in Colorado, and you are stunned by the beauty of the mountains. You sit at the Thanksgiving dinner table with your family, and you feel a great surge of gratitude for — everything. You're weary, bone-tired, and discouraged after a grueling meeting about a work project that's in trouble, and you feel an assurance that everything will be OK. You think about a neighbor, a woman who is waiting for the results of a cancer screening, and you feel an urge to connect with her.

You have feelings like these all the time. Some you remember; some you don't. Some call for a response; some don't. Recognize them for what they are — ways that God is trying to catch your attention.

Walk with Me

Being saved, I was taught when I was a child, was a way of saying, sinner that I am, sinner that I will ever be, I relinquish control of my life to He who knows more than I, he who knows everything. It is not a magical moment of becoming sinless, blameless, but rather it's a way of saying, "walk with me."

— Yaa Gyasi, *Transcendent Kingdom*

"Amazing Grace" is one of the great Christian hymns, an anthem of the experience of "being saved": "Amazing grace, how sweet the sound, that saved a wretch like me / I once was lost but now am found, was blind, but now I see."

It was written by John Newton, an English sea captain who had a long career in the slave trade. Newton renounced his past, became a leader in the abolitionist movement, and served for years as an Anglican priest. It's an impressive conversion story — with a twist. All these changes happened years after Newton was "saved." Newton became a Christian in 1748, but he continued to sail slave ships and invest in the slave trade after he retired from the sea. He had to walk with God for a good long while before his conversion was complete. It took years for God's "amazing grace" to change him.

Conversion takes time. It unfolds in the course of a relationship with God.

February 19

Let Your Imagination Go

Imaginative prayer makes the Jesus of the Gospels our Jesus. It helps us develop a unique and personal relationship with him. We watch Jesus's face. We listen to the way he speaks. We notice how people respond to him.

— DAVID L. FLEMING, SJ

Ignatius *imagined* his way to God. His heart was stirred by stories of the great saints. He dreamed about walking with Jesus in the Holy Land. He wondered what it would be like to give up his life of privilege and ease and go wherever God led him. He liked the way these dreams felt. He realized that these feelings pointed him to the life he really wanted.

Ignatian imaginative prayer engages "right-brain" faculties — sensation, intuition, holistic perception. We don't just *read* the gospels; we put ourselves *in* them as an onlooker/participant. We feel the heat of the sun, smell the sweaty bodies of the crowd around us. Above all we observe Jesus very closely: How does he treat people? What kind of man is he? The point of it all is to involve our "hearts" in the effort to know God.

Try it. Read a favorite sacred story and put yourself into it. A suggestion from the New Testament is Mark 10:46–52 — the healing of a blind man. Put yourself into it as a bystander at the side of the road and let you imagination go.

February 20

Look for Thin Places

We should be aware of the thin places in our lives, because they make experiences of God's creative desire for each one of us, and our correlative desire for God, more possible, by capturing our attention and pulling us out of our ordinary routines and concerns.

— WILLIAM A. BARRY, SJ

There's an Irish saying that heaven and earth are only three feet apart, but in thin places the distance is even shorter. "Thin places" are where the sacred breaks through. The wall collapses, the veil becomes transparent, and we glimpse the divine. The Irish find thin places in their island's rugged landscape. Shrines and churches and temples can be thin places. So can holy texts and moments with loved ones.

Almost anything can be a thin place. William Barry recalls a woman on a retreat who found a thin place in a mass of ugly seaweed clinging to a rock on the ocean shore. As she gazed on it, she saw beautiful, subtle colors; it reminded her of the goodness and grace she saw in the troubled boys she worked with. Says the poet Mary Oliver:

> It doesn't have to be
> the blue iris, it could be
> weeds in a vacant lot, or a few
> small stones; just
> pay attention.

God Is Like a Tangent

It could be a meeting on the street, or a party or a lecture, or just a simple, banal introduction, then suddenly there is a flash of recognition and the embers of kinship glow. There is an awakening between you, a sense of ancient knowing.

— JOHN O'DONOHUE

The Jesuit Gerard Hughes compares God to a tangent. In geometry, a tangent is a line that touches the edge of a curve but never crosses it. Our human experience is the circle. Every part of our experience touches God in some way, but it remains *our* experience. A tangent is also a thought or action that goes off in a different direction. God does that, too. He touches our experience and opens it to something new.

Karl Rahner calls these moments of "everyday mysticism." Examples: moments of silence and peace that feel more "real" than normal life; feeling wonder at being in this time and place; a sudden experience of being completely accepted in love.

Sparks of Holiness

What is that which gleams through me and strikes my heart without hurting it?

— St. Augustine

The collection of Jewish mystical commentaries on the Bible known as the Kabbalah tells a story about the creation of the world. In the beginning there was nothing at all besides God. God had to contract in order to make space for the new creation, and when he did, a great shattering occurred. Fragments of the Divine remained in place, scattered throughout the universe. These "sparks of holiness" are lodged everywhere, sometimes deeply hidden, sometimes in plain sight. Our job is to find them, collect them, and return them to God.

It's said that Baal Shem Tov, founder of Hasidic Judaism, would make it a habit to ask every Jew he met, "How are you?" in order to hear them say, "Well, thank God." The very mention of God's name would free the spark of holiness trapped in that place.

February 23

Praying for Things

Why ask God for something if he is all-knowing and loving? He does not need information, e.g., that my best friend is sick and I want him to get well. But if prayer is relationship, the issue is not information, but whether I believe he cares how I feel, and whether I am willing to let him know what I feel and desire, that is, to reveal myself.

— William A. Barry, SJ

Your first spontaneous prayer was probably a prayer of petition that sprang naturally to your lips in middle school: *God, please help me pass this test. If you do, I'll stop teasing my brother.* Prayers like these continue as life gets more complicated: *Please heal my sick daughter. I really need this job; please make this interview go well. God, please give me a good night's sleep.*

These prayers can begin to sound pretty childish. After all, adults don't go running to their parents all the time with pleas for help. And why am I telling God things he already knows? He *knows* I need a job.

But think about praying this way as the kind of thing that goes on in a relationship. People in a relationship tell each other what's going on in their lives. Your friend may know all about your troubles at work, but you want to tell her about them anyway. You grow closer that way. It's the same with God. Telling God what's on your mind takes the stiffness and distance out of the relationship. We want our prayers to be answered, but even more we want to be connected to God.

February 24

White Fire

Never have I heard contemplation more excitingly described: a long loving look at the real.

— WALTER J. BURGHARDT, SJ

An old Jewish saying holds that scripture is "black fire written on white fire." The black fire is the words of scripture; the white fire is the spaces between them. The white fire is sacred, too. Without the white fire — the emptiness, the white space — there wouldn't be any words. Ignatian prayer is mostly in the "black fire" camp. It has "content" — imagery, memories, words, and symbols. Other prayer traditions are more "white fire." They seek to empty the mind of ideas and simply rest in the presence of God. It turns out that Ignatian prayer dips into this tradition, too.

In *The Spiritual Exercises*, Ignatius recommends a method of prayer involving concentrating on a single word while breathing in and out. It's similar to contemporary centering prayer, where a focus on a "mantra" — a single word or sound — aids meditation. It's a style of prayer that reminds us that our bodies as well as our minds can be part of prayer. It slows us down and gives space for God to enter.

"Black fire" prayer is like talking to a good friend. "White fire" prayer is simply enjoying being together with a friend in wordless silence.

What Wasn't Said

Ignatius encourages prayer that puts us into the passage from scripture. We are instructed to use all our senses — hearing, sight, smell, touch, even taste. We are also instructed to contemplate what wasn't said, that is, what isn't written in the Gospels. What would I have said? What side conversations might be going on? What would Jesus have said to me had I been there?

— Lisa Kelly

We have an instinct to fill in the blanks. We want to know what wasn't said as well as what was. *What was he thinking when he did that? What isn't she telling me?*

That's one reason Ignatian imaginative prayer is so powerful. When we try to grasp a gospel story or other sacred text imaginatively, we envision conversations, events, details other than those described. Our imagination fills in the gaps. We can hear God in both what is said — and what isn't said.

Work Is Prayer

Jesus did not leave us a list of truths to affirm but a task to carry out.

— William A. Barry, SJ

Work doesn't get much respect in many religious traditions. The first Christian monks were men and women who fled the cities to live in the desert. They saw work as a distraction from the serious business of denying the senses and punishing the body. Work got some grudging respect with St. Benedict's template for monastic life — *ora et labora*, pray and work. But *ora* had priority. At best, *labora* — what most of us spend most of our time doing — had a supportive role in the spiritual life.

Ignatius took the next step; he sanctified work. "Love ought to be expressed in deeds rather than in words," he said. He perceived God as a worker, saving and healing the world. He said that Christ invites each of us personally to work beside him — "work with me by day and watch with me by night."

In the Ignatian view, work is no distraction; it's a big part of the *way* we have a relationship with God. *All* work has great dignity if it is freely chosen. This is true whether we empty bedpans or run the hospital. Work can be a "thin space" where the Holy Spirit crosses the barrier between heaven and earth.

Pilgrimage

Pilgrimage means a patient willingness to find God through the journeying. It also means a willingness to risk a process of trial and error, of successes and failures, of some triumphs but also many humiliating defeats.

— HOWARD GRAY, SJ

In the Ignatian metaphor, life is a pilgrimage. Pilgrimage is subtly different from a journey. The point of a journey is to get somewhere; the trip is something you put up with. The point of a pilgrimage is the trip itself. You're on the way to an unknown destination. There's no script. You'll be continually surprised. You'll go places you weren't planning to see.

A pilgrimage takes effort; pilgrims *do* things. Pilgrims have realistic expectations: They don't expect perfection; they're content with partial successes; they take failure in stride. A pilgrim is comfortable with ambiguity. A pilgrim is alert for the next challenge, the next opportunity. The pilgrim understands Kierkegaard's insight: "Life is not a problem to be solved but a mystery to be lived."

Ignatian Optimism

Ignatius was impressed by the fact that God spoke to him despite his sinfulness. That implied a liberality to God's giving and forgiving. If God would speak to him, he would speak to anyone.

— RONALD MODRAS

When God caught his attention, Ignatius was no one special — an indifferent Christian, a proud man with a bad temper and an eye for the ladies. Yet God sought him out and remade his life anyway. This filled him with joy and gratitude and shaped his worldview. Thus it's no surprise that the Ignatian spirit radiates optimism and hope. Ignatius saw God as nearby, present everywhere in the world, and generous with his gifts.

Plenty of people are pessimistic, including religious people — sometimes *especially* religious people. Things are bad, getting worse, and God is stingy with his grace.

Which view is more convincing? Consider the fact that God has reached out to *you*. Look at the material and spiritual blessings in your life. What have *you* done to deserve this? Not much. Most likely, you're like Ignatius — an ordinary person who has been touched by grace.

God is generous, not stingy. His grace is abundant, not scarce. God wants to meet everyone — even the likes of you!

March

LOVE

We are put on earth a little space,
that we may learn to bear the beams of love.

— William Blake, "The Little Black Boy"

More by Deeds than Words

Love ought to manifest itself more by deeds than by words.

— *The Spiritual Exercises*, 231

Words are important to spiritually minded people. We talk a lot, pray a lot, talk about praying. But Ignatius was impatient with big talk. In one spiritual exercise, he considers the sad spectacle of people with generous intentions who talk and talk about giving money away but never get around to actually doing it. You can imagine Ignatius listening to someone talk about their wonderful insights and inspiring plans, drumming his fingers impatiently on the table, "Yes, yes, but what have you *done*? What *are* you doing? What *will* you do?"

How about you? Do you do what you say you're going to do? Love is what you *do*, not what you say.

March 2

Love Is Sharing

Love consists in a mutual sharing of goods. In love, one always gives to the other.

— *THE SPIRITUAL EXERCISES*, 231

This is Ignatius's second rule of love: Lovers share. They share something of value.

Your time and attention are the most valuable things you have. Which is harder: donating a lot of money to your favorite charity through an app on your phone, or volunteering your time? Shopping for a gift online and sending it to your partner, or listening patiently to them while they describe a wretched day at the office?

The principle applies to God, too. Loving God means sharing something of value with him — mainly your time and attention. In fact, God *needs* that from you.

March 3

Self-Surrender

Whenever we find that our religious life is making us good — above all, that we are better than someone else — I think that we may be sure that we are being acted on not by God, but by the devil. The real test of being in the presence of God is that you either forget about yourself altogether or see yourself as a small, dirty object. It is better to forget about yourself altogether.

— C. S. LEWIS

Self-surrender goes against the grain. It's out of sync with the me-first, never-give-up, keep-pushing, can-do spirit of modern life. But religious thinkers across the board — Christian, Buddhist, Jewish, Hindu, Muslim — attest that the self is the problem. To know God, we must surrender ourselves.

Perhaps the most famous prayer of surrender is Ignatius's "Suscipe," named for the Latin word for "receive":

Take, Lord, and receive all my liberty, my memory,
my understanding, and my entire will — all that I
have and possess. You gave it all to me; to you, Lord,
I return it. All is yours; do with it what you will.
Give me only the love of you, together with your
grace, for that is enough for me.

"Suscipe" comes at the end of *Spiritual Exercises* and completes the circle of love that's at the heart of the world: All things come from God and all things go back to God. This cycle will be finished at the end of history; in the meantime, we return to God all that he's given us.

March 4

Too Good to Be True?

You are not as good as you have worked hard for years to make yourself seem, but you are much more loved than you could ever have imagined.

— GEORGE ASCHENBRENNER, SJ

In his short story "The Repentant Sinner," Tolstoy tells of a man, a great sinner, who calls out to God for mercy just before he dies. He arrives at the gates of heaven, but they are locked. The Apostle Peter explains that a sinner like him can't enter heaven, but the man reminds Peter of *his* sins — he denied Christ three times after swearing to be loyal. Peter goes away and is replaced by King David, who also says that sinners can't enter heaven. The man reminds David that God had mercy on him despite his many sins — including adultery and murder. Finally, the Apostle John arrives. In essence, the man says: "You are the beloved disciple. You wrote that 'God is love' and 'Brethren, love one another.' Surely you must let me in." And sure enough, John embraces the man and escorts him into heaven.

It sounds too good to be true. Surely Peter and King David have a point: A sinner can't call out for mercy at the very end and just walk into heaven. But this is what Christians believe — that God's love really is unconditional, and all we need to do is ask for it.

March 5

A Light in the Dark

Feed the hungry, clothe the naked, succor the sick and the frightened and lonely: that is the inarguable assignment, the blunt mission statement, the clear map coordinates — that is what we are here for: to bring love like a searing weapon against the dark, and to do so without fanfare and applause, without a care for sneers. Do what you know to be right, though the world calls you a fool.

— BRIAN DOYLE

Here's another way to look at love: It's light in the darkness, challenging the dismal lie that power, fame, and wealth are the forces that make the world go round. People who live for others are declaring that love is what matters most.

There's a paradox at the heart of the gospel. The weak are strong, mercy is greater than justice, and earthly power is powerless in the end. The arc of human history points one way; Christ points in the other. Love is our destiny. Love is the force at the heart of all things.

Live in Love

If we think that God loves us only if we act in a certain way, we will see our lives as a time of testing. We need to rise to the challenge, to avoid mistakes, to labor to do the right thing. But if God is Love loving, our life is a time of growing and maturing. Lovers don't test each other. Lovers don't constantly demand that the other measure up. Lovers give to those they love.

— DAVID L. FLEMING, SJ

Ellen Oglethorpe, a character in Walker Percy's comic novel *Love in the Ruins*, is described as "a strict churchgoer and a moral girl" who does not believe in God. "She is embarrassed by the God business. But she does right. She doesn't need God. What does God have to do with being honest, hard-working, chaste, upright, unselfish, etcetera."

Not much. "The God business" isn't about being a solid, upright citizen. God's love is unconditional; "God is Love loving," as the Jesuit David Fleming puts it. God loves us; he doesn't demand that we first pull ourselves together and clean up our acts. Life is a sacred journey. We're getting better at it as we go along, accepting the shortcomings, attentive to new opportunities, all the while growing closer to the One who has given us everything we have.

March 7

Sinners

I see myself as a sinner — bound, helpless, alienated — before a loving God and all the love-gifts of creation. I let pass before my mind all my sins and sinful tendencies which permeate my life from my youth up to the present moment.

— THE SPIRITUAL EXERCISES, 56

In one of his first interviews after becoming pope, Pope Francis was asked, "Who are you? Who is Jorge Mario Bergoglio?" He replied, "I am a sinner."

The pope's answer came straight from his Jesuit formation. Ignatian spirituality strips away our delusions. One of the biggest is that we are righteous, clear-headed creatures, prone to occasional mistakes, but basically OK. Ignatius wants us to understand how deeply entangled we are in sin. It clouds our minds, erodes our will, distorts our desires and dreams. Sin makes us stupid. The world is full of people who do cruel, selfish, callous things thinking they are right. That includes all of us.

But we are loved sinners. You don't have to change for God to love you. God loves you even in your weakness and faults.

Cut Rancor Off at the Roots

Whenever this rancor in the heart begins to burgeon, cut it off at the roots and do not rest until you have pulled it out stem and all.

— PETER FABER, SJ

Among the most frightening creatures in the *Star Wars* universe are rancors, giant two-legged reptiles with a salivating, tooth-filled maw. They roam the jungles of the planet Felucia, devouring prey and terrifying would-be settlers.

Rancors aren't ordinary predators, and rancor in the heart isn't ordinary anger. It's big, strong, and scary. It tends to take over; it begins with resentment and envy and grows into anger and finally into dark, miserable bitterness and comprehensive ill-will. The word has its roots in the Latin word for "stinking smell" and "rottenness." It rhymes with "canker," as in canker sore — that painful burning in the mouth that never seems to go away.

If you spot rancor in your heart, get rid of it *now*, Peter Faber says. Pull out the roots. Otherwise, it will take over the garden.

March 9

Impossible to Hate

When you visualized a man or woman carefully, you could always feel pity — that was a quality God's image carried with it. When you saw the lines at the corners of the eyes, the shape of the mouth, how the hair grew, it was impossible to hate. Hate was just a failure of imagination.

— GRAHAM GREENE, *THE POWER AND THE GLORY*

In Graham Greene's novel *The Power and the Glory*, a woebegone priest, an alcoholic and fornicator, spends a night in jail with some of the seediest and most corrupt people in town. One in particular is hard to bear: a self-righteous woman, a Christian, who is disgusted by the people around her and complains that the priest won't condemn their behavior. In the darkness of the jail the priest is repelled by her, but he imagines what the woman looks like. When she's vividly present in his imagination, he finds it impossible to hate her.

Are there people you strongly dislike? Even hate? Do what the priest does. Visualize them carefully. Imagine what it's like to be them. Can you hate them now?

Love Is the Lens

Love was the glue that unified the Jesuit company, a motivating force that energized their efforts. More profoundly, love was the lens through which individual Jesuits beheld the world around them. Loving their superiors, their peers, their subordinates, their enemies, and those they served changed not only the way Jesuits looked at others but what they saw.

— CHRIS LOWNEY

Research psychologists have documented many ways that mood, setting, and tone shape what we believe to be true, often unconsciously. It's called the "framing effect." Voters who cast their ballots in polling places in schools are more likely to vote for school bond issues. People who are instructed to frown while listening to a debater's argument are more likely to disagree with it.

For the early Jesuits, the great frame was love: warm affection, generous spirit, an optimistic outlook, a confidence in God's grace. Not only did it bind the Jesuits together, it caused them to see more clearly and deeply. It enabled Jesuits to see hidden opportunities and discern talents in others that others overlooked.

What's your frame? Is it love...or something else?

March 11

God Wants Something from Us

This is God's humility: God wants my trust, my love, my friendship. Let it sink in.

— WILLIAM A. BARRY, SJ

It's a remarkable claim: God wants something from us. He has created a universe where much of what he wants to accomplish depends on us. God is all-mighty and all-powerful, but there's something he doesn't have, something he badly wants. This is our love, our trust, and our friendship. He has work for us to do. He wants us to get on with this work, together, in partnership with him.

In his book *An Invitation to Love*, William Barry writes, "It gives God pleasure, you might say, when we trust God, tell God our secrets, our dreams, our hopes, and when we love God with all our heart, and with all our soul, and with all our mind, and with all our strength."

Let that sink in.

March 12

Friendship

They say that love is blind, but the affection friends have for each other is the opposite of blind. It is ferociously attentive. You are vulnerable, and your friend holds your vulnerability. He pauses, and you wait for him. You err, and she forgives.

— DAVID BROOKS

The Ignatian tradition extols friendship. The Jesuits were founded by a group of friends who loved one another fiercely. Ignatius, their leader, was the kind of guy who could connect with you immediately, remember your name, and win your trust. Francis Xavier missed his friends so much in faraway Asia that he cut their names out of their letters and carried them close to his heart. "If there were no friends in the world, there would be no joy," said Matteo Ricci, another Jesuit missionary in Asia.

The Jesuits cultivated their friendships in imitation of Jesus, who called his disciples "friends." Friendship was their metaphor for a relationship with God. One of the most popular forms of Ignatian prayer is the colloquy — an honest, intimate, personal conversation between you and God.

For a fresh experience of love, cultivate your friendships.

March 13

Really Love Your Opponents

*If we want to be of help to our opponents, we must be careful to re-
gard them with love, and to banish from our own souls any thought
that might lessen our love and esteem for them.*

— PETER FABER, SJ

Peter Faber, one of the founders of the Jesuits, was talking
about Protestants — Luther, Calvin, and their followers.
Sixteenth-century Catholics thought Protestants were the
worst people in the world. They were wrecking the unity
of the church. They were teaching things that Catholics believed would send people to hell. They were feared, hated,
denounced, burned at the stake when the authorities could
get their hands on them. Yet Faber was saying that his fellow
Catholics needed to regard them with love.

What's the contemporary equivalent? Terrorists, mug-
gers, rapists — people who threaten our safety? How about
crooked competitors: people who cheat and lie and bully?
Personal enemies: someone who spreads lies about us, tries
to get us fired from our jobs? Faber says: Treat them with
genuine respect and love.

You can't fake this kind of love; it's not just being polite
when you want to throttle the person you're talking to. It's
real love that has to come from the heart.

All Are Beloved by God

Every speck of creation, everything that happens, every kid kicking a soccer ball down a road in Guatemala, each office worker in New Delhi, every ancient great-grandmother in a rest home in Boynton Beach, every baby swimming in utero at this moment around the world — all are beloved by God.

— AMY WELBORN

According to an ancient Jewish midrash, the angels throw a party in heaven after the Egyptian army is destroyed and the Israelites are saved at the Sea of Reeds. But they notice that God is not joining the party; he's off to the side weeping. They protest: "Why are you sad? Your people have been saved. The Egyptians have been destroyed." And God says, "The Egyptians are also my people."

Who are the "Egyptians" today — those who supposedly lie outside God's love?

March 15

A Harsh and Dreadful Thing

Love in action is a harsh and dreadful thing compared to love in dreams.

— FYODOR DOSTOYEVSKY, *THE BROTHERS KARAMAZOV*

Dorothy Day, the Catholic social activist, loved to quote a line from a scene in *The Brothers Karamazov* where the holy elder Father Zossima exhorts a woman to a life of active love as a remedy for her doubts. The woman hesitates because she thinks she'll hate it when people are ungrateful for her help. Zossima agrees that, yes, that's going to happen, and, yes, it's going to disturb you very much, and then he says (according to another translation): "Active love is a harsh and fearful thing compared to love in dreams."

Everyone has felt the sting of ingratitude. Often we see it in the people closest to us. Keep walking down that road and we'll reach the end of our patience. This is why Ignatius insisted that love should be expressed in deeds. Out there in the world is where we meet the limits of our abilities and learn to depend on God.

Father Zossima told the woman that harsh and dreadful active love will take her to the God who loves her. His advice for the journey: Always tell the truth. Avoid contempt of others and yourself. Avoid fear. And especially, don't be frightened by your own bad actions.

You *Don't Mind Waiting*

Act yourself as you know how Jesus would act.

— PETER FABER, SJ

One afternoon Peter Faber spent six hours waiting for a young man to show up for an appointment. He became quite annoyed; the guy had already missed two appointments. Faber, a person of some standing in the community, felt slighted. His valuable time was being wasted.

Then the Lord reminded Faber of a couple of things. "You, Peter, have calmly waited hour after hour for great noblemen and princes to see *you*. *You* didn't complain. You looked forward to the favors you were likely to receive." The Lord went on, "How often have you made *me* wait for *you*? I stand next to you, ready to speak, ready to love you, and you are busy with other matters. You don't want me to be annoyed. So treat this young man as I treat you, with compassion, and understanding, and patience."

Show the mercy toward others that God has shown you.

March 17

Loved Sinners

Examining himself carefully and preparing to die, he could not feel afraid for his sins or of being condemned, but he did feel embarrassment and sorrow, as he believed he had not used well the gifts and graces which God our Lord had granted him.

— The Autobiography of Ignatius Loyola

Ignatius describes a near-death experience in this story from his *Autobiography*. He was on a ship sailing from Spain to Italy when a fierce storm came up. The wind howled, the waves broke over the little vessel — and everyone on board prepared to die. In this extremity, Ignatius's main feeling was sadness that he had to leave this life without making more use of the gifts and graces God had given him. He was mindful of his sins, but not overly bothered by them.

A year or so earlier, Ignatius's attitude was very different. He had fallen gravely ill and feared for his life; he was tormented by his sinfulness. He would confess the same sins over and over, unable to receive God's forgiveness. He was terrified that his soul was lost.

In the interim, Ignatius had come to see that he was a loved sinner — profoundly damaged and yet, by a miracle of grace, redeemed and set free. It's a paradoxical truth: We are deeply flawed yet called to be companions of Jesus and his partners in his ongoing work of healing the world.

Blind Eye to Imperfections

Father Ignatius says that God deals with us differently than do worldly human beings. They look to find whatever is bad or imperfect in our actions, they take note of it and then hold it against us. God, however, looks to see what good we have done, and closes an eye to our imperfections.

— Jerome Nadal, SJ

We're drawn to flaws and faults. We notice people's flaws more readily than their strengths. We experience pain but not painlessness. Negative product reviews on Amazon are twice as likely to be read than positive ones.

It's the other way around with God. He turns a blind eye to our imperfections, according to Jerome Nadal, Ignatius's chief deputy. This doesn't mean that we can ignore our faults. Nadal was a big advocate of regular self-reflection and disciplined work to eliminate one's faults and shortcomings. The fact that God turns a blind eye to our imperfections doesn't mean that we can, too.

Nadal's comment is about what God is like. He's not an accountant-in-the-sky keeping track of our sins and failures in a giant ledger. God is love; fault finding isn't one of his interests. Nadal's comment is also about what human beings are like. *We* are the accountants; we make careful note of others' failures and we hold it against them. Let's try to be more like God, letting others' faults go unnoticed.

March 19

A Hard Truth

One of the hardest truths about God for many of us to stomach is that Jesus died for the ungodly as well as the godly. Jesus died for everyone, including the worst sinners we can think of. And thank God that this is true. Each one of us knows that there are dark places within us that make us capable of great evil. Jesus died for those parts of us as well as for the serial killers and rapists of our world.

— WILLIAM A. BARRY, SJ

Some Christian thinkers think that everyone will ultimately be saved. They dissent from the mainstream Christian teaching that some people, perhaps many, will be lost to hell or oblivion. They point out that Jesus died for everyone. Certainly it was his desire that everyone be saved. Can God's desire be thwarted?

The idea that all will be saved has great appeal — at least initially. But it loses some of its charm when we realize that "everyone" includes the greatest monsters in history — mass murderers, terrorists, architects of genocide, serial killers, and rapists. What about justice? Surely the really bad people won't be saved because they don't deserve it. That implies that some will be saved because they *do* deserve it. But no one is in a position to make that claim. We're all sinners, saved by the grace of God. We are sinners, but we're loved anyway. The miracle isn't that Hitler is saved. It's that *anyone* is saved.

"All Possible Love, Modesty, and Charity"

The Jesuits took the road of love, to their great success and the benefit of those they served.

— CHRIS LOWNEY

Machiavelli thought that human beings were "ungrateful, fickle, liars and deceivers, fearful of danger and greedy for gain." To rule such people, Machiavelli said that leaders should follow the axiom that "it is better to be feared than loved."

Ignatius took the opposite approach: It's better for leaders to be loved than feared. He wanted his Jesuit brothers to be bound together with warm affection. He instructed superiors to govern with love and sympathy — with "all possible love, modesty, and charity," as he put it in the *Constitutions* of the Jesuit order. This was at a time when members of religious orders were often judged by how well they observed a myriad of rules. Many religious houses had a jail cell where recalcitrant members were punished.

Apply the "love test" to your circles. If you are responsible for others, do you govern with "all possible love, modesty, and charity"? Do they love you? Does love and sympathy characterize your family, your church, your associations and workplace?

March 21

Cold and Bitter Zeal

The love of many is growing cold. Those in charge of charitable works are impatient and unkind; they have little faith or hope. In both church and secular society many people would utterly suppress abuses, but they are moved more by a glacial impatience and a bitter zeal for justice than by the tender zeal that comes from love.

— Peter Faber, SJ

We know the people Faber is talking about. The progressive reformer who operates ruthlessly. The caustic teacher. The dogmatic therapist. The heartless administrator of a non-profit agency. The indifferent pastor who mails it in week after week. Their love has grown cold.

Perhaps Faber's complaint is naïve idealism unsuited to the real world. People say: "That's the way people are," "You have to crack a few eggs to make an omelet," "Who cares about motives so long as we get the job done?" But the Ignatian view is that motives and fervor matter a lot. Love drives the pursuit of justice. Love sustains good works in the long run.

Master Your Thoughts

The only thing we can do about people is to love them.
— DOROTHY DAY

Ignatius's friend Peter Faber had a two-pronged strategy to deal with bad thoughts about other people. Don't let such thoughts into your mind, but when they come, as they will, turn them into good thoughts. It's an application of Ignatius's principle of *agere contra*: desire the opposite. If you're feeling possessive of your stuff, give some of it away. If you're angry at someone, do something nice for them. If you think poorly of someone, find a reason to think well of them.

Try it. The aunt who won't talk to half the people in the family? Well, she talks to the other half, and her children love her. The colleague who doesn't like your ideas? He's a hard worker and has some pretty good ideas himself. The politician whose ideas you loathe? Grappling with those ideas has helped you clarify your own.

Master your thoughts. Don't let them master you.

Not Necessary but Wanted

I have never had such a clear experience of living on borrowed time, of living by sheer grace, and wish that I could keep it before my eyes always.

— WILLIAM A. BARRY, SJ

The Jesuit spiritual director William Barry tells a story. He was a provincial superior burdened with many responsibilities. He took a walk one day, anxious about his problems, unsure of himself, wishing he was doing something else. Then God spoke. Writes Barry:

> *"You are not necessary, but wanted,"* is what I heard God saying to me. The thought flashed through my mind, "You could be dead now." I broke out in a smile. It was true. I could have been dead, and someone else would be provincial; the province would go on without my so-called leadership. I am not necessary, but, for God's own reasons, I was wanted at that time not only in this position but in this world.

It's a terrible burden to be necessary. If you're the indispensable person the world can't do without, you're in big trouble. You'll be plagued by anxiety and dogged by looming failure because you think the success of the venture depends on you. The truth is that success or failure doesn't depend on you. You are not *necessary*. Instead, you are *wanted*. God wants you to do the work you're doing, to love the people he puts in your life. You're here because God wants you to be here.

The Conversational Apostle

Private spiritual conversation is an excellent method of helping our neighbor. It is the special quality of the conversational apostle to quietly and slowly win over his neighbor, to deal with him gently and light the flame of charity in his heart.

— JEROME NADAL, SJ

People learning a new language and settling into a new culture won't feel at home until they learn the skills of conversation. In ESL classes, people learn the arts of small talk and chitchat: Nasty weather, isn't it? How was the traffic? Any plans for the weekend? Gradually they learn how to talk about things that really matter.

Simple conversation is the grease for the wheels of social life. It turns strangers into acquaintances. It opens the door to friendship. It creates the atmosphere where serious discussion is possible. The early Jesuits took conversation seriously. The "conversational apostle" had a genuine regard for the other person. Conversation focused on what *they* were interested in.

This is one of the small ways we express love. Don't stay silent in a group. Reach out to the shy guy at a party. Make conversation an opportunity to get to know others and not just a chance to express your own views.

March 25

Spending Time

Haven't we all spent time with a close friend who was ill or depressed, even when the time was painful and difficult? Such time spent cannot be explained on utilitarian grounds. We spend that time because we love our friend for his or her own sake.

— WILLIAM A. BARRY, SJ

Your friend is sick, grieving, depressed, afflicted. The situation can't be fixed. You can't say anything that hasn't already been said. Yet here you are, at their side, listening to them, or just sitting together in silence. Why? Not because you're getting much out of it. Not because it will make you feel better; not even because it will make your friend feel better. You're there because you *want* to be there and your friend wants you to be there. You are drawn together by the bonds of love.

It's an analogy to our relationship with God. In the Ignatian view, we pray because we want to be with God. Prayer might make us feel better. It might fill us with energy and insight. But the essence of it is simply being with each other, spending time because you want to spend time.

Only Compassion, Not Judgment

For the virtues and good deeds of others let there be sweet rejoicing; for the opposite, if they be known for sure, let there be only compassion, not judgment.

— JEROME NADAL, SJ

Nadal made this comment in a treatise about how Jesuits should work together. *When someone screws up, have compassion*. It's pretty good advice for any workplace, any family, any marriage — any enterprise involving two or more people. Compassion is the ability to feel for other people, to understand what it is like to be them. It's hard to judge someone harshly when you can see things through their eyes.

Notice Nadal's caveat: Have compassion for shortcomings *if they be known for sure*. Your judgment could very well be wrong. You almost certainly don't have the whole picture. You view the part of the picture you *do* have through filters of bias and cognitive errors. It's wiser to suspend judgment and have compassion instead.

Compassion is an everyday virtue. It's not just for special hard times.

March 27

The Joy of Work

In their work they should find an inner joy, a serenity in judgment, a relish, a light, a reassuring step forward, a clarification of insight.

— Jerome Nadal, SJ

Nadal sounds a little like a typical CEO mouthing platitudes at a company meeting: "Here at Transformative Tech Corp., our people find joy, serenity." But Nadal sincerely believes it, and it's actually a quite striking claim about our work. Our work is an integral part of our spiritual lives. We should experience the same joy, peace, and wonder in our work that we do in our prayer.

This is a key Ignatian idea. There's no separation between work and the spiritual life. We don't experience God quietly at home and then encounter "not God" in the workplace. What we do all day is part of our spiritual life. We might say it *is* our spiritual life. Our work is where we encounter God.

We find God everywhere. He is present in all things, including our work.

Where Is Your Treasure?

"Heart" refers to our inner orientation, the core of our being. This kind of "heart" is what Jesus was referring to when he told us to store up treasures in heaven instead of on earth, "for where your treasure is, there also will your heart be."

— David L. Fleming, SJ

Jesus didn't care much about external signs of piety. He scorned the pious Pharisee making a big show of his devotion in the Temple: "God, I thank you that I am not like other men — thieves, adulterers." When you pray, Jesus said, do it at home where no one else can see you.

Jesus was much more concerned about the heart — our inner essence. This is the "heart" we mean when we say to a friend in distress, "My heart goes out to you." This isn't simply sympathy or understanding. It means something like, "I stand with you in this." This is also the "heart" we mean when we say, "My heart's not in it."

Is your heart in it? What do you love? What do you want?

March 29

A Search for Truth and Love

Being a Christian is more of a search for genuine truth and love than a secure position of certainty from which to survey the world and pass judgment.

— DAVID LONSDALE

One approach to being a Christian emphasizes thinking: Get it figured out, settle on the correct beliefs, and all will be well. Trouble is, this approach often makes little difference in how we live.

The other approach emphasizes action: Let the gospel shape the way you live, and all will be well. This approach also clarifies your thinking. The gospel is full of paradoxes and mysteries. The weak are strong, the poor are rich, the humble are honored, the meek will inherit the earth. None of this makes much sense until love rules your life.

Being a Christian is action, not ideas — a journey, not a place.

Love Will Decide Everything

Nothing is more practical than finding God, than falling in Love in a quite absolute, final way. What you are in love with, what seizes your imagination, will affect everything. It will decide what will get you out of bed in the morning, what you do with your evenings, how you spend your weekends, what you read, whom you know, what breaks your heart, and what amazes you with joy and gratitude. Fall in Love, stay in love, and it will decide everything?

— ATTRIBUTED TO PEDRO ARRUPE, SJ

We don't usually think about falling in love as something *practical*. Quite the opposite: Falling in love is utopian, visionary, romantic — blue-sky stuff compared to the nitty-gritty of ordinary life.

But what could be more practical than love? If you love someone, every single thing about your life is different because of it: where you live, what you do for work, what time you go to bed and get up in the morning, what you eat for dinner, who your friends are, and what you watch on TV. Love is a feeling and a commitment; it's also a way of life.

Ordinary Love

There is nothing we can do but love. Dear God, please enlarge our hearts to love each other, to love our neighbor, to love our enemy as our friend.

— DOROTHY DAY

"Love" can be abstract — a thought, a concept, a tad impersonal. But it's as close as the people you live and work with — in the next room, the next cubicle, at the receiving end of the next text message you send. "I really only love God as much as I love the person I love the least," said Dorothy Day.

April

FREEDOM

We try to be formed and held and kept by him,
but instead he offers us freedom. And now when I try to know
his will, his kindness floods me, his great love overwhelms me,
and I hear him whisper, Surprise me.

— RON HANSEN, *MARIETTE IN ECSTASY*

April 1

Free to Choose Well

You desire freedom from anything that prevents you from following along the way. You want to free yourself from any excess baggage. You want, as Ignatius said, to be free of "disordered attachments."

— JAMES MARTIN, SJ

Ignatius invites us to imagine our life as a journey, a path, and not necessarily a linear one. It's more like a meandering spiral, with tangents and digressions and an occasional cul-de-sac, a journey driven by reflection, choice, further reflection, more choices, all the while taking us into deeper experience of God. To walk this path, we need to make good choices, and to choose well we need to be free. That's the essence of the Ignatian idea of freedom.

The specific freedom we seek is freedom from "disordered attachments" — those cravings and passions and yearnings that cloud our minds. This makes freedom very concrete. It's not a philosophical abstraction or a political slogan. It involves our deepest yearnings. It affects our life choices: who we live with, what we do. It affects our everyday choices. Freedom is important, and there's nothing easy about it.

April 2

A Strange Error

The logic of worldly success rests on a fallacy: the strange error that our perfection depends on the thoughts and opinions and applause of other men! A weird life it is, indeed, to be living always in somebody else's imagination, as if that were the only place in which one could at last become real!

— THOMAS MERTON

Ignatius thought that our hunger to be noticed, to gain others' esteem and admiration, was a great spiritual hazard. It's not all bad; everyone wants others to think well of them. But to pursue honor, to make it a prime factor in our choices, leads to bad decisions and a life warped by vanity and pride. This is what "success" means in our world, says Thomas Merton — being seen as special, better than others. And it's a judgment rendered according to the values of others, not our own values, or God's.

This is something to regularly consider when we're deciding what's worthwhile. Are you doing something because it reflects your deep desires or because you hope it catches the attention of someone you're trying to impress? Have you chosen it freely? Or are you trying to win someone's favor?

April 3

Who Is Pushing Me?

Oh, the painstaking process of coming home to oneself, of being aware of what is going on! Where are these drives coming from? Who is pushing me?

— Anthony de Mello, SJ

One of the things that's pushing us is a defective idea of personal freedom. C. S. Lewis called it "my monstrous individualism." He wrote, "No word in my vocabulary expressed deeper hatred than the word Interference." He correctly saw that this idea of freedom was seriously at odds with Christianity. Christ, he said, was "a transcendental interferer." Ignatius thought that this hunger for personal freedom was one of the "disordered attachments" that stood in the way of true freedom.

Achieving real freedom is a complex, lifelong task. The Indian Jesuit teacher Anthony de Mello says it begins with awareness of what is going on inside. Where are these drives coming from? What is pushing you?

I Want It so Badly

The "I want it so badly" virus can infect any of us, in all sorts of decisions: I so wanted to get to the top of the company, or to attract that attractive person, or to be rich, or to be recognized as important, or to have the best house, or to have a more exciting life. In fact, we sometimes delude ourselves into thinking that the object of our affection (the job, the car, the partner, the house) must be right for us precisely because we want it so badly.

— CHRIS LOWNEY

Ignatius had two names for the ties that bind us: disordered attachments and disordered affections. These are the things that we are in love with, the ends we pursue, the things we spend our money on and that take up our time. They are *affections*; we love them, crave them, cultivate and nurture them. They are also *attachments*; they bind us, they come with us wherever we go. They are the things we *must* have.

Almost any desire or yearning can become a disordered attachment: to make money, to be admired, to give the orders instead of following them, to be physically fit, to enjoy sexual pleasure, to be in the know, to be cool. These are not necessarily *bad* things. The problem comes when these desires and affections become *disordered* — literally out of order. They crowd everything else out. Our truest, deepest desires — the things we *really* want — are buried under a pile of yearnings for money, success, luxury, sex, honor, power, or whatever it is we think we can't do without.

Ignatius would have us bring those desires into the light for scrutiny.

What Do You Really Want?

"Why do you want to get a PhD?" "I want to be as educated as possible." "Why do you want to be as educated as possible?" Is a PhD a condition of your worth? Do you need it because you will then be accepted and worthwhile and looked up to? Or is it because you wish to minister to others through teaching? In other words, do these and other decisions flow from freedom and love or from fear and compulsion?

— GERALD FAGIN, SJ

It's like peeling an artichoke. Or panning for gold. You sift through great heaps of dross to get to the nugget of your truest desire.

You've been offered a new job in another state, more money but more risk, not exactly your thing, but close. Why do you want this? *It's a step up, a challenge.* What's so important about a step up? *I've got to think about my career.* What *is* your "career"? *It's [fill in the blank].* Why are you doing this work? *I'm trained to do it. I've been doing it a long time.* What drew you to this work? *I found out I was pretty good at it.* No, what *drew* you to it? What deep desire does it satisfy?

When you know what you really want, you know what God wants.

April 6

Our Freedom Is Important to God

The freedom we have comes from God. We have it for a purpose. Your choices matter. God cares about them.

— J. MICHAEL SPAROUGH, SJ

One of C. S. Lewis's great literary creations was the devil Screwtape, whose thirty-one letters to his nephew, the demon Wormwood, are collected in *The Screwtape Letters*. Screwtape's job is to explain the ways of God (the Enemy) to his nephew, who is just getting started in the business of temptation. Here, Screwtape explains why God doesn't simply overwhelm human beings with a constant sense of his presence:

> He cannot ravish. He can only woo....He wants them to learn to walk and must therefore take away His hand; and if only the will to walk is really there He is pleased even with their stumbles. Do not be deceived, Wormwood. Our cause is never more in danger than when a human, no longer desiring, but still intending to do our Enemy's will, looks round upon a universe from which every trace of Him seems to have vanished, and asks why he has been forsaken, and still obeys.

In Lewis's (and Ignatius's) view, God goes to some pains to assure that our choice for him is free. The most important question is, What will you do with your freedom?

April 7

Ignatian Indifference

Therefore, we must make ourselves indifferent to all created things....
We should not prefer health to sickness, riches to poverty, honor to
dishonor, a long life to a short one.

— THE SPIRITUAL EXERCISES, 23

We've all seen a statue or a picture of the "scales of justice" — a blindfolded woman with a sword holding up a set of scales. The image symbolizes the ideal of impartiality. It promises that evidence will be weighed carefully and justice will be rendered fairly, without bias.

Ignatius says that we want to be the blind woman holding the scales but coolly detached from them. She has no stake in the outcome. This is what Ignatius means by indifference — the impartial stance we take when making an important decision or rendering a weighty judgment. Indifference is the solution to the problem of disordered attachments. It is detachment from one's biases and the willingness to carefully balance alternatives. It's a willingness to go wherever God wants to take us. Indifference is freedom to pursue what we most deeply want, which is what God wants.

April 8

Hidden Disabilities

The gospel invites us to enter the mystery of our own disabilities, hidden or otherwise. We need not fear those parts of our being we hide away and lock up: our failures and sins, our vanities and deceptions, our jealousies and fakery. He will reach out to touch us there.

— JOHN KAVANAUGH, SJ

Jesus healed eleven lepers in the gospels: a single man who approached him (Luke 5) and, later, a group of ten (Luke 17). Lepers were social outcasts. They were driven out of the community and condemned to loneliness and a miserable life of begging. They were doubly disabled — visibly with disease, and inwardly by their neighbors' fear and rejection. Jesus healed both kinds of damage, and the gospel stories make it clear that the greater healing was the healing of the spirit.

So it is with us. Our invisible wounds are usually more painful than the visible ones. And they are easier to hide. The visibly marred have an advantage; they can't hide their weaknesses. They can't pretend that all is well when everyone can see that they are impaired, ill, old and frail, homebound and limited. But we can bury our inner wounds pretty easily — or try to.

Freedom comes from admitting our innermost wounds and asking for healing. It's counterintuitive; it doesn't feel like freedom to expose our inner flaws. But it is true freedom. To do otherwise, to hide our weaknesses, is to remain in bondage.

April 9

Freedom from Influence

If [the candidate] says that he was not moved by any member of the society, the examiner should proceed. If the candidate says that he was so moved, give him a period of some time, in order that, by reflecting on the matter, he may commend himself completely to his creator and Lord as if no member of the society had moved him.

— The Constitutions of the Society of Jesus, 51

Ignatius took freedom so seriously that he wrote a stringent rule into the constitutions of the Jesuit order: If another Jesuit had ever encouraged a man to apply for the order, the candidate was to take some extra time to reflect and pray on the matter. Ignatius worried that the encouragement might influence his decision. That's a pretty tough rule. Probably most of the young men thinking about entering the Jesuits had been encouraged by other Jesuits at some point. In fact, you'd think that Ignatius would *want* Jesuits to spot and recruit new talent.

Ignatius wanted candidates to make a perfectly free decision to join the order. He knew that they were influenced by their teachers, family, friends, social norms, love of learning and adventure, and a host of other things. He wanted them to be sure these things didn't unduly influence their decision. He wanted them to achieve a posture of neutrality, aware of pressures but free of their influence.

The Tech Monster

I know of no other force so pervasive, so strong, and so seductive as the consumer ideology of capitalism and its fascination for endless accumulation, extended working hours, the drumming up of novel need fulfillments, the theologizing of the mall, the touting of economic comparison, the craving for legitimacy through money and possessions, and unrelieved competition at every level of life.

— JOHN KAVANAUGH, SJ

Some of the smartest people in the world are working hard to develop apps and games and social networks so useful and attractive that we'll become addicted to them. We can stream more entertainment than we can ever watch right into our living room. We can look up anything on our phone. We can visit museums, listen to concerts, take courses at the best universities online. We can be with our friends, express our opinions, and explore odd interests without getting off our couch. We can fritter away all our time in countless pleasant ways. It doesn't seem like a fair fight. If you worry about your freedom, worry about this.

To begin to deal with the tech-enabled monster that is our culture, try to at least become *aware* of the extent of these influences on you. Then decide to be *intentional* about your exposure to the online world. Engage it on *your* terms.

April 11

Façades

In our own attempts to fit in and find some semblance of acceptance by others, we create façades that, paradoxically, prevent ourselves from ever truly being known, ever truly being accepted by others in any honest way. Our attempts to fit in and to connect lead us to create external appearances that serve only as barriers to being truly known, truly accepted, to truly fitting in.

— JOSEPH WAGNER, SJ

It's a dilemma. We adapt ourselves to the social worlds we inhabit, but in doing this we create façades that hide who we really are. Our friends don't really know us. We're strangers to the people we work with. Even the people closest to us wonder who we are sometimes.

The dilemma is that making these façades is often the right thing to do. It's right to drag our surly selves out of the house and into the society of others. We put a smile on our face, show up when we'd rather be home, and work on a project that's not as interesting as the one we had in mind. This is what's necessary to live life. But the façade has a price, and it's a steep one if the façade extends into our most intimate relationships. And because the façade covers the more disagreeable and unpleasant parts of ourselves, we can start believing in the façade ourselves.

That's why we have to be careful not to be fooled by our adapted selves.

April 12

Hold It Lightly

I gladly and sincerely offer to turn over to you the office I now hold.

— IGNATIUS LOYOLA

Ignatius never wanted to be the superior general of the Jesuits. He initially refused the job when his brother Jesuits elected him in 1541. He turned out to be a brilliant leader, one of the greatest in the history of the church, but he never thought of himself as the Indispensable Man. He was genuinely detached from his job even though he did it well. A few years into Ignatius's tenure, Nicholas Bobadilla, one of the senior Jesuits, objected to his management style. Ignatius calmly replied that he would gladly turn over the job to Nicholas or anyone else the society named. "My desire is to have a lowly station and be without this weight of responsibility," he wrote. Ignatius had a big job that he held lightly.

Imagine you've just been told that today is your last day on your job. How attached are you to it?

A Time to Let Go

When a householder gets to see wrinkles on his body, white hair on his head, and his grandchildren, he should retire to the forest.

— MANU SAMHITA, 6

Classical Hindu philosophy says that a good life unfolds in four *ashramas*, or stages: student, householder, retired, and ascetic. The third stage is called *Vanaprastha*, whose name comes from two Sanskrit words meaning "retiring" and "forest." This is the stage starting in midlife in which we turn away from worldly success and become more interested in spirituality and service. The Manu Samhita, an ancient Hindu text, says this of the person who is retiring into the forest: "Let him be always industrious in privately reciting the Veda; let him be patient of hardships, friendly toward all, of collected mind, ever liberal and never a receiver of gifts, and compassionate toward all living creatures."

This is the time to move from "resumé virtues" into what the writer David Brooks calls "eulogy virtues." "Resumé virtues" are oriented to worldly accomplishment and success. "Eulogy virtues" are the qualities you'd want people to mention at your funeral: compassion, generosity, kindness, spiritual depth. You want people to say: "She loved her family and friends," not "She made a lot of money for the shareholders," or "He racked up a million frequent-flyer miles."

April 14

Slow Down, Be Smart

We will try not to have made our minds up before we have to. We will be alert to having deep-seated prejudices and to making implied or even overt demands on God....We will wait when alternatives are emerging. We will try not to favor one over the other until we are clear whether God is telling us something.

— Joseph Tetlow, SJ

Tetlow's description of the "indifferent" Ignatian state of mind highlights two points: *slow down* and *be smart*.

Slow down: Don't rush to make an important judgment or decision. Don't act until you have to. Sit with the ambiguity for a while. See what turns up.

Be smart: Especially be smart about your biases. You'll never be free of them. You will always be vulnerable to "confirmation bias" — the tendency to look for reasons to do what you've already decided you want to do. You're vulnerable to self-delusions. Take your weaknesses into account when you are making a decision; do what's necessary to compensate for them.

Indifferent to What Others Think

Stop wishing to catch the notice of men.

— PETER FABER, SJ

Ignatius thought that our hunger to be admired by others is a pernicious form of bondage. It invites others to set the agenda for our life, causing us to chase money and power, suppress our true opinions, do work we don't like, hang out with disagreeable people — all because other people think these things are important.

Ignatius lived in an age that was obsessed with status. The worst thing imaginable was to be thought a person of no account. But Ignatius thought this was the *best* thing imaginable. He wanted people to be able to say, "I desire to be accounted as worthless and a fool for Christ, rather than be esteemed as wise and prudent in this world." A person who is indifferent to what others think is a person who is free.

April 16

No Assumptions

These people desire to get rid of the attachment, but in such a way that there remains no inclination to either keep the acquired money or to dispose of it. Instead such a one desires to keep it or reject it solely according to what God Our Lord will move one's will to choose.

— THE SPIRITUAL EXERCISES, 155

Most religions admire their strictest practitioners. A Hindu spiritual ideal is to become a *sadhu*, an ascetic who has renounced worldly life. Many Christian saints are men and women who embraced penances and strict bodily discipline. There's a notion, often not explicitly stated, that the hardest path is the best one — that God prefers that we do the most difficult, most disagreeable thing.

This isn't the Ignatian attitude. Ignatius laid out his view in a parable about three people who must decide what to do about a great fortune they've unexpectedly received. Two take positions that allow them to keep some control of it. The third resolves to follow wherever God leads — "to rid himself of it so that he has even no liking for it, to keep the fortune or not to keep it."

Most of us assume that God probably wants the third person to give the fortune to the poor and walk away. That's the Christian ideal, isn't it? Not necessarily. God might want them to keep it and be known to all the world as a lucky Christian who has stumbled into wealth through no effort of their own. True freedom allows for that possibility.

April 17

Do the Opposite

You can help yourself by using the "Act against It!" method. This is far from a dubious ascetic practice: It is a strategy for surviving and overcoming desolation and getting moving again on the journey home to wholeness.

— MARGARET SILF

Several important Ignatian ideas are given extra gravitas for a modern audience by being rendered in Latin. One is *agere contra*, which means "do the opposite."

This is a bit of spiritual psychology to deal with troublesome desires. Don't just resist them and hope they go away; do the opposite. If you're feeling sorry for yourself and want to be alone, get together with your friends. If you're worried about money, give some of it away. If you're angry at someone, tell others how good they are.

"Do the opposite" means *doing* something. It illustrates the vigilant assertiveness that permeates the Ignatian outlook. Don't get comfortable. Beware of settling in. Always be alert for the next thing the Lord is calling you to do.

April 18

Sensible Simplicity

The Ignatian approach to a simple life does not ask you to become a half-naked, twig-eating, cave-dwelling hermit. It simply invites you to live simply. It is a sensible simplicity. A moderate asceticism. A healthy poverty.

— JAMES MARTIN, SJ

Christian attitudes toward lifestyle run the gamut from prosperity gospel luxury to monastic poverty. The Ignatian view is somewhere in the middle; it advocates a simple lifestyle: adequate housing, healthful food, modest diversions and entertainments. Nothing fancy, nothing that says "look at me." It's a practical mindset. A simple lifestyle frees you for the work you're doing. It takes a lot of work to acquire more than you need, and more labor to maintain and protect it. A simple lifestyle is freer.

April 19

Scruples

Although he was practically convinced that those scruples did him much harm and that it would be good to be rid of them, he could not break himself off.... He shouted out loud to God, saying, "Help me, Lord, for I find no remedy in men nor in any creature."

— *The Autobiography of Ignatius Loyola*

In the year after his conversion, Ignatius wandered in the hell of morbid scrupulosity. He was obsessed by memories of his sins. He compulsively examined the details of them. He couldn't shake a feeling of pathological guilt. He confessed the same sins over and over again, thinking that God had not truly forgiven him. Ignatius *knew* all this was wrong, that his scruples were lies, that God *had* forgiven him, that he was not an evil person. But his heart couldn't accept what he knew to be true.

The problem was Ignatius's defective idea of God. He clung to the old mental model of God as a harsh celestial accountant looking for sins and failures even though he had experienced a God of forgiveness and peace. Ignatius mastered his scruples when he made a decision to throw in his lot with the loving God. He decided to act as if God had forgiven his sins. He stopped confessing them. He dwelled on the many ways God had blessed him. He had to make a choice. He acted in faith. This was the breakthrough that freed him from scruples.

Doing God's Will

God's will, therefore, becomes not something remote and unknow-
able (that I will be punished for not carrying out!) but something as
close to me as the deepest desire of my own heart.

— MARGARET SILF

"God's will" is often thought to be something outside ourselves — a blueprint, a plan devised by a cosmic engineer.
But in the Ignatian view, "doing God's will" is a mutual thing.
It occurs within a loving relationship. God's will is implanted
in our hearts, and there is no one right answer. The good is
plural. God is abundant, not limiting. Most of our choices
are among the good, better, and best — not right and wrong.
Doing God's will is a matter of growing into the kind of person we're meant to be. The question to ask is: Is this action
consistent with who I am and who I want to become?

We don't seek out the will of God; we create it. When we
freely choose what seems best in this time and place, *that's*
what God wants to happen.

April 21

Give People Space

The one who explains to another the method and order of meditating or contemplating should narrate exactly the facts of the contemplation or meditation. Let him adhere to the points, and add only a short or summary explanation.

— THE SPIRITUAL EXERCISES, 2

The spiritual marketplace is full of teachers, gurus, sages, and other spiritual authorities who are happy to take us under their wing and explain the mysteries of God. In the Ignatian world, though, teachers (usually called spiritual directors) are remarkably hands-off. The first rule is: Don't lay down any rules! The second: Don't explain too much!

In his autobiography, Ignatius says that God taught him directly, like a schoolmaster teaches a child. He thought everyone should learn this way. Spiritual directors are warned not to explain material for contemplation at great length. People are to find the meaning for themselves. He explains: "This brings more spiritual relish and spiritual fruit than if the one giving the Exercises had lengthily explained and amplified the meaning of the history."

Parents, teachers, managers, experts, "helpers" of all kinds — take heed. Give people freedom to find the meaning for themselves.

April 22

Seeing God's Back

Moses said, "Show me your glory, I pray." And the LORD said, "I will make all my goodness pass before you. But," he said, "you cannot see my face; for no one shall see me and live." And the LORD continued, "See, there is a place by me where you shall stand on the rock; and while my glory passes by I will put you in a cleft of the rock, and I will cover you with my hand until I have passed by; then I will take away my hand, and you shall see my back; but my face shall not be seen."

— EXODUS 33:18-23

What a disappointment! Moses wants to experience God directly, to "see" him — something all of us want — but God says no, that's not possible. "You're not permitted to see my face. But I'll do this. Hide behind this rock here and avert your eyes while I'm passing through. But then after I've passed by, open your eyes and you'll be able to see my back."

The point of this enigmatic story is that we find God indirectly. We see him most clearly in retrospect, when we reflect on our work, our relationships, our desires. This is the characteristic flavor of Ignatian prayer. We can find God when we take the time to examine the life we lead. We don't see his face directly, but we can always see his "back" — the unmistakable signs of his loving presence.

April 23

Ashamed

Many people do not get the help they need because they are ashamed to ask for it. The reality is that most people react with admiration when someone admits the truth that will set him or her free. The requirement for membership in the Christian church is similar to that of AA. One need only say, "I'm Joe, and I'm a sinner in need of salvation."

— WILLIAM A. BARRY, SJ

Shame. Nothing is more debilitating. You look repulsive in a bathing suit. Someone smirks when you mispronounce a word. You show up for a meeting on the wrong day. You wish you could sink into the ground and disappear. Shame is worse when you've really done something wrong. You've broken a promise. You've lied. You've spread nasty gossip about a friend. You're hiding a drinking problem. Your marriage is falling apart. The message shame sends is directed at the self: *I'm a defective person, a failure, and asking for help would just let others in on the dirty little secret.*

But it's a false story. You're not a bad person but a sinner in need of salvation like everyone else. Don't let shame prevent you from getting the help you need.

Training in Freedom

The third experience is to spend another month in making a pilgrimage without money, begging from door to door at times, for the love of God our Lord, in order to grow accustomed to discomfort in food and lodging.

— THE CONSTITUTIONS OF THE SOCIETY OF JESUS, 67

As part of their training, Jesuits go through assignments designed to make them uncomfortable. They do lowly jobs in Jesuit communities and spend extended periods of time living with poor people. The most rigorous of these "experiments" is what Ignatius called a "pilgrimage" — a long journey without enough money to finish it. A young Jesuit in Los Angeles might be given a bus ticket, a hundred dollars, and told to show up at a Jesuit house in New York in a month's time. The person will have to find work, make friends, bed down where they can at night, and generally learn to depend on God and the kindness of strangers.

These "experiments" strip away status and redefine "necessities." They teach trust and freedom. In Ignatius's words: "This so the candidate, through abandoning all the reliance on money, may with genuine faith and intense love place his reliance entirely in his creator and Lord."

April 25

Freedom Takes Time

It is a measure of our megalomania, but also of our helplessness, that we often feel that even the grace of God cannot overcome our resistance to love and to forgive as Jesus loves and forgives.

— WILLIAM A. BARRY, SJ

Jesus's command is simple — "love one another" — but human hearts are complex. How can a rape victim forgive the rapist? How can someone love the unlovable? We think we have forgiven someone and repaired a relationship, but doubts and bad feelings persist. We are flawed creatures with hearts that are capable of loving and hating the same person, of wanting to forgive and not to forgive at the same time. We need God's help to love, and since God usually works through the ordinary processes of human psychology, we can expect that this will take some time. We must allow the spirit of love to work through all the layers of unloving, especially that last layer where we hold the memories of past hurts close.

April 26

Biased Judgment

You're a slave, a bound helpless slave to one thing in the world, your imagination.... You let your imagination shinny on the side of your desires for a few hours, and then you decide. Naturally your imagination, after a little freedom, thinks up a million reasons why you should stay, so your decision when it comes isn't true. It's biased.

— F. Scott Fitzgerald, *This Side of Paradise*

The speaker is Clara Page, a shrewd young woman who takes the measure of Amory Blaine, the charming and feckless protagonist of Fitzgerald's novel. Amory agrees with her criticism and blames his lack of willpower. Clara, whose name means "bright and clear" replies: "This has nothing to do with will-power; that's a crazy, useless word, anyway; you lack judgment — the judgment to decide at once when you know your imagination will play you false."

"People aren't rational, they rationalize," wrote the psychologists Daniel Kahneman and Amos Tversky. Many of our choices aren't free at all. They're determined by deep desires, often operating unconsciously. Our imagination steps in to think up a million reasons to do what we want to do. Finally, our "reason" makes up a story about why we act the way we do.

The remedy is to employ our good judgment. You *know* how easily your desires can mislead you. Act on what you know.

Strip Away the Vanity

Almost everything in life was vanity — success a vanity, privilege a vanity, Europe a vanity, beauty a vanity. When you stripped away the vanity and stood alone before God, what was left? Only loving your neighbor as yourself. Only worshiping the Lord, Sunday after Sunday.

— JONATHAN FRANZEN, *CROSSROADS*

Ignatius's program for good decisions and a happy life has two parts: Keep your eye on what matters most and get free of disordered attachments. To achieve this perspective, he suggests imagining yourself on your deathbed. What matters now? Not success, status, beauty, or power. It's the people in your life and how you loved them. It's your integrity. It's God. Did you become the person you were meant to be?

April 28

Freedom in Suffering

Are we responsible for our unmerited suffering? The answer is no. And yes. We are not responsible for our predicament as its cause — whether it be cancer or job loss or the death of a child or spouse. But we are responsible for what we do with the effects, for what we build from the rubble that fate has made of our lives.

— WILLIAM J. O'MALLEY, SJ

We can't do anything about the storms in our lives, but we can choose how we respond to them. In his classic memoir *Man's Search for Meaning*, the psychiatrist Viktor Frankl saw people exercising freedom in concentration camps, in the extremity of suffering, where everything had been stripped away. Even there, people possessed "the last of human freedoms — the ability to choose one's attitude in a given set of circumstances."

We suffer in many circumstances, but God is always there. That's the point of the gospel story about Jesus and his disciples in a storm on the Sea of Galilee. The disciples were terrified, fearing for their lives. Jesus calmed the storm with a word, then he asked, "Why were you afraid? *I* am with you." What matters is not Jesus's miracle-working power over nature but the comforting power of his presence. We can turn to him no matter how terrible the circumstances.

April 29

No Illusions

I've heard contemplation defined as "anything that dismantles illusions." To sit in honest contemplation with my actions or wants, hard as it is to admit, reveals their disordered nature. It also reveals their true nature as well. Rather than completely deny the object of my attachment, I seek only to hold it openly, in ways that free my soul from fear.

— LISA KELLY

Our disordered attachments are seldom completely disordered. There's usually something genuine and valid about them, too. Honest reflection will take both facts into account.

You're thinking about the need to make more money. On the one hand, you feel considerable anxiety about your finances, and if anxiety rules, you realize that this could lead to bad choices. On the other hand, it looks like you really *do* need to make more money. The bills are coming in. *Some* anxiety doesn't seem out of place. In sorting this out, ask what's illusory and what's real. Here the disorder is anxiety, not the concern for money. You may not be able to completely rid yourself of anxiety, but at least you can understand that it's *your* creation — the way you are responding to the problem.

April 30

What Freedom Is For

The really important kind of freedom involves attention and aware-ness and discipline, and being able truly to care about other people and to sacrifice for them over and over in myriad petty, unsexy ways every day.

— David Foster Wallace

Freedom is prized in many circles today as an end in itself, but in the Ignatian perspective, freedom is a means to an end — the service of God and other people. Says the Jesuit *Constitutions*, "The ideal is an unconditional consecration to mission, free of any worldly interest, and free to serve all men and women." That's why we do all the hard work of achieving indifference and becoming free of disordered attachments — to make good choices so we can serve freely and effectively. As the Jesuit philosopher John Kavanaugh says, "Our freedom is only realized when we give ourselves away in love."

Our service might involve big, visible projects like the schools, refugee camps, and other ministries that the Jesu-its are known for. But as the novelist David Foster Wallace reminds us, the most important service is taking care of the people in our lives in small, humble ways. That's why we want to be free.

REFLECTION

May

WORK

Everywhere there is good to be done,
everywhere there is something to be planted or harvested.

— PETER FABER, SJ

May 1

Repairing the World

Before God created this world, he created worlds and destroyed them, created worlds and destroyed them. He said, "These I don't like. These I don't like." Then he created this world. He said, "This one I like."

— Midrash Rabbah, Kohelet 3:14

God gives us plenty of work to do. The early Jewish rabbis spoke of *tikkun olam* — "repairing the world." God's creation is not a one-time thing; it continues and we are charged with doing the work. It's also been damaged and needs to be repaired; we are the fixers, the engineers, the reformers, the craftspeople, the helpers, the inventors, the tinkerers. Our job is to repair a broken world where evil too often overshadows the good, and where too many people lack what they need to live in dignity.

Ignatius imagined God as a laborer hard at work in the world, and Christ as the leader calling his people to join him in the sacred task of fixing what is wrong. "Whoever wishes to come with me must labor with me," he said. We do our work *with* Christ. We're his partners, working alongside him in the trenches.

May 2

Jesus Knows about Work

Christ our king calls us to be with him. The essence of the call is not to do some specific work, but, above all, to be with the One who calls. We are to share Christ's life, to think like him, to do what he does.

— DAVID L. FLEMING, SJ

Jesus was a worker, a *tekton*, usually translated as "carpenter," but also "craftsman" and "stonemason." He ran a small business: He estimated jobs, negotiated deals, figured out how to make a profit, paid his suppliers, and went after customers who owed him money. He went to sleep exhausted at night and got up before dawn to do it all over again. Jesus knows work intimately.

Ignatius thought that we need to know Jesus as a worker if we're to know him at all. In work, we learn gratitude, patience, generosity, and courage. In work, we learn about our limitations. In work, we encounter God every day, because God is a worker like we are.

Where Is Your True Calling?

You will know your vocation by the joy that it brings you. You will know. You will know when it's right.

— DOROTHY DAY

Your calling isn't synonymous with your career. What you do from nine to five might not be your biggest contribution to repairing the world. In fact, it probably isn't.

If you have children, being a parent and grandparent is more important than anything you'll do at the office. Your true calling might be coaching youth sports teams, sitting on the school board, tutoring, making your community cleaner, more inclusive, more just. It might lie in volunteer work in churches, soup kitchens, hospitals, schools, museums, and arts organizations. Your calling might be to paint, make music, or perform in community theater. Your calling might be to be a great aunt or uncle, cousin, friend.

Heed Dorothy Day's advice: You will know your vocation by the joy it brings you. In Ignatian language, you'll know your calling when you know what you really want.

May 4

Doing the Lowliest Tasks

My nine friends in the Lord arrived here from Paris in mid-January. They came braving the wars and the biting cold of winter, and on arrival they settled in two hospitals to serve the sick and the poor in the lowliest tasks.

— IGNATIUS LOYOLA

In the winter of 1537, the young men who were to become the first Jesuits joined Ignatius in Venice; they immediately started serving the sick and poor "in the lowliest tasks." This isn't what educated clerics and teachers ordinarily did, then or now, but Ignatius's friends were just following the example of their leader. While he was a student, Ignatius spent a good deal of time working in hospitals. He often begged for his daily bread. All his life he avoided the trappings of wealth and comfort. No work was too menial. In fact, humble work and lowly people were to be preferred.

Ignatius and his companions did this in conscious imitation of Christ. Since Jesus was poor, preferred the company of poor people, and healed the sick and afflicted, they wanted to do those things, too.

What "lowly tasks" are available to you?

Fake It till You Make It

Always serve Christ the Lord with gladness.
— PETER FABER, SJ

If you want a mood lift, spend a few minutes looking at Norman Rockwell's paintings. They are suffused with joy and sly humor. Look at *Freedom from Want*, his scene of a happy family sitting down to Thanksgiving dinner. Or *Girl with Black Eye* — a smirking girl, clearly the winner of a fight, waiting outside the principal's office. No wonder he is perhaps America's most beloved artist.

Rockwell also battled chronic depression his entire life. Sometimes he had to be hospitalized. His therapist, the famed analyst Erik Erikson, told him that he painted happiness but did not live it. Rockwell seems to have made a deliberate decision to depict a joy that he didn't feel as a strategy to counter his depression. It's a remarkable accomplishment and it worked; he had a productive career despite serious mental illness.

"Fake it till you make it" is actually a sound psychological principle. If you want to feel happy, act as if you already are. In time, your emotions will adjust to your actions and you will feel happier.

The World as It Is

I don't have it all worked out, but I'm ready. I want to try working with what I've got instead of wishing I had something else.

— MARK SALZMAN, *LYING AWAKE*

The speaker in Salzman's novel is Sister Miriam, a young novice who wants to become a better person — holier, more generous, more loving — before committing to her religious order. She finally sees this dream as a fantasy; she faces herself as she really is, flawed and destined to stay that way, and takes the step she has been wanting to make for a long time. Sister Miriam adapts to the world as it is — a pretty good place, but one in which she is something less than the paragon of perfect virtue she wants to be.

We're often told that we'll find our calling in life by following our dreams. But our dreams need to be adjusted to reality. It does no good to dream of playing major league baseball when our level of skill is more suited to a weekend beer league.

The Ignatian counsel is to reflect, reflect, reflect. Examine your dreams. Ask if they express your deepest desires or some superficial fancy. Examine the world around you — the world as it is. What opportunities does it offer for service that means something?

The Link between Anxiety and Laziness

Laziness causes a lifetime of anxiety. So rouse yourselves. Work with energy.

— IGNATIUS LOYOLA

Ignatius often warned about the dangers of laziness — and not just because the slothful person doesn't get important work done. He shrewdly noted the connection between idleness and anxiety. A lazy person is often an anxious one, restless and uneasy because they're aware of life passing them by. It works the other way, too. An anxious person is often idle because they're overcome by doubts about their ability to accomplish the task at hand. Ignatius didn't like excessive zeal either. White-hot fervor brings many problems; one of them, ironically, is sloth. The zealot gets burned out. The slothful person napping on the couch is the shell that's left over after the zealot has crashed.

Sloth is one of the seven deadly sins. The other six involve doing bad things; sloth is failing to do good things. Your neighbor needs your help. Rouse yourself and give it.

May 8

Love the Swamp

It is not enough to begin. We must, as far as possible, finish.

— IGNATIUS LOYOLA

Some call it the Dip. Or the Dark Swamp. It's the point where things get tough after you start something new. The new project or the new relationship is exciting for a while, and then problems crop up. Your ideas are met with resistance; your friend's quirks aren't so endearing; you work harder to accomplish less. As you slog along, the idea of quitting starts to seem like a good idea. Other projects, other people start to seem more promising than this muddle you're in now. So you quit, start something new, get excited, enter the Dark Swamp, and the whole process repeats itself. The danger is that you'll end up with a pile of regrets as you look back on years of bright ideas that somehow never made it.

Ignatian practice offers two remedies for this problem. The first is to identify your deepest, truest desires and make sure that new ventures flow from them. The second is to fall in love with the Dark Swamp. If you're doing what you really want, you'll enjoy solving the challenges, problems, and setbacks.

May 9

Go for It

We cannot choose correctly all the time. That plain fact inhibits many of us from making as many choices, and bold choices, as we ought to.

— CHRIS LOWNEY

The data shows that football teams should take more chances than they do. They should try to score touchdowns instead of settling for field goals. They should go for it on fourth down instead of punting. But too often coaches will make the cautious choice, even though the riskier option is objectively the better one. They're afraid of looking bad, thinking, *Something bad might happen, and I'll be blamed.*

Football coaches are no different from the rest of us. We'll go to great lengths to avoid looking bad. We'll settle for something safe instead doing the bold thing that might not work.

Ignatius would say, first, set aside worries about your reputation. You might be criticized; so what? Then look at the choice dispassionately; detach yourself from the emotions associated with either outcome. Be guided by a desire to do something good instead of avoiding something bad. Then make the best choice, understanding that the outcome isn't up to you.

One Foot Raised

The world is our house. Jesuits are in their most peaceful and pleasant house when they are constantly on the move, when they travel throughout the earth, when they have no place to call their own.

— JEROME NADAL, SJ

Many statues of Ignatius Loyola show him with "one foot raised" — toes planted, heel elevated, striding into an unknown future. It's an homage to his belief that Jesuits must always be on the move, ready for anything.

This attitude isn't just for Jesuits. It suits all of us, living as we do in a world of constant change. Sociologists say we can expect an important change in our lives every twelve to eighteen months. Really big changes, what author Bruce Feiler calls "lifequakes," happen five or more times in everyone's life. Then there are unpredictable disasters: the Covid pandemic, the 2008 financial crisis, the 9/11 terrorist attacks.

So it's not a bad idea to learn to live with "one foot raised." You're probably living that way already, whether you like it or not.

The Obstacle Becomes a Means

The revolution accomplished by St. Ignatius showed that that which appeared to be an obstacle could become a means.

— JEAN DANIELOU, SJ

The conventional wisdom in Ignatius's time held that a busy life was an obstacle to spiritual growth. It was thought that the best way to pursue holiness was to focus one's whole life on prayer, contemplation, and devotion, as monks and nuns were able to do. People with jobs and families and obligations in the community were out of luck.

Ignatius challenged these assumptions. He asked, Isn't God present in our experience of everyday life? If so, then maybe an active life in the world could be a *means* to holiness, not an impediment. If holiness means being like Christ, why not imitate the *active* Christ — the Christ who traveled all over the place with his friends, enjoying their company, meeting strangers, contending with enemies, attending weddings and festivals, healing the sick, and feeding the hungry? The new Ignatian spiritual ideal was the contemplative in action — the prayerful, reflective person who is fully engaged in the affairs of the world. Monks could pursue holiness, but so could busy, worldly people, finding God in places where he was thought to be absent.

How can you turn obstacles into means as Ignatius did? A tedious daily commute is an opportunity to pray and reflect. A baffling work problem is an occasion for humbly asking for help. The tedium of the daily grind is an invitation to patience and persistence. Find your way to God in your life as you live it.

May 12

Good Intentions Aren't Enough

You seem to hold that the use of natural helps for ends that are good is to bend the knee to Baal. The man who thinks this way has not learned how to use all things for God's glory.

— IGNATIUS LOYOLA

Ignatius insisted that Jesuits use every resource — worldly as well as spiritual — to advance their work. This didn't sit well with some critics. They thought that a fervent faith was sufficient. Raising money, enlisting the help of influential friends, honing one's secular skills — these sorts of things were "bending the knee to Baal," that is, leaning on dark spiritual forces to advance the work of God. We'll succeed because we trust God alone, they said.

A secular version of this attitude persists in our age. It's called the "planning fallacy" — the notion that all will be well because we have such a good plan. We don't need to anticipate troubles and prepare for contingencies because we're so smart, our enthusiasm is high, and our intentions are pure.

The Ignatian view is that we need all the help we can get. We should be especially skeptical of exalted claims about the strength of our faith and the purity of our intentions. These aren't sufficient — and they're not as impressive as we think they are.

May 13

God Is Already Here

The best Jesuit missionaries asked not, "Can we bring God to you?" but rather, "Where in your culture, in your profession, in your occupation, in your religious experience, in your life, does God already exist?"

— HOWARD GRAY, SJ

When the Jesuit missionary Matteo Ricci got to China in 1583, he ditched the traditional somber clothing of a European priest and dressed like a Chinese sage: "in violet silk, with the hem of the robe and collar and the edges bordered with a band of blue silk a little less than a palm wide." He dressed this way because he wanted to talk to Chinese scholars and learn from them. Since Ricci's Ignatian training told him that God could be found in all things, he asked: Where is God already working in China?

Most Christian missionaries thought they were bringing Christ to the unbelievers. The Ignatian view was that Christ was already working there. They were to find him and join him in that work. It's an attitude of thoughtful humility we would do well to emulate. God is already working in that muddled situation you find yourself in. Find him, and join him.

May 14

Finding God in a Dismal Job

I tried to explain that the pride I took in my work differed from the pride a communist might take in building up the new society. The difference lay in the motivation. As a Christian, I could share in their concern for building a better world. I could work as hard as they for the common good. The people who would benefit from my labors would be just that: people. Human beings. Families in need of shelter against the arctic weather.

— WALTER CISZEK, SJ

If you labor at a dismal job in a spirit-crushing workplace, be inspired by Walter Ciszek. He was an American Jesuit, unjustly accused of spying and imprisoned and exiled in Soviet Russia for more than twenty years. He spent many of those years building shelters in a Siberian prison camp. It was a truly miserable job. The work was brutal; the living conditions deplorable. Yet Ciszek found great meaning in his work. It benefited real flesh-and-blood human beings in the most direct way: by giving shelter from the cold.

Many of us are stuck in less than satisfying jobs. But, like Ciszek, we can always connect to a larger purpose. People benefit from the dreariest work in tangible ways. Such work provides money to live and support others. You can be kind to the people you work with. It's no small accomplishment to bring goodness and integrity to a workplace where these virtues are scarce. No task is truly thankless.

Go Home and Relax

Do what you can calmly and gently. Do not be disturbed about the rest. Leave to God what you cannot manage yourself.

— IGNATIUS LOYOLA

Workaholism is a danger for those with an Ignatian outlook. If work is so important — after all, we're supposed to help repair the world and find God there — the temptation is to overdo it. If eight hours at the office is good, ten or fifteen is better. We think: *Things will fall apart unless I finish this. This can't wait another day. I'm in the zone; I can't stop now.* But this is a delusion. Things won't fall apart. Things *can* wait. We're not indispensable. Anyway, what are the chances that the busiest person you know is the most productive? Practically nil.

That's what Ignatius thought, too. In a famous letter he admonishes some Jesuits who exhaust themselves on prayer and devotions. He compares them to horses who sprint out of the gate but fade long before the end of the race. They are like sailors who sink their ship by overloading it with cargo. "God is not pleased with that anxiety which afflicts the soul, because he wishes our limitations and weakness to seek the support of his strength," he said. In other words, you are not God. You are not the star of the show.

May 16

The Focusing Illusion

Nothing in life is as important as you think it is when you are thinking about it.

— DANIEL KAHNEMAN

We're inclined to think that people who live in a region with good weather (Southern California) are happier than people in a bad climate (northern Michigan). We think that paraplegics are mostly unhappy and that lottery winners are happy. None of these things is true. We can convince ourselves that marginally lower taxes or a modest expansion of health care benefits will make a huge difference in the quality of life for millions of people. It hasn't, and it won't.

Psychologists call this the "focusing illusion" — a tendency to place too much importance on one detail of a larger, complicated picture, namely, the detail we happen to be thinking about at the time. Ignatius was alert to this problem centuries ago. He worried about people's tendency to exaggerate the benefits of an option that seems attractive: *An exciting new regimen of prayer and fasting will cure my spiritual lethargy. I'll be more creative if I can get a new job. I'll be happier with a change of scenery.* These are likely misleading illusions that will disappoint us.

The worst thing, he said, is that they "prevent us from taking advantage of what is at hand" — a complex reality that will thwart our good plans.

God's Family Business

God invites us human beings into the family business to be partners with God. God's family business is this world which God wants to be a place where human beings live in harmony and friendship with God, with one another and with the whole creation. God needs our adult cooperation to bring about this dream for our world.

— WILLIAM A. BARRY, SJ

A well-run family business can be a great place to work. Your ties to your coworkers are bonds of affection and loyalty. You have a deep personal stake in the business. You're helping the family when you do a good job and help the business grow.

William Barry extends the metaphor to our working partnership with God. God's family business is repairing the whole world. The firm does every conceivable kind of work. There's work for everybody; the HR department accepts all applications. We're all adults. We're expected to take the initiative and use all our talents and energy. The goal is a world where everyone lives in freedom and harmony.

What's your part in God's family business?

"Help Souls" at Work

One of the simplest ways we can find meaning in work is by being kind to those who are struggling — the mother working two minimum-wage jobs; the secretary beleaguered by her tyrannical boss; the underappreciated janitor. To put it in Ignatian language, can you see yourself as someone who could "help souls" at work?

— JAMES MARTIN, SJ

When he was a teenager, James Martin worked for a summer on the assembly line at a packaging plant. His job was to put little boxes into big boxes and cover them with plastic shrink-wrap from 7 a.m. to 4 p.m. — standing in front of a noisy machine. "I hated it. Everyone hated it," Martin writes. Everyone was miserable, he says, except for three women on the line who laughed and chatted the entire day. They were close friends, and their time at work was a time to take delight in each other's company. "They hated their jobs but they loved each other," Martin writes.

Almost everyone has friends at work. When you're looking for meaning in your work, begin there — with the people you work with.

Meaning Comes First

The common wisdom about career choice often runs as follows: fig-ure out what sort of lifestyle you want to have; then estimate the level of income that it will take to live in this way; finally, find a career that will deliver that income. I fear that there could hardly be a worse way to discover a meaningful life.

— WILLIAM C. SPOHN, SJ

Jesuit William Spohn quotes the lament of a lawyer friend: "I hate spending sixty hours a week making rich people richer." His friend became a lawyer because he was adept at lawyerly skills and the money was good. He didn't think much about the nature of the work or its purpose.

Ignatius says that's the main mistake people make about their life choices: They decide what they want to do, and then try to fit their other goals into that. Instead, Ignatius says we should identify our deepest desires. What do you *really* want? This isn't wealth, renown, or a comfortable retire-ment. It will be to serve God and other people. The question then becomes, how do I best pursue that end in my work?

Sweat the Small Stuff

We should never delay doing something good now because we might do something better later, even if the good we can do now seems small.

— IGNATIUS LOYOLA

Football coach Nick Saban has achieved great success following an approach he calls "the process." He breaks down complicated projects like football games into hundreds of small actions. The average football play takes seven seconds. Saban wants players to focus on precisely what they are supposed to do in those seven seconds. They're not to think about what just happened or what might happen next. "The process" says: Do what's in front of you and do it well and the game will take care of itself.

Process thinking runs contrary to the way our minds work. Most of the time, we're morbidly ruminating on the past or speculating about the future. "If only," "what if?" — especially "what if?" We think: *I may be bored or frustrated now, but I'll do something great tomorrow.*

This is a great sinkhole of illusion, Ignatius says. Do what's in front of you now, and do it well. Most of the time, what's in front of us now is small stuff: small talk. A household chore. An email to write. Traffic to drive in peacefully. Sweat the small stuff, says Ignatius. Do the good you can do *now*.

Laborers in the Vineyard

One who works in a vineyard is an optimist, a laborer committed to the long haul, to patient, respectful cooperation with fellow laborers and with the Lord of the harvest. We are here to tend the garden and bear fruit that will last.

— PETER SCHINELLER, SJ

How do you *imagine* your work and workplace? Some see it as a battlefield; they sally forth each morning to struggle against the forces of darkness. For others it's a pilgrimage; they move from place to place, experiencing new things, meeting new people, developing their skills, seizing the possibilities that circumstances offer. For some, sadly, work is a prison, a place of drudgery to be endured in order to pay the bills.

Ignatius's favorite image for work was the vineyard or garden. God is already at work, giving life to the fruits and plants, making them grow. Our job is to help — to water and weed, clear brush, till the soil, plant new seeds, fertilize, harvest the crops. There's plenty of room for creativity.

Laborers in the vineyard are partners with God, who is Lord of the harvest.

It Gets Harder

Can you become a good logician? Then become one! A good theo-logian? Then become one! The same for being a good humanist. Do not be satisfied with doing it halfway!

— JEROME NADAL, SJ

Here's a paradox about work: It gets harder, not easier, as you go along. You'd think it would be the other way around; it should get easier as you get better at teaching or writing or coding or whatever your craft may be. But it doesn't. As you get good, you realize how hard it is to get *really* good. Some great thing you did when you were starting out will later be seen, correctly, as a minor accomplishment. You see imperfections you didn't see before. The great solo violin-ist making Mozart's violin concerto look easy is working harder than they ever have, and they probably go home with a list of flaws to correct.

This is why great saints like Paul and Ignatius said that they were the greatest of sinners. An obvious exaggeration to us, mere beginners, but not to them. They saw their faults more clearly than they ever had.

Win or Learn

I never lose. I either win or learn.

— NELSON MANDELA

The wide receiver drops a touchdown pass in the end zone. The client chooses someone else for the big job. The student fails a big exam. Conventional wisdom says: Put it all behind you, declare it "yesterday's news," and move on to the next opportunity with confidence. Ignatius says: Figure out why things went bad. "Review it carefully," he says, all the way back to the beginning. Were you thinking clearly? Did you overlook something? Maybe not. In that case, you simply had bad luck or were tripped up by factors out of your control. Most of the time, you'll find something you can do better next time.

We learn more from failure than success. When we succeed, we are inclined to chalk it up to our skill and brilliance, but maybe we were just lucky. When we fail, we can learn something.

A Better Person Isn't Here Right Now

I often find myself, as an administrator, in situations with students and colleagues that I would very much prefer to avoid. I know that I do not have the wisdom or experience that I should have to be dealing with the issues at hand; but nevertheless there they are, and here I am. There may be someone better out there, but that person is not here right now, and the work still needs to be done.

— Ann Garrido

Sometimes we get into a tough spot, what's known in basketball as "a bad matchup." Our opponent looks bigger, quicker, more skilled than we are. We're not confident about the outcome of this play. In these situations we need to embrace our responsibility, rely on our training and experience, and forge ahead. There might be someone out there who's better able to handle a problem like this. But that person isn't here. It's up to us.

Bill Belichick, the legendary coach of the New England Patriots, constantly tells his players: "Do your job." The job is yours — you've practiced it, we're counting on you to do it, and it fits into a larger whole. Do *your* job — not someone else's. And *do* it. Don't put it off.

Do What You're Doing

A well-known phrase in Jesuit life is age quod agis — *"do what you're doing!" We tend to obsess over what we wish we were doing, or what we might be doing instead of our boring jobs, or what we would like to be doing that someone else is doing, or what we would have been doing if our luck had been better. Such preoccupations distract us from whatever real opportunity lies right in front of us.*

— CHRIS LOWNEY

Leonardo da Vinci wrote a fable about a stone that lay underground for many years until it was uncovered by rain and wind. It found itself in a pleasant grove surrounded by flowers above a busy road. The stone grew bored and restless. "Why am I with these herbs?" it asked. "I want to be with my fellow stones down on the road." So the stone let itself fall to the road — and that was a mistake. The stone was miserable in its new home. It was trampled by horses and wagons, covered in dung, chipped and bumped all day long. In vain the stone longed for the peaceful grove it had abandoned.

"What if …?" "If only …?" These two questions occupy our minds all day long. But what's real is what we are doing now. God is found in all things, Ignatius says. Certainly, the first place to look for God is in what we are doing right now.

Don't Wear Yourself Out

Work is what horses die of. Everybody should know that.

— ALEKSANDR SOLZHENITSYN,
ONE DAY IN THE LIFE OF IVAN DENISOVICH

No Christian thinker had a higher regard for work than Ignatius, but he was also alert to work's hazards. There's "mission creep" — a successful project gradually expands until it takes on too much and fails. There's workaholism — the more work the better. There's the spiritual error of believing that our value as a human being comes from the work we do. Ignatius's letters are full of warnings about the dangers of overwork. He constantly reminded Jesuits not to try to do more than they could do. "There is no need to wear yourself out, but make a competent and sufficient effort, and leave the rest to God," he wrote.

You're not responsible for the outcome of your efforts. God is.

Glamorous Jobs

To lift up the hands in prayer gives God glory, but a man with a dung fork in his hand, a woman with a slop pail, gives him glory too.

— GERARD MANLEY HOPKINS, SJ

God can be found in all things. There's no division between the sacred and secular. All work is holy. Jesuit poet Gerard Manley Hopkins expresses these Ignatian ideas in the arresting image of people glorifying God by digging manure and carrying the contents of an indoor toilet. No one has a glamorous job. When you dig into the details of what people do all day, you'll find that most of it is burdensome and boring. But it's meaningful because all of it advances Christ's work of service and healing.

If you think about your work that way, all of it is glamorous.

May 28

Adaptable

There was nothing predetermined in Ignatius's outlook; he was al-
ways adapting his plans to new situations, never considering his de-
cisions as standing for all time; the principles of the apostle were to
be applied with prudence and regard for the particular situation.

— Philip Caraman, SJ

One of the hallmarks of an Ignatian approach is flexibility. Plans need to be adjusted if circumstances call for it. New situations need to be studied and understood. Decisions need to be taken carefully. Rules aren't much help. This attitude is both liberating and worrisome. It's liberating because it gives room for creativity and makes it more likely that a suitable solution will be found. It's worrisome because there's more room to make mistakes. It's scary to operate in the dark, without the guidance of rules.

But if you believe that God can be found in all things, you don't have much choice. God is lurking in the new, unexpected, troubling situation. To find him, you need to be ready to change your mind and alter your plans.

May 29

Magis

The question we seek an answer for is "What more does God want of me?" More is the magis of Ignatian spirituality — the aspiration to always grow in service.

— David L. Fleming, SJ

Ignatian spirituality is flavored with the spirit of *magis*, a Latin word meaning "more." It means a striving for excellence, a willingness to change, an openness to new ideas. The word comes from a challenge Ignatius issues in *The Spiritual Exercises*: Be willing to do *more* than the usual. You can do what most people do, or you can go all in. A person committed to the *magis* isn't satisfied with the current state of things. They look for ways to do things better. If given a choice between something that's working pretty well and something riskier but better, they would be inclined to take the risk.

Magis means that you keep your bags packed and your opinions open to revision. Always be looking for new knowledge and a better way of doing things.

What Isn't Being Done?

The Society cares for people who are being neglected or being cared for badly. This is why the Society exists. This is its strength.

— JEROME NADAL, SJ

The early Jesuits took care of plague victims and people locked up in prison. They set up houses that offered prostitutes a different way of life. They worked to end violent vendettas between Italian clans. They defended Jews from ill treatment. They ministered to poor people and others on the fringes of society. The Jesuits made a deliberate choice to do important work that no one else was doing.

That's still a good approach: Notice what isn't being done and do that. What isn't being done right now in your home, your office, your community? Do that.

God Is Already at Work

A pebble cast into a pond causes ripples that spread in all directions. Each one of our thoughts, words, and deeds is like that. No one has a right to sit down and feel hopeless. There is too much work to do.

— DOROTHY DAY

Ignatian service is "to help." "To help" recognizes that God is already working in your corner of the world; you're there to help it along. It started before you arrived on the scene. You're not the star of the show. You have a supporting role.

The possibilities for helping are limitless. The Jesuits took an expansive view of the kinds of help they gave. Help for the body as well as the spirit: food and shelter, medical care, education, companionship and friendship. We do likewise. We proceed "one brick at a time, take one step at a time," as Dorothy Day put it, remembering that the impact of the help is incalculable.

June

DESIRE

I should ask for what I desire.

— *The Spiritual Exercises, 65*

Let's Not Be Too Hard on Desire

Without desire we would never get up in the morning. We would never have ventured beyond the front door. We would never have read a book or learned something new. Desire is energy, the energy of creativity, the energy of life itself. So let's not be too hard on desire.

— MARGARET SILF

In the Ignatian view, desire is the engine that drives the train. Love happens in the heart, not the mind, and the key to the heart is desire. What do you want? When you know what you want, you know what God wants.

Many religious traditions view desire with deep suspicion. For Buddhists, desire is the source of suffering. Christian moralists shake a stern finger at sexual desire. Stoics, both ancient and modern, shun desire. The Stoic Diogenes said, "It is the privilege of the gods to want nothing, and of godlike men to want little." But Ignatius said that a desire for goodness is at the core of our being, and that the point of spiritual growth is to cultivate desire, not suppress it, and direct it toward its proper objects. Our problem isn't desiring too much but rather desiring too little.

God's Desires for Us

It's freeing to say, "This is what I desire in life."

— JAMES MARTIN, SJ

When he was in seminary, James Martin went to the doctor complaining about migraine headaches. A scan revealed a "suspicious spot" under his jaw, and soon Martin found himself on a gurney, tubes snaking out of his arms, being wheeled into an operating room. As a nurse put a mask over his face and started the anesthesia, "suddenly an incredible desire surged up from deep within me. It was like a jet of water rushing up from the depths of the ocean to its surface. I thought, 'I hope I don't die, because I want to be a priest!'"

Martin had been preparing for the priesthood for years, but he had never wanted it so much as he did then. The surgery was successful, and Martin went on to fulfill the desire he felt most deeply on the operating table. It was the key to his life: the force that moved him, the love that gave meaning to everything else. For Ignatius, these deep desires are holy desires, expressions of God's desires for us. They show the path to joy.

Fire in the Heart

To discover what we deeply, truly desire forces us to wade into a swamp of needs, expectations, demands, casual wishes, moods, obligations, and much more. Your deepest, truest desire may coincide with one or another of these interior experiences but will always cut deeper into your heart than any of them. True desire is fire in the heart.

— GEORGE ASCHENBRENNER, SJ

Some of our desires are to *possess* things — the nice home, the big job, the attractive person, the well-deserved vacation. Other desires lead us out of ourselves. We desire to share our life with another person, to create something that doesn't yet exist, to make a home, to help others satisfy their desires. These are the deeper desires — to give, not possess; to share, not to hold.

Ask for What You Want

I should ask for what I desire.
— THE SPIRITUAL EXERCISES, 65

Don't be timid. Speak up. Ask for what you want. It's a message Ignatius often repeats in *The Spiritual Exercises* and in his letters. Tell God what you want. Put it into words. Don't suppress your desires. Bring them out of the murk of the unconscious into the light of day, where you can understand them and fulfill them.

It's a key Ignatian theme that's similar to the aim of psychoanalysis. Both the therapist and the Ignatian spiritual director urge us to put words around our wordless longings, to bring unconscious desires into awareness so that they can be understood, mastered, and if need be, healed.

We'll discover what our desires really mean. A desire for a job is really a desire for security and peace. Prayers for material needs are really about a closer relationship with God. Our deepest desires are what we really want.

Made for Another World

It is difficult to find words strong enough for the sensation which came over me; Milton's "enormous bliss" of Eden ... comes somewhere near it. It was a sensation, of course, of desire, but a desire for what?

— C. S. Lewis

C. S. Lewis never forgot the glimpse of glory he had as a young man standing before a flowering currant bush in a garden — a moment of indescribable longing for the pure and holy. This is the world he was destined for, he thought. "Creatures are not born with desires unless satisfaction for those desires exists," he wrote. "If I find in myself a desire which no experience in this world can satisfy, the most probable explanation is that I was made for another world."

Lewis thought that human love, friendship, sex, aesthetic satisfaction, and other earthly pleasures give us a taste of this transcendent joy that awaits us. That's why we desire them; they hint at what we're made for.

June 6

Wants and Needs

Distinguish between wants and needs. Is it "nice to have" or "need to have"? Do you "need" a bigger television or the latest phone or the newest computer?

— JAMES MARTIN, SJ

Warren Buffett, the billionaire investor, lives in the same house he bought for $31,500 in 1958. NBA superstar Kawhi Leonard, who makes $34 million a year, often drives a rehabbed 1997 Chevy Tahoe. "It runs and it's paid off," he says.

Arthur Brooks, an economist who studies happiness, offers a simple equation for a happy life: Satisfaction = what you have ÷ what you want. The secret is to work on the denominator of the equation: what you want. Don't obsess about what you have; manage what you want. If the house you live in suits you, stay there. If your old car gets you around safely and efficiently, be content with it. The fewer your wants, the greater your satisfaction.

Hidden Desires

You have made us for yourself, O God, and our heart is restless until it rests in you.

— ST. AUGUSTINE

Often, we need to dig into our desires to find out what they really mean. Consider Rick Blaine, the cynical proprietor of Rick's Café Américain in the movie *Casablanca*. Rick loves Ilsa Lund. He thinks love means that he is to have her for his own; he discovers that truly loving her means giving her up.

Or take Ebenezer Scrooge, the bitter miser in *A Christmas Carol*, who desires peace of mind. He thinks this means being left alone, without the nuisance and pain of relationships; the three ghosts show him that the peace he desires is to be found in human warmth and affection.

Says the great Jesuit psychologist William Barry, "Scratch any of these desires a little, even the seemingly most self-centered and materialistic, and we will find that we want to know something about God and his relationship to us." Desires are in essence pleas for assurance that God loves us, hears us, and that all is well between us.

June 8

Know That God Hears You

Often we tell ourselves, or we are told, in an effort to quell our desires, to look at all the good we already have. We can be made to feel guilty and ungrateful for desiring what we want. But if we suppress our desires without being satisfied that God has heard us, we pull back from honesty with God.

— WILLIAM A. BARRY, SJ

I want a better job. I want my children to love each other. I want my brother to get well. Desires like these well up from a deep place in our hearts. Sometimes, though, we suppress them because we think, or are told, that there's something wrong with them: *Don't make too much of this. Be grateful for what you have. Stop complaining. You can't do anything about it, so it's time to move on.*

Go ahead and talk about what you want. Your friends might not want to listen, but God does. He wants to hear from you, and he'll listen as long as you want to talk. Don't stop talking to God until you are satisfied that he has heard you.

Information Doesn't Help

We are drowning in information, while starving for wisdom.

— Edward O. Wilson

More information is supposed to be a good thing: The more we know, the smarter we are; more information means wiser choices, better decisions. Sadly, this doesn't seem to be true. We're bombarded with information; we're the best-informed people in history; and yet there's no evidence that we're wiser, more balanced, smarter about what matters most. In fact, studies show that more information seldom changes minds, but it makes people more confident about what they already believe, which is often false.

Ignatius was skeptical about the value of information in spiritual matters. He wanted people to meet God, not learn *about* God. He didn't want spiritual directors to spend a lot of time explaining things. "Knowing much doesn't satisfy the soul," he said. He wanted people to think for themselves.

Put down your phone, close your browser, and reflect on what is moving your heart.

Boredom

Let the little things that would ordinarily bore you suddenly thrill you.

— ANDY WARHOL

In the movie *Groundhog Day*, a smug and dislikable character played by Bill Murray is forced to relive the same day over and over hundreds of times. Nothing new happens. He's nearly driven mad by the tedium of it. But then he starts to notice things: his shortcomings, the needs of other people, his desire to be a better person. He's been oblivious to these things, but they've always been there. Noticing what's really going on opens the door to a new life.

Ignatius didn't believe it when his friends said that "nothing's happening" in their spiritual lives. That simply meant that they weren't paying attention. Something is always happening in your inner life, he said. Powerful currents of desire and feeling are moving inside. You need to pay attention, be aware of them, and ask what they mean.

Disordered Desires

Many spiritual writers of Ignatius's day spoke of desires as obstacles to God's will. A person was supposed to suppress his desires — to eliminate them whenever possible. But Ignatius held the radical notion that God dwells within our desires. Not only are desires not evil; they are one of God's primary instruments of communicating with us.

— MARK E. THIBODEAUX, SJ

In the Ignatian view, desires are not good or bad, trivial or substantial, unworthy or worthy, harmful or helpful. They are *ordered* or *disordered*. They are in the right place or they are out of place. It's a simple distinction that's hard to put into practice. What's the place of money in your life? You need to make money. How much do you need? How much effort should you spend to get it? Good health is important. How important? How much time should you spent on fitness? On healthy food? On avoiding infections?

A rule of thumb is to look at the direction the desire takes us. A desire is ordered when it takes us outside ourselves. We make money so we can do something other than make money. A desire is disordered when it turns inward and narrows our lives. It becomes something that feeds our ego and crowds out relationships.

A Reverse Bucket List

There was a disturbance in my heart, a voice that spoke there and said, I want, I want, I want! It happened every afternoon, and when I tried to suppress it it got even stronger. It only said one thing, I want, I want! And I would ask, "What do you want?" But this was all it would ever tell me. It never said a thing except I want, I want, I want!

— SAUL BELLOW, *HENDERSON THE RAIN KING*

A man wants to be married but only looks for dates on hookup websites. A woman wants a better job but never gets around to looking for one. An investor pursues two different strategies at the same time. No wonder everyone's disappointed. The source of the confusion is our contradictory desires. Wanting everything, we want inconsistent and conflicting things.

One way to discover what you really want is to make a list of the attachments in your life that you could do without. Make a bucket list in reverse — the stuff you *don't* need, the things that waste your time, the amusements that aren't so much fun, the ways you waste money, the things that cause you to say, "Why did I do that?" A list like this will help you see what's most important.

What Is Your Treasure?

What is our treasure that, once found, is worth all we can sell or trade? What is the pearl of great price for which we would sacrifice everything? This is what the gospel's reign of God is about: our hearts' desire, our deepest existential longing.

— JOHN KAVANAUGH, SJ

A wizard appears and invites you to ask for anything you want. What do you want the most?

Aladdin in the Disney movie thinks his treasure is the princess Jasmine, so he asks for the wealth and status that he believes will give him a shot at wooing her. It turns out that what he *really* wants is to be a good person, not a thieving street urchin. He achieves this with his final wish — freeing the genie from bondage. For King Solomon, the treasure is wisdom — the ability to know the truth. His treasure allows him to know what is truly valuable in every situation that comes up for the rest of his life. Solomon's treasure is to keep finding treasure. It's hard to think of a better thing to wish for.

How would you answer the wizard? What would you sacrifice everything for?

"Clothes, Shoes, Diamond Rings"

Superficial desires — such as those linked to consumerism — demonstrate all too graphically our cultural narcissism, but more authentic desires always lead us out of ourselves and into the human community.

— EDWARD KINERK, SJ

In the song "I Want" by the English boy band One Direction, the singer is discouraged by his girlfriend's superficial desires for "clothes, shoes, diamond rings / stuff that's driving me insane." His desire is deeper — to love her and be loved by her.

Ignatius asks, Where is your desire taking you? Superficial desires — for clothes, shoes, diamond rings, and the like — point inward. They are things you possess. They are about *you*. Deep desires point outward — toward others and the community. There's a paradox here: Our desires are uniquely personal, yet the deepest desires lead us out of ourselves. The question "Who am I?" means "Who am I in connection with others?"

Think Big

We hope for more than ordinary results from you. We don't expect commonplace achievements.

— IGNATIUS LOYOLA

Ignatius thought big. He wasn't satisfied with modest goals. He invented a new kind of religious organization, jettisoning a centuries-old model of religious life. His Jesuits reinvented the educational system of Europe and exported it to the rest of the world. They excelled as scholars, explorers, scientists, artists. They developed a new kind of everyday spirituality. The key to this program was desire. Ignatius urged Jesuits to "elicit great desires." Great desires led to ambitious goals; ambitious goals demanded fierce, single-minded commitment. When your goal is big enough, it will demand everything you have.

What's your desire? What task will satisfy it? Maybe you won't explore new lands or reform a school system, but you can be a great partner, a great parent, a great friend, a great volunteer. You can take on great tasks at work. Think big.

June 16

Seven Tough Years

I had not a single day when I wasn't deeply anxious, fretful, and gloomy... and was utterly unbearable to myself.

— JEROME NADAL, SJ

To see how conflicting desires can wreak havoc in our lives, consider the case of Jerome Nadal, Ignatius's chief deputy, probably the most important of the early Jesuits after Ignatius himself. As a young man Nadal had twice encountered Ignatius and his companions; both times he was strongly attracted to the group and just as strongly repulsed by the idea of joining it. He fled from Ignatius and endured seven years of depression and misery, torn between a desire to join the Jesuits and a desire to pursue a conventional ecclesiastical and academic career. In a memoir he wrote:

> During the whole seven years I then spent at home
> I had not a single day when I wasn't deeply anx-
> ious, fretful, and gloomy. I had perpetual headaches
> and stomach pains, and was in constant depression.
> I lived surrounded by doctors and medicines and
> was utterly unbearable to myself.

Nadal resolved his dilemma by dramatically confronting it. He wanted to serve God in the best possible way, but he was paralyzed by his misgivings about the ways to do that. He understood that his deepest desire was to become a Jesuit, so he acted. He wrote a letter to Ignatius asking to join the order. At once his depression lifted; he was able to pursue what he really wanted.

Think Hard about What Matters Most

Weigh matters carefully and think hardest about those that matter most. Fools are lost by not thinking. Some ponder things backward, paying much attention to what matters little, and little to what matters much.

— BALTASAR GRACIÁN, SJ

Celebrities, sports trivia, puzzles, recipes, jokes — they wash over us all day in our connected world, the petty and trivial, the ephemeral and inconsequential. It's easy to waste time "paying much attention to what matters little," as Baltasar Gracián put it four hundred years ago, long before the internet arrived to engulf us in Twitter rants and cat videos.

Unplug yourself for a few hours and spent some time thinking about what you *really* want. What are the desires beneath your desires? Which matters most: the desire to be recognized for your accomplishments, or the ability to take quiet satisfaction in what you've done with the opportunities you've been given? A life of pleasure and ease, or the patience and fortitude to bear the turbulence in the life you actually lead?

Maybe your prayers have already been answered. You just need to recognize it.

No Blueprint

God's will for us is that we should learn to respond in freedom to God's love for us, and to give shape to our individual and common lives in freedom by the choices that we make. There is a sense in which we create, in terms of concrete action in given circumstances, the will of God in this exercise of freedom. There is no blueprint in God's mind with which we have to comply.

— DAVID LONSDALE

One model for "doing God's will" is the engineer metaphor: God has devised a detailed blueprint for how he wants our lives to unfold; we read the design and follow the instructions. Another is the mystery model: God has sprinkled clues about his intentions all over the map; we play detective and try to sniff them out.

The Ignatian model is the loving partnership: God has desires for his creation and for us; we desire to know what they are so we can do them. It's something we do together. Ignatius's view of it is summed up in a meditation note: "To imagine myself as standing before God and all his saints, that I may desire and know what will be more pleasing to the Divine Goodness."

Doing God's will occurs within a loving relationship. There's a mutuality about it. It's fueled by desire.

June 19

Checking Desire

Two questions always worth asking ourselves in the examen are: (1) What am I desiring? and (2) What do I desire to desire?

— Edward Kinerk, SJ

To get the most out of your desires, reflect on them regularly. On the micro level: Which of the things you desire are needs and which are wants? Which consume too much time? Which are satisfying and which are not? On the macro level: What "great desires" are you pursuing? What's the purpose of your work? What needs to be done in your family? What do you want to do to make your community a better place?

Lastly, what do you desire to desire? Are you "stuck" somewhere — torn between conflicting desires?

June 20

Iron Hearts

God, it would seem, is madly in love with us and is always attracted to us. The problem is that most of us do not really believe it.

— WILLIAM A. BARRY, SJ

Our hearts are divided. We love God but we're afraid of him, drawn to God but repelled by him, too. In Holy Sonnet 14, John Donne describes the problem as a romantic triangle. The poet is in love with God but engaged to someone else: "Dearly I love you," but he is "betrothed unto your enemy." To break the impasse, God has to take the initiative: "break that knot again, / take me to you, imprison me." Elsewhere, Donne writes, "thou like adamant draw mine iron heart." The poet's heart might be a cold hunk of iron, but God is a magnet, drawing the iron to himself.

Do You Have the Desire for This Desire?

Ignatius would ask, "Do you have the desire for this desire?" Even if you don't want it, do you want to want it? Do you wish that you were the kind of person that wanted this?

— JAMES MARTIN, SJ

There are many things we *should* want but *don't* want — or don't want badly enough to make them happen. Simple things: We should eat a healthier diet. Get more exercise. Get to bed earlier. Graver things: Live more simply, break off a bad relationship, forgive someone who has wounded us. We'd like to do it, but we have no desire to do it.

Experts are divided about what to do in this case. Some pounce on the *should*. Who says you *should*? Don't do things that others say you *should* do. Others advise patience. See what happens with this desire; meanwhile don't get upset about it. Others will say you should do the thing anyway even if you have no desire to do it.

Ignatius takes a different approach. If you lack the desire for something you're drawn to, pray for the desire for that desire. Pray to become the kind of person who wants it.

What Fairy Tales Tell Us

Fairy tales take us right to the heart of our desiring by way of pictures, symbols, and metaphors, and help us to connect these deep and universal desires (and fears) to the feelings we are experiencing.

— MARGARET SILF

Fairy tales aren't just stories for children; they endure through the ages because they express the deepest human desires and longings. A good way to get in touch with your deepest desires is to reflect on which fairy tales move you and why.

Are you especially touched by "Cinderella" and "The Ugly Duckling" — stories revealing the beauty hidden inside? How about "Sleeping Beauty" and "Beauty and the Beast" — the redeeming power of love. Do you admire plucky Little Red Riding Hood and brave Jack cutting down the beanstalk? If you had one wish, like King Midas, what would it be?

Extend the exercise beyond fairy tales. Why do you like your favorite movies, novels, songs? Which stories from the gospels especially stir you?

June 23

Who Do You Imitate?

A conversion of heart means rejecting a false triangulation of desire (me, a rival, and an object of competition) for a new triangulation: God, the poor, and my deepest self.

— TIM MULDOON

The philosopher René Girard suggested that desire is "triangular." That is, we desire things because other people desire them. We want nice clothes, a new car, and a big green lawn because we've learned from the people around us that these are desirable things. You might love opera, enjoy avocados, shun Facebook, and despise football not because you've thought deeply about these things but because that's the taste of the group you hang out with.

That's why Ignatius thought it very important to imitate the right things. "Keep before your eyes those who are active and energetic," he said. Ignatius thought that the best model is Christ. *The Spiritual Exercises* are an immersion into the personality of Christ. Those who follow the *Exercises* strive to think like Christ thinks, act like he acts, value what he values.

Joy Comes through Desire

Joy comes to me when my attitude concerning God and humility turns to one of desire rather than of burden.

— ALCOHOLICS ANONYMOUS, *DAILY REFLECTIONS*

This reflection is about a turning point in the Alcoholics Anonymous 12-step program. Recovering alcoholics find joy when they deeply *desire* God. This typically happens after they spend a great deal of time doing the hard work of disciplined self-reflection required for recovery. They learn that, as this *Daily Reflection* continues, "being truthful and honest... results in my being filled with serenity, freedom, and joy."

This is true beyond the context of a recovery program. Our deepest desire is for God, but often it takes a long time and a lot of hard work to uncover it and express it.

The Desire to Please

I believe that the desire to please you does in fact please you.

— THOMAS MERTON

One of the most famous prayers of the twentieth century begins with a frank confession of complete uncertainty. "I have no idea where I am going," wrote Thomas Merton in *Thoughts in Solitude*. "I do not see the road ahead of me." It's an updating of Psalm 23 for the age of doubt. In the Bible, the psalmist prays, "Even though I walk through the darkest valley, I fear no evil; for you are with me." Says Merton: "Therefore will I trust you always though I may seem to be lost and in the shadow of death."

Merton trusts God because he trusts his desire. "I believe that the desire to please you does in fact please you," he tells God. He prays that this desire will animate everything that he does. If he can do this, he says, God will lead him by the right road, "though I may know nothing about it. ... I will not fear, for you are ever with me, / and you will never leave me to face my perils alone."

Who's in Control?

If someone were to be so captivated by food, drink, affection, or knowledge that any one of these realities claimed ownership over that man or woman, Ignatius would see this as a kind of slavery.

— HOWARD GRAY, SJ

Psychologist Jonathan Haidt likens the acting self to a rider perched atop an elephant. The rider is the steady, rational part of our psyche; the elephant is the irrational part — big, powerful, and prone to swings of emotion and instinct. The rider can see the path ahead; the elephant provides the energy to get there. The rider thinks they are in charge of this partnership, and that's how it looks as long as the elephant moves steadily down the road. But the elephant is much bigger and more powerful than the rider. In an argument about which direction to take, the elephant will be able to overwhelm the rider and go where it wants.

In Ignatian language, the rider is the person's core desires — what they *really* want. The elephant is the roiling mass of longings, wants, and needs that sometimes stay in their place and sometimes take over. The risk is that the rider will grow complacent; sitting high above the landscape, reins in hand, admired by onlookers below, thinking they are in control. We are not. The steady, rational self can be quickly overthrown.

Is Your Heart in It?

Today we commonly say about someone who shows no enthusiasm for a project that "his heart isn't in it." We usually say this when someone is behaving in a way that is at odds with their deepest desires.

— David L. Fleming, SJ

A regular event in professional football is the "surprise retirement." A star player at or near the top of his game will abruptly announce that he's done; he's hanging up the cleats and going home. They always say, "My heart isn't in the game anymore," or words to that effect. Most fans nod in understanding. If you're going to play a game where your body gets pummeled and crushed all the time, your heart had better be in it.

Coaches want players whose hearts are in the game. So do employers, friends, and romantic partners. If your heart isn't in it, if you're mailing it in day after day, people will notice. They'll avoid you, give the exciting jobs to someone else, maybe even replace you with someone whose heart *is* in it.

Regularly ask yourself whether you're living in a way that's consistent with your deepest desires. If you're not, do something about it. Have you truly grasped what your deepest desires are? Are you willing to do what it takes to fulfill them?

June 28

Praydreaming

Good discernment consists of prayerfully pondering the great de-
sires that well up in my daydreams.

— MARK E. THIBODEAUX, SJ

We spend a lot of time daydreaming — almost half our
waking hours according to one study. Not all daydreaming
is a waste of time. Psychologists think daydreaming can be
a source of creative energy and can help develop skills of
self-reflection.

The Jesuit Mark Thibodeaux thinks that daydreaming
in a reflective, prayerful mode — what he calls "praydreaming" — is a great way to find out what our desires are all
about. Let your thoughts drift to your desires: What do you
want? Why do you want it? What do you think will happen
if you get it? What if you don't get it? Ask God to direct
these musings. Eventually the deepest, truest, most authentic desires will come to mind.

Daydreaming is how Ignatius discovered his mission in
life. He fantasized about possible futures. One was becoming a great saint like Francis of Assisi; another was becoming a swashbuckling hero at the court of the kingdom of
Castile. Praydreaming led him to understand that a life of
service to God would give him the most joy.

June 29

Take a Drink

If we wish to quench our thirst, we must lay aside books which explain thirst and take a drink.

— JEAN-PIERRE DE CAUSSADE, SJ

There's a tendency in spiritual matters to sit back and wait for something to happen. "Wait on the Lord" is the gist of much spiritual counsel: Be patient, pray, pray some more, and wait. And wait. And wait. Waiting can become calm acceptance of things as they are without an effort to resist or change them. We can wait too long and miss our chance. Meanwhile, our passivity can look an awful lot like real spiritual depth.

Passivity is not the Ignatian way. Ignatian spirituality is biased toward action. Ignatius believed that God is intensely active in our everyday lives, inviting us into a deeper relationship and greater joy. The grace is there; we need to respond to it. Take a drink.

June 30

Last Words

I should have bought more crap.

— *New Yorker* CARTOON OF A MAN ON HIS DEATHBED

Toward the end of her life, Mother Teresa was asked why she had spent her life caring for the poor and the dying. "Because I like doing my own thing," she said. Her thing turned out to be God's thing, too. She did what St. Augustine suggested: "Love God and do what you will."

What's your "thing"? How would you like to be remembered? Ignatius suggested that people making an important decision imagine looking back on this decision at the end of the lives, on their deathbeds. How does this decision look from that vantage point? Extend the exercise further: What do you think will be written in your obituary? Further still: What would you *like* to be in your obituary?

July

HUMILITY

I do not know You, God, because I am in the way.
Please help me to push myself aside.

— FLANNERY O'CONNOR

Blessed Are the Uncool

It takes a long while before we sense the wild genius of the Beati-tudes — blessed are those who do not think they are cool, blessed are those who abjure power, blessed are those who deflate their own arrogance and puncture their own pomposity, blessed are those who quietly try to shrive their sins without calling attention to their over-weening piety, blessed are those who know they are dunderheads but forge on cheerfully anyway.

— BRIAN DOYLE

"Blessed are the meek," "blessed are the poor in spirit," "blessed are the peacemakers" — the Beatitudes are among Jesus's most beloved teachings. They are also among the most radical. The claim is not merely that God loves lowly and humble people, or that things will turn out all right for them in the end. Jesus is saying that weakness and meekness are the way to live. Turn away from power and celebrity and riches. The weak are strong. Humility is the path to glory.

We're ambivalent about humility. We admire restraint and self-effacing humor; we like it when a public figure displays a touch of modesty. But we admire proud self-confidence even more. Don't overdo this humility thing, we say. But Jesus says, overdo it. Humility is the way to go.

July 2

What Humility Is Not

You must therefore conceal from the patient the true end of Humility. Let him think of it not as self-forgetfulness but as a certain kind of opinion (namely, a low opinion) of his own talents and character.... By this method thousands of humans have been brought to think that humility means pretty women trying to believe that they are ugly and clever men trying to believe they are fools.

— C. S. Lewis, *The Screwtape Letters*

In *The Screwtape Letters*, C. S. Lewis imagines the devil Screwtape advising an apprentice about the best ways to tempt a Christian man from the path of righteousness. One way is to confuse him about the meaning of humility: Get the Christian to think that humility means thinking poorly of oneself, that appreciating one's talents is boastful pride and that denigrating them is wise and virtuous.

To think that we're talentless and insignificant is false humility. It makes us passive; we take a back seat and let dominant people push us around. It causes us to avoid new challenges for fear of making mistakes. It breeds resentment; absorbed in our weakness, we come to dislike those who are strong.

Real humility is a true opinion of one's gifts, not a low opinion of them.

Pride and Humility

During synagogue services one Yom Kippur, the rabbi was overcome with religious feeling and threw himself to the ground proclaiming, "Lord, I am nothing!" Not to be outdone, the cantor prostrated himself and exclaimed, "Lord, I am nothing!" The temple janitor, working in the back of the sanctuary, joined the fervor, prostrating himself and crying, "Lord, I am nothing!" Whereupon the rabbi nudged the cantor and whispered, "Look who thinks he's nothing!"

— CLASSIC JEWISH JOKE

This joke pinpoints another problem with the virtue of humility. Our efforts to grow in humility can be an occasion of pride. We can find ourselves taking unseemly satisfaction at having done such a good job of being humble. Is pure humility even possible with mixed motives?

Probably not. Our motives are *always* mixed. Pride will always leak into our bigheartedness; we'll always wonder how we're coming across when we're doing our best to be generous and kind. When we feel sad about our shortcomings, some of the sadness is about falling short of our cherished image of ourselves. We're not perfect. All the more reason to cultivate a humble heart.

July 4

Oppressive Humility

"I enjoyed your homily," a female student told me earnestly one day last year, after I had celebrated a school liturgy, "but I really disagree with your statement that Christian discipleship means 'self-emptying service.' That's just another name for subjugation!"

— BRIAN E. DALEY, SJ

The student isn't wrong. Over the centuries, countless weak, powerless, oppressed people — especially women — have been told that Christian humility requires them to accept their lowly lot in life. This is a gross distortion of what Jesus meant by humility, but it's still often heard. The strong piously invoke humility to keep people in their place. People who conspicuously lack humility can use it as a weapon to protect their privilege.

That's one reason why Christian humility can appear to be strange and even dangerous to the secular mind. Another reason is that it runs contrary to the constant message of affirmation: Take control, do what you want, there are no limits to what you can do. Humility is countercultural in the social sense, counterintuitive in the intellectual sense. We'd best speak of humility carefully. It's easily misunderstood.

We Know Just a Little

To speak about finding God in all things is to admit that no doctrine, no tradition, and no Scripture can exhaust the mystery that is God. It is to remember that our theology, our prayer, and our teaching are limited in their ability to convey this mystery.

— TIM MULDOON

Everywhere we hear strong opinions being asserted with great passion and conviction: *This is what's wrong with... [the world, politics, kids today, baseball]. This is how to fix... [schools, my company's problems, Hollywood].* It's all bluster. We don't know these things. Not really.

The Ignatian principle that God can be found in all things gives us another reason to be humble. "All things" is a lot of things — more than we can ever know. Our knowledge will always be partial. It's impossible to know with certainty the best way to do anything.

This is humbling and exciting. The fact that God can be found in all things means that something will always come along to teach us more.

Pride Is the Cause of Our Illness

How is it that wickedness is so abundant? Through pride. Heal pride and there will be no wickedness. That the cause of all our illness — our pride — might be healed, the Son of God came down and was made humble.

— St. Augustine

Pride was a virtue in the ancient world, which believed that the ideal man (women counted for little) was the *megalopsuchos* — the "great-souled" man who is better than everyone else and knows it. The virtuous man was independent, completely self-sufficient, and benevolent. The ancient world was like high school — a place where the strong and beautiful were glorified and the humble and weak were mocked.

Into this world of power and pride came a ragtag band of Jews who claimed that God came into the world as a peasant in a province on the empire's borderlands, lived as one of the humble ones, and died a criminal's death. They turned the moral edifice of the ancient world upside down; pride was the problem, not a virtue — a disease that infected the spirit and corrupted the community. The cure is humility — the virtue of the common people.

It's Not about You

It's not about you. The purpose of your life is far greater than your own personal fulfillment, your peace of mind, or even your happiness. It's far greater than your family, your career, or even your wildest dreams and ambitions. If you want to know why you were placed on this planet, you must begin with God. You were born by his purpose and for his purpose.

— RICK WARREN

The Ignatian idea of humility is not a feeling. It's not a virtue attained by self-discipline and prayer. It's not a habit of thinking about oneself as being less skilled or less worthy than others. Humility in the Ignatian mode is a recognition that we are not the ultimate source of meaning.

"The first way of being humble," writes Ignatius, is to desire "that in all things I may be obedient to the law of God our Lord." In other words, humility means recognizing that we don't make our own rules. The moral order comes from elsewhere. The purpose of life isn't to manipulate the world to advance our own interests. It's to grow into the creature God created us to be.

July 8

Forget about Yourself

If you meet a really humble man, he will not be thinking about humility: he will not be thinking about himself at all.

— C. S. Lewis

It's not much fun to converse with somebody who's immersed in their own concerns. They rattle on about their worries, their opinions, their plans, their experiences. They're sitting right in front of you, but they are not really "there." It's also tense and awkward when you're self-conscious in the middle of a conversation: *How am I coming across? How did that sound? Am I making a good impression?*

The most satisfying conversations are those when the parties have lost themselves in the flow of the talk. You're not thinking about yourself, and neither is the other person. You've lost yourselves in the world of the other person. Humility is freedom from the disease of self-absorption. It's liberation from the self.

Humility doesn't mean undervaluing yourself. It means valuing other people.

July 9

Doing "Important" Work

When I had made a decision to spend my whole life doing nothing else but work that is looked on as particularly contemptible and trivial, there followed a great strengthening of the spirit of humility.

— PETER FABER, SJ

One day Peter Faber was bored and annoyed by the work he was doing in the household of a nobleman. Faber was a man of some consequence — a founder of the Jesuits, a confidant of popes and princes — yet in this home he was spending most of his time with the servants and children. He thought he should be doing something more important. Faber saw the pride in this attitude. He decided that it would be okay with him if he spent the rest of his life doing such humble work. In fact, he decided he'd be happy if he spent the rest of his life with the lowly ones.

Faber came to see that humble work was important work. Hearing the confessions of children was just as important as counseling princes. His pride had blinded him to that fact.

What makes your work important?

The Safer Path

The hypersensitive are subject to paralyzing self-doubt and second thoughts that keep them from translating sound inspirations into action. They spontaneously ask themselves questions like, "Am I really seeking my own glory?" "Will this cause scandal?" "Would the safer way be to back off, or at least wait?" "Couldn't x, y, or z go wrong?"

— DEAN BRACKLEY, SJ

There are good reasons to be cautious: It's smart to do your due diligence, understand what you're getting into, and think through the implications. Then there are bad reasons: It's easy to think something might go wrong, you'll get blamed for it, and it's safer to wait.

Ignatius thought that spiritually sensitive people were geniuses at finding reasons not to do things. Ignatius's counsel is to make a reasonable decision and stick to it. Resist the temptation to entertain second thoughts. Unless there is a clear reason to question one's original plans, resist doubts and fears and follow through on the original decision. Above all, don't take the safer path just because it's safer.

July 11

Things Fall Apart

Ignatius was obsessed with self-awareness: "Am I on the right track? What does God want from me? Am I fervent or am I in desolation?" We have to know where we are going.

— ANTHONY DE MELLO, SJ

Steven Pinker, a Harvard psychologist, says that the second law of thermodynamics punctures our illusions that we've got things under control. The law, as you may remember from high school physics, states than the energy in any closed system will eventually reach a state of static equilibrium. Without input, the system will become less organized, less active, less able to do anything until, eventually, nothing is happening. In other words, trouble is built into the very nature of things. Without constant attention, the things we build, the relationships we cherish, the projects we launch will run down, fall over, go off track, stop.

The law applies to our inner life as well. We will regularly experience what Ignatius called "desolation" — alienation from our true selves, separation from God. We'll get confused and mistrustful. That's why Ignatius insisted that we pay attention to these inner movements of the spirit.

Your spiritual practice will deteriorate unless you pay attention to it.

It Was All Pride

Pride was what made the angels fall.

— GRAHAM GREENE, *THE POWER AND THE GLORY*

Graham Greene's novel *The Power and the Glory* is about a priest who becomes trapped in a quagmire of pride, but who nevertheless does good. The priest (who is unnamed) lives in a part of Mexico in the 1920s where Catholic worship was forbidden and priests were hunted and killed. The priest decides to stay with his people — an admirable decision made for the wrong reason, out of pride, so that he would appear good before God and his people. He suffers and fails: He drinks too much, he fathers a child. He despairs over his weakness — but he continues to help his people as best he can. It's a redemptive suffering: He's never complacent. He exemplifies humility — all the while thinking he is consumed by pride.

Finally the priest reaches a place of safety but returns to danger because someone needs him. It's the priest's greatest act of heroism, and the key to the essence of humility. He puts the needs of others before his own.

The Undiscovered Ocean

For now we see through a glass darkly.

— 1 CORINTHIANS 13:12

Isaac Newton was one of the greatest scientists who ever lived, yet at the end of his life he suspected that his accomplishments might not amount to much in the larger scheme of things. "I seem to have been only like a boy playing on the seashore," he said, "finding a smoother pebble or prettier shell than ordinary, whilst the great ocean of truth lay all undiscovered before me."

Many scientists believe that it's only a matter of time until humankind sails the whole ocean and learns all of nature's secrets. But not all do. A school of thought called "mysterianism" holds that the human intellect has limits. Consciousness, time, the origin of life, the full story of the universe — these and other mysteries will never be fully understood by us. The idea that we'll one day know everything is an illusion, a trick of the overconfident human mind. Every other creature in nature has a limited intellect: The smartest dog will never be able to solve differential equations; the cleverest monkey will never grasp the laws of physics. Why should humans be any different?

There's much we don't know, much that we'll *never* know.

July 14

We Can't Be Sure

When the enemy of our salvation sees that we are humble, he tries to draw us on to a humility that is excessive and counterfeit.

— IGNATIUS LOYOLA

Epistemic humility is knowing that our knowledge is always incomplete and provisional. We don't know everything about anything, and what we think we know might be wrong. It's a good point to keep in mind when you're forming opinions and making decisions. You can't be sure. Don't be overconfident, and be ready to change your mind if new facts come out.

However, the reasonable axiom that "we can't be sure" can lead to an insidious form of false humility. "We can't be sure" — therefore it's okay for me to do nothing, or whatever I want. "I can't be sure that being careful about what I eat will do me any good, so I'll eat what I want" (even though I'm diabetic). "A new job might be better than this one, but I can't be sure, so I'll stay put." "I won't check my answers on the math test because I can't be sure I'll catch all the mistakes."

This isn't real humility. It's a cloak for pride.

July 15

Failure Is Your Teacher

Times of spiritual desolation are exercises in humility; they remind us that we cannot make, summon, or control grace.

— KEVIN O'BRIEN, SJ

"Learn from your mistakes" may be a cliché, but it's still wise advice. Unless you fail, you won't learn how to do things better. Failure is your teacher.

When things go well, it's easy to go one's merry way without a second thought. Why bother to go back and analyze a success? Your decisions were obviously correct. You were ready for problems when they arose. It happened just the way you thought it would. Bring on the next challenge! But what if your decisions were actually bad ones — and the project succeeded anyway? What if you were just lucky, and the disaster you weren't prepared for never happened? It's only when we fail that we ask the hard questions.

That's why Ignatius thought so highly of failure. Failure brings objectivity. It causes you to ask why. It gives you a reason to ask what you could have done, and what you can do better in the future.

July 16

Speak Up

The devil is ready to suggest that a good person sins if he speaks of the graces our Lord has given him.

— IGNATIUS LOYOLA

There are lots of good reasons to keep one's mouth shut. You might not know what to say in this situation. Maybe you're silent so that others may speak. Maybe you're silent because you know you're tempted to talk to show off. But there are also bad reasons to keep silent. One of them, according to Ignatius, is hesitating to mention the good things that have happened to you because you're afraid that someone will think you're proud. It's false humility to be silent when you have a chance to talk about how good and generous God is.

If you stay silent because you think that makes you look modest and humble, that's pride, not humility.

July 17

When You Must *Speak...*

Be slow to speak. Be considerate and kind, especially when it comes to deciding on matters under discussion. If you must speak, then give your opinion with the greatest possible humility and sincerity, and always end with the words salvo meliori iudicio — *with due respect for a better opinion.*

— IGNATIUS LOYOLA

Sometimes it's best to listen for a while. In 1546 Ignatius instructed some Jesuit theologians about how they were to conduct themselves at the Council of Trent, which would chart the future of the Catholic Church. The stakes couldn't have been higher. Ignatius thought this was a time for discretion in speech and humility in expressing opinions.

- Speak only after you've listened to others "so that you may understand the meaning, leanings, and wishes of those who do speak."
- Understand the reasoning behind the opinions expressed.
- Don't join factions, stay independent, "deal with everyone on an equal basis."
- Speak humbly. Acknowledge that a better opinion might come along.

This is pretty good advice for participating in any discussion of important matters.

The Problem Lies Within

You are mistaken in thinking that the cause of your disquiet is due to the place, or your superiors, or your brethren. This disquiet comes from within and not from without.

— IGNATIUS LOYOLA

Recovering alcoholics and addicts talk about "doing a geographic" — short for "geographic cure." This is the effort to fix an unhappy life by packing one's bags and moving to a new city for a fresh start. It's an attractive option for many alcoholics and addicts who've often lost their jobs and alienated their friends and family. Sometimes the geographic cure works — for a while, until the old problems emerge again. They've been there all along, lodged in the addict's wounded spirit. As the saying goes, everywhere you go, there you are.

That's what Ignatius is telling the complaining Jesuit: The problem is *you*. You can change your residence, find different work, get a different boss, and you will *still* be unhappy, and it's your pride that prevents you from seeing this. Pride says that my miserable job, my boring apartment, my nagging spouse are making me unhappy. Humility reveals the truth: The problem lies within.

To fix unhappiness, look inside first.

July 19

Frozen

Many let themselves be persuaded that they don't count for much, that they don't have much to say or much of a mission in life. They stifle their inner voice; they fail to speak and act when they should do so.

— DEAN BRACKLEY, SJ

In Dante's *Divine Comedy*, the poet journeys through the circles of hell until he comes upon Satan himself in the depths of the ninth circle. Dante depicts him as a creature frozen from the waist down. He flaps his wings in the frigid air; the breeze keeps the ice from melting. Satan is frozen in place — in ice of his own making. It's an arresting image of monstrous pride.

Many people are frozen in place, unable to act. Dean Brackley suggests that fear is at the core of their paralysis — fear of failing, fear of looking bad, fear of ridicule. The fear is actually pride shrouded in the appearance of humility.

Simplicity Is a Flame

"Be at peace," I told her. And she had knelt to receive this peace. May she keep it forever. It will be I that gave it her. Oh, miracle — thus to be able to give what we ourselves do not possess, sweet miracle of our empty hands! Hope which was shriveling in my heart flowered again in hers; the spirit of prayer which I thought lost in me forever was given back to her by God.

— GEORGES BERNANOS, THE DIARY OF A COUNTRY PRIEST

Georges Bernanos's novel *The Diary of a Country Priest* takes up a paradox of humility: Any conscious attempt to attain it is self-defeating. We reach it only when we've forgotten about it. The main character is an awkward, sickly young priest with meager intellectual and pastoral gifts. He accomplishes little in his village parish. Children mock him. Adults ignore him. He thinks little of himself. But he loves the people in his parish. He notices their suffering and tries to help them. Time and again people experience God's love and forgiveness through him, even though he thinks he's a failure.

The priest is a symbol of Christ. Because he is empty of self, he becomes a channel through which God's love flows to others. A friend tells him, "Your simplicity is a kind of flame which scorches them. You go through the world with that lowly smile of yours as though you begged the world their pardon for being alive, while all the time you carry a torch."

July 21

Tentative Judgments

Those who are united with God have the humility to recognize that their judgments are at best indicative, not definitive.

— WILLIAM A. BARRY, SJ, AND ROBERT G. DOHERTY, SJ

A story from the Platform Sutra, a text of Chinese Chan Buddhism, addresses the puzzle of knowledge and humility. One of the master's followers had become very knowledgeable about a difficult point of Buddhist doctrine, but he had become proud of what he knew. The master rebuked him for arrogance, commenting that knowledge had fettered the man's mind rather than liberating it.

Ignatius had great respect for learning, but he insisted that one gained knowledge and skill for the sake of serving others. He noticed that arrogant smart people — persons of "great talent exerting great labor" — often didn't accomplish very much. They fell short because they didn't let themselves be moved by God; they acted out of self-love. "They achieve results proportioned to their own weak and feeble hands," he wrote.

Great knowledge and great humility often don't mix well.

Humility and Hubris

Humility says, "How can I serve you?" Hubris says, "Here's how you fix yourself."

— GREGORY BOYLE, SJ

Hubris is a hard word. It's worse than pride. To the ancient Greeks, hubris was a breaching of limits that had been set by the gods and usually brought swift punishment. Icarus tumbled into the sea when he ignored instructions and flew too close to the sun. In the Bible, hubris is pride mingled with cruelty. It's arrogant contempt for the rights of others. The biblical proverb "pride goes before destruction" is talking about hubris.

So it's a bit startling that the Jesuit Greg Boyle, founder of the Homeboy ministries to gangs in Los Angeles, says it's hubris to tell troubled people what they need to do to fix themselves. After all, this happens all the time. Whole professions, whole bureaucracies, are devoted to telling people what they should do to straighten themselves out. You've probably done it yourself.

What's needed instead is humility, asking: How can I serve you? It respects other people. It acknowledges limits; we don't really know how someone else should live. Hubris is telling people what they ought to do. Humility is sharing a life with them.

July 23

Humility as a Healer

A great turning point in our lives came when we sought for humility as something we really wanted, rather than as something we must have.

— BILL W.

The first step in the Alcoholics Anonymous program of recovery is an admission of powerlessness. The alcoholic is defeated. They can't stop drinking and they can't keep drinking. There's no way out. Their only hope is to admit defeat and cry out to God for help. It's a humility born of desperation.

A turning point in the program comes with step seven: "Humbly asked Him to remove our shortcomings." Bill Wilson, AA's founder, says that alcoholics can take this step after seeing how it has transformed others' lives: "Everywhere we saw failure and misery transformed by humility into priceless assets. We heard story after story of how humility had brought strength out of weakness. In every case, pain had been the price of admission into a new life. But this admission price had purchased more than we expected. It brought a measure of humility, which we soon discovered to be a healer of pain."

It's a profound insight into the nature of humility. Humility brings healing as we face pain instead of running from it, accept responsibility instead of blaming misfortunes on circumstances and other people. The humility of desperation is a humility of healing.

Who Do You Worship?

Here's something else that's weird but true: in the day-to-day trenches of adult life, there is actually no such thing as atheism. There is no such thing as not worshipping. Everybody worships. The only choice we get is what to worship.

— DAVID FOSTER WALLACE

One of our most cherished illusions is that happiness consists in doing what we want to do. *I* call the shots. *I* am in control. The truth is that "you're gonna have to serve somebody," in the words of Bob Dylan. We all do someone's bidding. We dance to their tune. The only choice we have is *who* to serve.

Make sure you choose wisely because you'll come to value what your master values and think how your master thinks. A bad choice has bad consequences. If you serve riches, you'll always be poor. If it's honor, someone will always be sneering at you. If you want health above all, you'll always be sick. If beauty is your aim, you'll always be ugly. If it's power, you'll always be fighting those who want to take it away from you. If it's all about you, *you* is what you'll get — lonely, anxious, wondering what trick the boss will pull next.

Ignatius says that the wise choice is to "imitate Christ our Lord better and to be more like him here and now." We're to imitate Christ's humility: his simple life, his indifference to what others thought about him, his devotion to his mission.

Imitating Christ

What does the LORD require of you but to do justice, and to love kindness, and to walk humbly with your God?

— MICAH 6:8

The ancient philosophers had nothing good to say about humility. Humble people were the despised, poor, and lowly. They lacked the strength, independence, and command that people should have. The Stoic philosopher Epictetus even frowned on prayers of petition. He thought that the only thing we should ask the gods for is the power to make ourselves what we want to be.

The Jews came along and said that the lowly people were especially beloved by God. God took care of the humble; their poverty and weakness put them in a good position to love God in return and to keep his law. To be humble came to be seen as a central part of recognizing the power and mystery of God. Moses, the great leader of the Hebrews, was "the humblest man on earth."

With the Christians, humility was no longer an idea but a virtue embodied in a person, Jesus Christ — God himself, who took on the form of a slave and was born into human flesh. "He humbled himself." At the core, being a Christian means following a person and trying to become like him, and Jesus's outstanding characteristic is his humility.

July 26

Praying for the Interrogators

Gradually, too, I learned to purify my prayer and remove from it all the elements of self-seeking. I learned to pray for my interrogators, not so they would see things my way or come to the truth so that my ordeal would end, but because they, too, were children of God and human beings in need of his blessing and his daily grace.

— WALTER CISZEK, SJ

Walter Ciszek's interrogators were not nice people. Ciszek was an American Jesuit who spent twenty-four years in confinement in the Soviet Union for conducting clandestine missionary work. Five of those years were spent in the infamous Lubyanka prison in Moscow where he was treated harshly, often brutally. His interrogators would often wake him up in the middle of the night and accuse him of being a spy. It was a terrible ordeal, but Ciszek overcame pain and resentment to grasp an essential truth: His captors were children of God as much in need of God's grace as he was.

This seems extraordinary, but Ciszek probably didn't think so. He was simply following the implications of Christian humility. Humility means thinking about other people instead of yourself. Ciszek did this in extreme circumstances, where the other people were especially unlovable.

When your grievances build up, think of Walter Ciszek.

July 27

Exercises in Humility

The second experience is to serve for a month in a hospital. The candidates should help and serve all the sick and the well, in conformity with the directions they receive, in order to lower and humble themselves more.

— THE CONSTITUTIONS OF THE SOCIETY OF JESUS, 66

Men in training to be Jesuits are exposed to various "experiences" to see if they have what it takes. One is an assignment to do janitorial work or help with the cooking in a Jesuit community. Another is to take care of the sick and infirm in a hospital or rehab facility. The idea is to puncture egos. Jesuits are high-status men, accomplished, highly educated — in training to be leaders. Emptying bedpans and sweeping floors help keep the ego in check. It's humble work that humbles "important" people.

Humility isn't an abstraction. It is a virtue that's expressed in concrete acts. It's a matter of how you treat other people, of how you spend your time and where you direct your energy.

July 28

Litany of Humility

From the fear of being humiliated,
From the fear of being despised,
From the fear of suffering rebukes,
From the fear of being forgotten,
From the fear of being ridiculed,
From the fear of being wronged,
Deliver me, O Jesus.

— Cardinal Rafael Merry del Val y Zulueta

A litany is a repetitive list, often involving misfortunes. Your teenager has a litany of complaints. A litany of injuries to key players can decimate your favorite team. Cardinal Merry del Val's "Litany of Humility" is a list of bad things that might happen. He doesn't pray that they *won't* happen. He prays that he will be delivered from the *fear* of these things happening. *Fear* is the problem.

You deal with fear by facing it. Make a litany of humility part of your spiritual practice:

From fear of messing up my PowerPoint presentation,
From fear of sickness,
From fear of letting other people down,
From fear of missing my deadline,
From fear of my debts,
Deliver me, O God.

Some of these bad things might happen, but we don't need to be afraid of them. No matter what happens, God will be with you.

July 29

Christ Chose the Poor

Our Lord so preferred the poor to the rich that he chose all his apostles from among the poor. He lived and associated with them. He made them princes of His church. To such a degree has He exalted the state of poverty!

— Ignatius Loyola

In Ignatius's thinking, the root of pride is the desire for riches. "Riches" are money and the things money can buy, but it also includes intangible goods like our skills, reputation, and status. If these "riches" are what we really care about, we'll seek more of them. And more. And more. If riches make you who you are, wanting more of them means wanting more of yourself. Pretty soon, *you* is all you care about. The Jesuit Joseph Tetlow puts it neatly. At first you say, "Look at all this stuff I have." Then you say, "Look at me. I have all this stuff." Finally you say, "Look at ME."

If pride is rooted in riches, humility is rooted in poverty. Ignatius had a high regard for material poverty. He noted that Jesus had no possessions to speak of, that he preferred the company of poor people, and his chief disciples came from the class of tradesman and laborers he grew up with. Poverty, Ignatius thought, made it easier to avoid the mistake of defining yourself according to what you have and what others think of you.

A simple life, uncluttered by riches, makes it easier to think about yourself less and others more — the essence of humility.

Why Humility Is Hard

*O my God, make me to see things as they really are, that I may not
be deceived by any illusion.*

— St. Thérèse of Lisieux

The biggest illusion is that the world revolves around *you*.
It's an illusion that we're all hard-wired to believe. *You* are
the center of every experience you've ever had. You look out
at the world through *your* eyes, hear it with *your* ears, interpret it with *your* reason, and feel it with *your* feelings. Moralists complain about egocentricity as if it's a bad choice that
truly virtuous people don't make. Well, egocentricity is an
inescapable literal fact of consciousness. From the moment
you wake up in the morning, it seems obvious that you are
the center of things. But you're not. It's a trick of perception,
an illusion.

That's why humility is hard. It's the ability to see through
an illusion that looks very real.

July 31

Be the Person You Are

Humility consists in being precisely the person you actually are before God.

— THOMAS MERTON

There's a paradox at the heart of humility. Humility is forgetting about the self: thinking of others and working for their welfare. But only someone with a healthy sense of self can forget themselves. To be humble, you need to know who you are: a redeemed sinner, loved by God, someone of great dignity and worth. *Then* you can let yourself go.

August

COMPASSION
AND TRUST

If you want others to be happy, practice compassion.
If you want to be happy, practice compassion.

— DALAI LAMA

Therefore I will trust Him.
Whatever, wherever I am.
I can never be thrown away.

— JOHN HENRY NEWMAN

Practice Compassion

In the name of Allah the Compassionate, the Merciful.

— QURAN

Practice compassion — it's a universal ethical principal. The classical Buddhist tradition regards compassion as the noblest quality of the human heart. Compassion is one of the Three Treasures of the Tao Te Ching (the other two are simplicity and humility). According to the Hebrew scriptures, compassion is one of God's most outstanding qualities: "And He will give you mercy, and have mercy upon you and multiply you."

In the Christian view, God shows us compassion "so that we may be able to console those who are in any affliction with the consolation with which we ourselves are consoled by God" (2 Corinthians 1:4). In other words, the compassion shown us is meant to be shared with others.

August 2

Being There

Ignatian compassion is essentially our loving presence. There is nothing we can do. There is little we can say. But we can be there.

— David L. Fleming, SJ

The word *compassion* is made from two Latin words: *com*, meaning "with," and *passio*, meaning "suffer." A compassionate person is one who suffers with another. This is the particular emphasis Ignatian spirituality gives to compassion.

There is nothing we can do about much of the suffering we encounter. Our dying friend isn't going to get better. Aging bodies will continue to break down. Nothing can undo the pain and suffering that come with loss. All we can do is *be* with our suffering friends and neighbors.

The gift of our loving presence is the most precious gift.

August 3

Mercy Is Unreasonable

I learned that to show mercy to others is a very effectual means of finding mercy ourselves with God, and how easy it is to receive spiritual gifts from God if we give generously to others ourselves.

— PETER FABER, SJ

Compassion isn't based in reason. The Stoic moralist Seneca justified killing deformed and sickly babies, explaining that "it is reason which separates the harmful from the sound." Aristotle said masters were free to discard aged and injured slaves because "the slave is no different from a living tool, and what consideration can a tool receive?" Nietzsche condemned compassion because inducing the strong to feel bad for the weak just increases the amount of suffering in the world. These are observations based in reason.

Compassion comes from a place deeper than reason. It opens a conduit to God. It taps into a divine system of merciful exchange. Ignatius's friend Peter Faber wept when he realized that showing mercy to others made it easier for him to receive mercy from God. It was a "great knowledge," he wrote. As the Jewish Kabbalah puts it: "If a man does kindness on earth, he awakens loving-kindness above."

August 4

Seeing Things as They Really Are

Gratitude will keep us humble, compassionate, able to see things as they really are.

— WILLIAM A. BARRY, SJ

Peter came to Jesus one day with a question we've all had: How often do I need to forgive someone who won't stop doing the thing that offends me? "Seventy-seven times," Jesus replied, meaning: You forgive *all* the time, you never stop forgiving. Then he illustrated this with the parable of the unforgiving servant. The servant owed a gigantic debt to his master, which the master mercifully forgave. But the servant then went to the people who owed *him* money and demanded payment. He treated his debtors brutally; he threw them into prison until they paid up. When the master found out about this, he was furious. "I showed you mercy," he told the servant. "You should have done likewise."

The servant forgot how richly he had been blessed. He took it for granted; it slipped his mind. His ingratitude led to moral blindness and hardness of heart. Gratitude isn't seeing things through rose-colored glasses. It's seeing things as they really are.

August 5

No Us and Them, Just Us

How can we achieve a kind of compassion that stands in awe at what the poor have to carry rather than stand in judgment at how they carry it? For the measure of our compassion lies not in our service of those on the margins but in our willingness to see ourselves in kinship with them.

— GREGORY BOYLE, SJ

A key moment in the *Lord of the Rings* saga comes when Frodo and Sam capture the deranged creature Gollum, who has been stalking them, hoping to steal the One Ring, which he once possessed. Sam wants to kill Gollum, and indeed this seems to be the reasonable thing to do. Gollum is a mortal threat to their mission and their lives. But Frodo shows mercy. He understands the obsession that drives Gollum because he's experienced it himself. The Ring corrupts everything it touches. Frodo looks past the lies and ugliness and sees in Gollum someone very much like himself.

Gregory Boyle says that it's this kind of kinship — the recognition that we're the same kind of people belonging to the same community — that is the essence of compassion. Boyle works with Black and Hispanic gang members. He's seen members of rival gangs, who once used to hate and fear each other, learn mutual respect and affection. Says Boyle: "What we want to achieve is this sense of mutuality where we obliterate once and for all the illusion that we're separate. No us and them, just us."

August 6

The Qualities of Mercy

[Peter Faber] is unwilling to dwell on others' faults and sins, but would rather bring to God's attention any good he may have observed in the persons. He wants always to have a compassionate heart and feelings of mercy toward all.

— GERHARD KALKBRENNER

Peter Faber, a founder of the Jesuits, was renowned for his compassion. One of his friends, a monk named Gerhard Kalkbrenner, listed some of Faber's notably merciful attitudes.

- He had "no wish to have zeal for the execution of God's justice."
- He would rather offer excuses for other people's sins than to dwell on them.
- He would "bring to God's attention any good he may have observed in the persons."
- If he needed to mention someone's offenses, he would use "gentle words."
- He wouldn't say anything if he felt indignation, but would wait until he felt charitable.

August 7

Compassionate Feelings

Compassionate feelings, whatever their intensity, fall short of the true grace of compassion unless they contain the sense of involvement on our side.

— Michael Ivens, SJ

Compassionate feelings come easily for some people. Others — not so much. Ignatius was in the first camp — a weeper when he encountered suffering. One day he burst into tears when he heard that a poor beggar had been accused of stealing his clothes. Ignatius had given the man his clothes, but no one believed the beggar's story. Ignatius's imagination kicked in. He put himself in the beggar's place — mocked, abused, harassed, threatened with beating and jail. He wept in compassion.

Others can hear a story of woe and be emotionally unmoved. One of Ignatius's Jesuit friends complained to him that some fellow Jesuits were doing work with the poor and suffering without showing much visible feeling. This didn't bother Ignatius. Some people are put together that way, he said. It would be a mistake to try to change them. In any case, compassionate deeds matter more than compassionate feelings.

August 8

Notice the Person in the Ditch

The Good Samaritan noticed the man in the ditch. He included him in his circle of concern. Compassion means noticing the needs of others.

— GERALD FAGIN, SJ

Simply *noticing* that others are in need is the first step in compassion. This is harder than it seems.

In Jesus's parable of the Good Samaritan, we're shocked by the callousness of the priest and the levite who ignore the man wounded and bleeding in a ditch. What are they thinking? Probably: "I can't get involved," "I'm sure someone has called 911 already," "Nothing I can do will help," or "How sad, yet another tragedy on the Jerusalem-Jericho road." You've probably had such thoughts yourself when coming on a scene of pain and suffering. There are lots of ways to move the suffering of others to the backdrop of our lives, acknowledged but not *seen*.

The Good Samaritan reacted differently: "When he saw him, he was moved with compassion, came to him, and bound up his wounds, pouring on oil and wine." He acted compassionately, but first he *saw* the need right before his eyes.

August 9

Be Kind

Be among the disciples of Aaron, loving peace and pursuing peace, loving people and bringing them closer to the Torah.

— PIRKEI AVOT, 1:13

In Jewish tradition, Aaron, Moses's brother, was famous for his compassion toward people in conflict, especially quarreling spouses and friends who were angry with each other. He fervently believed that in their deepest core everyone desires peace. The medieval Jewish sage Maimonides extended compassion to include acts of loving-kindness. He thought that compassion includes paying attention to people, asking after their health, offering hospitality, and treating everyone with warmth.

Acts of compassion don't have to be as dramatic as the Good Samaritan's rescue operation. In fact, most of them are simple gestures of loving-kindness, the kinds of things we can do dozens of times every day.

August 10

Schadenfreude

Why do you see the speck in your neighbor's eye, but do not notice the log in your own eye?

— MATTHEW 7:3

Schadenfreude is a German word for the pleasure we take in the misfortunes of others. It's the opposite of compassion. Schopenhauer thought that its presence in a person's heart was a clear sign of evil. If so, we're in trouble; we seem to be hardwired for schadenfreude. It's at the heart of the popularity of "reality television," westerns, mystery thrillers, superhero blockbusters, Shakespearean tragedies, and other dramas that show the "bad guys" getting their deserved comeuppance in the end. We especially like it when people who are smarter, nicer, and holier than us are laid low by misfortune.

That's why compassion isn't easy. It challenges some powerful impulses in our divided hearts.

Compassion for Everyone

As he was setting out on a journey, a man ran up and knelt before him, and asked him, "Good Teacher, what must I do to inherit eternal life?"…Jesus, looking at him, loved him, and said, "You lack one thing; go, sell what you own, and give the money to the poor, and you will have treasure in heaven; then come, follow me." When he heard this, he was shocked and went away grieving, for he had many possessions.

— MARK 10:17, 21–22

When we hear the word *compassion*, what often comes to mind are tender feelings for people who've been battered around by life — the sick and suffering, the poor and the weak. But how about compassion for healthy, powerful, privileged people who are suffering? Consider the rich young man in Mark's gospel; he's turned his back on Jesus, yet Jesus looks on him with love and compassion.

How much compassion do you have for the politician you loath entangled in a sex scandal? How about the boastful CEO whose company goes bankrupt? Are you sad or secretly pleased when the coworker you don't like very much is "restructured" out of their job?

Compassion is for everyone, not just for those who seem to deserve it.

August 12

To Love Is to Suffer

Pain is so much a part of the love that the love would be vastly di-minished, unrecognizable, without it. To suffer in love for another's suffering is to live life not only at its fullest but at its holiest.

— FREDERICK BUECHNER

A thought experiment: Sometime in the future, a person you love deeply dies. You are given a choice. Grieve for a year or so, intensely at first, and then gradually less painfully as the months go by, until you reach a point of equilibrium and acceptance. Or you can take a magic pill and go straight to the acceptance, skipping all the pain. Would you take the pill?

Most people probably wouldn't. We understand that pain is part of love. Buechner takes it a step further. *All* the pain we experience in relationships is part of love. Having a family and friends means that at times we will be disap-pointed in them, angry at them; we'll lie awake nights wor-rying about them; we'll weep with them; we'll suffer with them in their misfortune and loss. If they die before we do, we'll grieve them.

To live is to suffer, said the Buddha. To love is to suffer is also true.

August 13

Through Thick and Thin

Sing for joy, O heavens, and exult, O earth;
*   break forth, O mountains, into singing!*
For the LORD has comforted his people,
*   and will have compassion on his suffering ones.*

— ISAIAH 49:13

The Hebrew word for compassion is *rachamim*. The root of this word is *rechem* — womb. Compassion means feeling for another the way a woman feels for an unborn child in her womb — protected, loved, as intimately close as it's possible to be. A woman loves her born children, of course, but not with the same clarity. Her sons and daughters might disappoint or anger her on occasion. But she doesn't feel that way about the child who is yet to be born.

The Bible is saying that this is the way God feels about us — with *rachamim*, "womb-love."

August 14

Compassion Is a Gift

Hope and trust that we will be given the gift of a compassionate heart for all our unfortunate brothers and sisters and not turn our gaze away from their plight. Compassion is the beginning of doing something.

— WILLIAM A. BARRY, SJ

It was a big day for the young writer Frederick Buechner. He was in New York and had just signed the contract for his first novel; he imagined himself on the brink of literary glory. But shortly after he left his publisher's office, he ran into a man he had known in college. His friend admitted that he was struggling. Currently, he was working as a messenger boy and hoping that he could find something more satisfying. All at once Buechner's good cheer vanished, replaced by a profound sadness at his struggling friend's bad luck. "Something small but unforgettable happened inside me," he wrote, "some small flickering out of the truth that, in the long run, there can be no real joy for anybody until there is joy finally for us all."

Buechner recognized the feeling as a gift. He felt compassion in the literal meaning of the word — *com-passio*, "suffering with" another.

August 15

Feel What Wretches Feel

Poor naked wretches, wheresoe'r you are,
That bide the pelting of this pitiless storm,
How shall your houseless heads and unfed sides,
Your looped and windowed raggedness, defend you
From seasons such as these? O, I have ta'en
Too little care of this.

— WILLIAM SHAKESPEARE, *KING LEAR*

Compassion can open your eyes. Compassion can heal.

Consider King Lear, an arrogant and very foolish monarch whose catastrophic mistakes wreck his comfortable world. In act 3 of Shakespeare's play, his power gone, homeless, despised by his daughters, Lear finds himself wandering on the heath in the midst of a raging storm. Lear suffers for the first time in his privileged life; he understands what it means to be poor and weak, and when he stumbles across a group of wretched people struggling to survive, he feels compassion. He regrets that he'd neglected the poor and needy in his kingdom when he had power.

You might follow Lear's example and "expose thyself to feel what wretches feel." You meet suffering people every day. Notice them; feel what it means to be like them, and see what happens.

August 16

Compassion Fatigue

The poor will always be with us. So also will the physical and moral evils that make them so. Our efforts are dwarfed before their immensity.

— JOHN KAVANAUGH, SJ

The Jesuit philosopher and ethicist John Kavanaugh loved Peter, Jesus's impulsive and often obtuse chief disciple. Kavanaugh thought about Peter when he got compassion fatigue in the face of human suffering.

Peter made lots of mistakes. He caught only glimpses of what Jesus was all about. Once, he ran his mouth at the wrong time and said something Jesus didn't want to hear. Jesus wheeled on him, rebuked him, and called him a devil for saying such a thing. That must have stung badly, but Peter carried on in faith, his knowledge feeble, his abilities shaky, but he was able to trust Jesus and do what he could. Writes Kavanaugh:

> In the end, it is not our task to end the sin and suffering of the world or to stop the mindless march of violence. It is, rather, to follow a different way: to take opportunities, small as they may be, to reduce hatred and carnage, to let go fears, and to entrust even our poor inadequacy to the hands of God. This is the taking up of our daily cross.

What Matters in the End

Come, you that are blessed by my Father, inherit the kingdom pre-
pared for you from the foundation of the world; for I was hungry
and you gave me food, I was thirsty and you gave me something to
drink, I was a stranger and you welcomed me, I was naked and you
gave me clothing, I was sick and you took care of me, I was in prison
and you visited me.

— MATTHEW 25:34–36 ·

Ignatius said that love is expressed more in deeds than in
words. That's the point of the great vision of the Last Judgment at the end of time in Matthew's gospel. The blessed
are rewarded for what they *did* — they fed the hungry, welcomed the stranger, bound the wounds of the injured and
sick. Those who are lost are condemned for what they failed
to do. They ignored the needs of others. They failed the test
of love.

In the end, what matters is the compassion in our
hearts — and the deeds of love that compassion inspires.

August 18

Trust in Someone

It is one thing to have faith or believe that *a statement is true or* that
someone is telling the truth. It is something else altogether — involv-
ing the whole person and not just one's intellect — to have faith in
someone or to believe in *something, in other words, to* trust.

— RONALD MODRAS

When Jesus said that faith could move mountains, he wasn't
talking about belief in the Trinity, the Incarnation, or other
creeds and doctrines formulated by the Christian churches
over the centuries. He was talking about himself — trust in
him and his teaching. This is what faith means in other religious traditions, too. Buddhists speak of *Śraddhā*, a commitment to a teacher and a teaching. The biblical Hebrew
word for faith, *emunah*, means trusting something solid and
firm. The Arabic *amoona* has the same meaning for Muslims.

This was Ignatius's idea of faith. He avoided the doctri-
nal controversies of the Reformation and molded his teaching on the biblical idea of faith: trust in God, confidence in
Jesus, and desire to mold one's life on his. Faith is trust. It's
personal. It's a relationship. Having faith takes everything
you've got.

God Will Supply What Is Lacking

Do what you can calmly and gently; leave to God's providence what you cannot manage yourself. God is well pleased with the earnestness and moderate anxiety with which we attend to our obligations, but He is not pleased with that anxiety which afflicts the soul. He wishes our limitations and weakness to seek the support of His strength and omnipotence, with the trust that in His goodness he will supply what is lacking to our weakness and shortcomings.

— IGNATIUS LOYOLA

Ignatius had a busy friend named Jerome Vines who seemed to have been prone to anxiety, and perhaps self-doubt, judging by the advice Ignatius gave him. Ignatius didn't tell Vines not to be anxious. He accepted "moderate" anxiety — it's normal, even useful. It's the anxiety that afflicts the soul that's the problem. Neither did he tell him to cheer up and think positive thoughts. In fact, he encouraged his friend to admit that his strength and skills were limited. His weakness was an invitation to trust in God "who will supply what is lacking."

It's good advice for us, too. The challenges of life are really beyond us, and we're anxious about this. Ignatius says this is an invitation to trust God.

August 20

A Friend You Can Trust

I mean by a friend one who will give as well as take; I mean one who will trust me far enough to let me see his weakness as I let him see mine, knowing that I too will not misunderstand, or misinterpret, or become impatient, or condemn, or turn upon my heel and walk no more with him, even as I know he will not do the like to me.

— ALBAN GOODIER, SJ

We all want a friend or two like the one Goodier is describing — someone who is open, who trusts us, and whom we can trust and rely on and know is always there for us. Now, you might be tempted to ask how your friends measure up to this ideal, but instead let's turn it around. What kind of friend are *you*? After all, the Ignatian practice is about scrutinizing what *we* do, not what other people do.

Are you candid with your friends? Do you lean on them in times of trouble? Or are you the "strong" partner in the relationship, the one who gives but never takes, the helper who doesn't need help? Are you generous with your time or do you ration it? Do you come when you're needed?

Be the kind of friend your friends can trust.

August 21

Don't Trust Everything You Hear

Be careful when you inform yourself about things. Much of our lives is spent gathering information. We see very few things for ourselves, and live trusting others. Seldom does truth reach us unalloyed. It is always blended with the emotions it has passed through.

— Baltasar Gracián, SJ

We need to be skeptical about the information that comes our way. As Gracián says, information sources are biased, colored by emotion, and agenda-driven. But that's only half the story. *We* are biased, colored by emotion, and agenda-driven. Consider the problem of "motivated reasoning." We will quickly accept new information that supports what we already believe, but we're much more skeptical about information that challenges our beliefs.

For example, if you're someone who enjoys alcohol, you'll be pleased to hear about a scientific study that says that drinking a glass of wine every day is good for the heart. But you won't be so pleased if the study says that alcohol is *bad* for the heart. Your impulse is to look for reasons to reject it. "It's only one study," "These studies contradict each other." "No one knows anything for sure about alcohol and the heart." "Correlation, not causation." In this way we pretend to be hard-nosed skeptics, but we've effectively screened out important information because we don't want to hear it.

All the more reason to be careful about what you hear.

As Good as Your Word

I wouldn't know what to do with someone whose word cannot be trusted. How would you drive a wagon without a yoke or a chariot without a crossbar?

— CONFUCIUS

"Trust no one" is the first rule of cybersecurity. Change your passwords. Use two-factor authentication. Never download a file unless you know who sent it. But "trust no one" is a terrible rule for social life. You can't get through the day unless you trust a host of people and organizations to do the work they say they're going to do. Even the money in your wallet is nothing more than trust.

Trust is the thread that holds families and communities together. It's the key to human relationships. If trust is ever broken, even unintentionally, it's very hard to restore it. That's why it's important to be someone whose word can be trusted. Always deliver on the commitments you make. Make the phone call you said you'd make. Finish the job you've been putting off.

August 23

Trust Your Colleagues

Those who are on the ground will see better what should be done.

— IGNATIUS LOYOLA

One of the biggest challenges of leadership is trusting subordinates to make decisions. It's easy to encourage people to take more initiative — until they actually do. People don't do things the way the boss would. Sometimes, they even make mistakes. It often takes great patience from the leader to support subordinates who've gone out on a limb.

Ignatius was very good at this. One of his outstanding qualities as a leader was his trust in his people. He thought that Jesuits on the scene were in a better position to know what to do than administrators in far-off Rome. He often declined to give direction to Jesuits who asked him what do about a problem, saying that the decision was up to them. It's a policy we can emulate. We have lots of opportunities to trust our colleagues, partners, children, friends — especially when they face trouble and look to us for support.

What We Do Matters

Our own harsh judgments of ourselves may be limited. In living out our vocations, we can only trust that God's call to us is greater than we can fully understand. Can we really know how we have made a difference?

— TIM MULDOON

"Life is but an endless series of little details, actions, speeches, and thoughts," said the Hindi teacher Sivananda. "The consequences whether good or bad of even the least of them are far-reaching." It's a humbling thought. What we do matters, but most of the time we don't know *what* will matter in the long run and *how* it will matter. We hope things will turn out well. But we don't really know.

It's a matter for trust. We forge ahead. Our efforts to be true to our calling will bring greater good than we can know.

What God Do You Believe In?

Ignatius came to the conclusion that he faced a choice. He had to decide what God he believed in. When he chose not to confess his past sins again, he had no guarantee that he was right. He had to act in faith, hope, and love that God was not an ogre ready to pounce on mistakes and forgotten sins.

— WILLIAM A. BARRY, SJ

In the months after his conversion, Ignatius was afflicted with terrible guilt about his past life. He didn't think he would ever be free from his sins and shortcomings. He was wracked with remorse over the things he had done. He couldn't believe that God had forgiven him. He was full of shame and fear. In his despair, he thought about ending it all by throwing himself into the fire. Ignatius *knew* that this was all wrong. God wasn't like this; these thoughts were doing him terrible harm. But his heart was captive to the false idea that God was a fierce judge who never forgave, never forgot, and perpetually held him to impossibly high standards. He was paralyzed, unable to live in freedom.

It came down to a choice: Which God would Ignatius believe in, the God of freedom and love or the God of guilt and anger? He chose by *acting*. He acted *as if* the God of love was the true God. When he did, his scruples melted away. His trust in a God of love and mercy freed him.

August 26

A Way of Proceeding

The earliest Christians were known as "people of the way." They lived according to "the way of Jesus." It was a way of living their daily lives, a distinctive way that others noticed.

— David L. Fleming, SJ

Ignatian spirituality has often been described a "way of proceeding." It's a set of attitudes and customs rather than a clearly defined set of practices and rules. The Ignatian way prizes flexibility and adaptability. It values work. It sees God as present in the world, seeking to communicate with us in the circumstances of our daily lives. It says we find God by reflecting on our experience and by exercising our imagination. It says we find meaning by finding the work we are meant to do. Ignatian spirituality works because this "way of proceeding" is aligned with the way God deals with human beings. It works better than a code of conduct.

What is your way of proceeding? What values and assumptions do you bring to the world every day? Are you cheerful or glum? Is the world a welcoming place or thicket of dangers? When you're perplexed, how do you regain clarity? When what you're doing isn't working, how do you regroup?

August 27

Trust Your Experience

If we are to listen for the God who creates and sustains us, we need to take seriously and prayerfully the meeting between the creatures we are and all else that God holds lovingly in existence. That "interface" is the felt experience of my day. It deserves prayerful attention. It is a big part of how we know and respond to God.

— DENNIS HAMM, SJ

Ralph Waldo Emerson disliked the way writers tiptoe up to their topic by quoting what other people have said about it. "I hate quotation. Tell me what *you* know," he said. It's a habit we can get into when reflecting on the spiritual life. We get absorbed in what other people have said about God, faith, virtue, and right living and neglect what *we* know about it.

The Ignatian perspective insists that we can trust our personal experience. After all, why *wouldn't* God be present in our everyday experiences? That's where we live our lives. Anxiety, peace, joy, irritation — these and the many other feelings we experience are signs. They say: Look here. Something important is going on.

August 28

Fear Is an Invitation to Trust

Fears rise as invitations to greater trust, if we only face them and move through them.

— JOHN KAVANAUGH, SJ

"Only the paranoid survive," proclaimed Andy Grove, former head of Intel. It's a famous saying from the world of tech, often quoted as wisdom. But is it true? Some paranoids survive, but many don't. They make terrible mistakes. Living in a state of perpetual fear and suspicion hardly seems like a good idea. In the Ignatian view, fear is an invitation to examine what Carl Jung called "our alleged trust in God." Is our trust in God, or is it in a comfortable status quo? Have we grown used to peace and serenity?

August 29

More than Ever

More than ever, I find myself in the hands of God. This is what I have wanted all my life, from my youth. But now there is a difference; the initiative is entirely with God. It is indeed a profound spiritual experience to know and feel myself so totally in God's hands.

— PEDRO ARRUPE, SJ

Pedro Arrupe didn't speak these words; he wrote them, and they were read to an assembly of Jesuits in 1983 as Arrupe looked on from a wheelchair, paralyzed and mute. Arrupe had suffered a terrible stroke two years before and had resigned as superior general of the Jesuits. His tenure had been full of controversy. The pope had lost confidence in him. Arrupe's circumstances were about as bad as could be, and yet he expressed a trust in God so breathtakingly deep as to be almost inexplicable.

So how to explain it? Christians understand themselves to be completely dependent on God, but for most, the experience of this dependence is mingled with the exercise of God-given talents and responsibilities in the world. Arrupe had exercised plenty of responsibility, and done it well, but now he had no responsibilities and could do nothing for himself. He was able to experience his trust in God in its purest form. The illusion of mastery was stripped away. He could do nothing for himself. All he had was God, and that was enough.

August 30

His Affair and Not Mine

This means accepting such limitations as may be placed on me by authority... out of love of God who is using these things to attain ends which I myself cannot at the moment see or comprehend. This is his affair and not mine.

— THOMAS MERTON

In 1962, Thomas Merton's religious superiors stopped him from publishing a book advocating pacifism as a moral imperative for Christians. The monk Merton's pacifist sentiments had stirred up considerable hullabaloo in the Catholic Church and the authorities had had enough. They told him to shut up.

An injustice for sure — but not much different from the injustices inflicted on ordinary people every day. You get blamed for someone else's mistakes. You don't get the job because someone who knows someone has the inside track. Your hard work is ignored. What's different here is that Merton's renown gave him leverage to fight back. He could have raised a huge stink that might have gotten the decision reversed. It would at least have embarrassed his oppressors. Instead, Merton acquiesced. He trusted the promise he had made when he became a monk to obey his superiors. He acknowledged that he didn't look at this situation the way God might look at it. God would bring good out of it. It took great humility to say, "This is his affair and not mine."

August 31

It's OK to Be a Little Frightened

Sometimes all we can do is live life on a daily basis, even in the midst of fear and confusion. Sometimes, even in the spiritual life, it is okay to be a little frightened.

— JAMES MARTIN, SJ

The story of Mary's Annunciation is traditionally told as a story of heroic trust in God. Mary is a young unmarried Jewish woman in a poor family in a backwater province of the Roman Empire. One day the angel Gabriel appears to her and announces that she will become the mother of Jesus, the Savior and Son of God, through God's miraculous conception and a virgin birth. Mary ponders this incomprehensible message for a moment, and agrees: "Be it done to me according to thy word." She faces a turbulent future with perfect serenity and trust. Today, her yes to God is held up as the model for the surrender we are all called on to make to God.

So goes the standard telling of the tale. The Jesuit James Martin has a different take. He thinks that Mary was very upset and faced the future with anxiety and fear. She had little peace. She trusted God, but there was a note of desperation in her trust. This, says Martin, makes Mary an even better model for trust than the serene Mary of the pious story. She was at least a little frightened — the way we're likely to feel when we need God the most.

ACTION

September

CHOOSING WELL

Knowing how to choose is one of heaven's greatest gifts.

— BALTASAR GRACIÁN, SJ

September 1

Decisions Gone Awry

There are many people with a fertile, subtle intelligence, rigorous judgment, both diligent and well informed, who are lost when they have to choose. They always choose the worst, as though they wanted to show their skill at doing so.

— BALTASAR GRACIÁN, SJ

The news from social scientists who have studied decision-making isn't good. On the whole, we make decisions thoughtlessly, impulsively, in a haphazard fashion, guided by biases, for reasons we can't articulate. Here's a summary of the problems from the Jesuit psychologist Michael O'Sullivan:

- We tend to avoid changing anything if at all possible.
- If we must make a decision, we either procrastinate or decide too quickly.
- Usually, we wind up choosing what we think our friends and relatives want.
- We're guided by proverbs and cliches from popular culture.
- We fall back on what we've chosen in the past and don't pay sufficient attention to the details of the present situation.

Life is messy. We can't map it out cleanly. We never have enough information. All the more reason to approach our decision-making with care. We have everything to gain if we pause for a minute, step back, and give some careful thought to how we choose.

September 2

What Port Are You Sailing To?

In the end, it's not about the decision. It's about your values, your character, your ideals. It's about your love — your love for God and for other people. If love is your aim, your decisions will be good ones, even when they don't turn out the way you thought they would.

— J. Michael Sparough, SJ

According to Ignatius, the decision you want to make is only a tool — a means to an end. The quality of the decision, the process of it, the timing — none of that matters unless you have a clear idea of what you hope to accomplish by making the choice. As Seneca put it, "If you don't know what port you're sailing to, no wind is favorable."

What do you really want? What work would satisfy your deepest longings? What kind of people do you want to be with? We must look at these questions deeply before making choices about careers, schools, and relationships.

A good way to scrutinize your goal is to examine your motives. These are some of the questions Ignatius would have us ask. Are you trying to accomplish something or avoid something? Are you driven by generosity or anxiety? Are you motivated by love, or does fear have the upper hand?

September 3

At the Balance Point

What Ignatius meant by indifference was freedom. The freedom to approach each decision afresh. The ability to be detached from one's initial biases and to step back, the willingness to carefully balance the alternatives. An openness to the working of God in one's life.

— JAMES MARTIN, SJ

Masters of the art of negotiation say that you won't get the best deal unless you're willing to walk away from it. If you *must* have the deal, you'll pay too much, or you'll agree to a deal that you shouldn't make at all. If you're able to walk away, you're detached enough to see the situation clearly. Ignatius's term for this attitude is indifference. By this he meant freedom from personal preferences, conscious and unconscious desires, biases, longings, and agendas overt and hidden — what he called disordered affections. We can make a good choice when we're free from their influence.

Ignatius describes indifference as the balance point between two weights: Think of a child's seesaw in a playground, perfectly level with equal weights on each side, poised in balance on the fulcrum. That's how we should stand before any significant choice.

September 4

Why Mergers Go Bad

Why is indifference so important to discernment? If I set out to make a decision without indifference, then I'll unconsciously be steering my discernment toward the option that I want.

— MARK E. THIBODEAUX, SJ

An astounding number of corporate mergers and acquisitions fail. They lose money, deflect companies from their true mission, and entangle executives in a morass of problems. People lose their jobs; stockholders lose money. Why should this be? The smartest analysts, lawyers, and corporate chieftains in the world labor over these deals, and yet they often make the wrong decision.

The answer, according to those who've studied the question, wouldn't surprise Ignatius. CEOs pursue unsound deals because they're blinded by disordered attachments: They want to feel important; they think they are smart enough to solve insoluble problems; they think that bigger is better; they make deals because other people expect them to make deals. They think they are coolly examining the facts, when all the while they are steering the decision in the direction they unconsciously prefer.

Don't fall into the "bad merger" trap. As you size up the next big thing, make sure you're seeing the situation clearly. Begin by examining your motives: Why are you pursuing this thing?

September 5

Hearing What You Want to Hear

The spirit that I have seen
May be the devil: and the devil hath power
To assume a pleasing shape; yea, and perhaps
Out of my weakness and my melancholy,
As he is very potent with such spirits,
Abuses me to damn me.

— WILLIAM SHAKESPEARE, *HAMLET*

The drama of *Hamlet* is the hero's procrastination: Hamlet can't decide whether or not to kill his stepfather in revenge for killing his father. One of the many reasons why Hamlet hesitates is doubt about the veracity of his father's ghost, which claims that he has been murdered and demands revenge. Hamlet is rightly suspicious. Should he believe this ghost? What if the ghost is the devil, telling lies? Hamlet, a smart guy, puts his finger on a big problem: He already hates his stepfather, and thinks the devil, by demanding that Hamlet kill him, might be telling him what he wants to hear.

Let's take the spirit of Hamlet's father as a metaphor for the many ways we can be misled and mislead ourselves. Bad ideas will always seem plausible. Poor decisions will seem like good ideas.

September 6

What to Do with a Windfall

For Ignatius, indifference means that a person is so passionately committed to God and to embracing God's plan that everything else is secondary to that one goal and one purpose.

— GERALD FAGIN, SJ

To illustrate what he means by indifference, Ignatius proposes a thought experiment. Three people suddenly come into a windfall fortune; imagine that one wins the lottery; one sells their tech start-up to Google for a billion dollars; one inherits a fortune from a rich uncle. They all want to be generous with this money. What do they do?

The first person talks about doing something but never acts. The second person comes up with a plan to do something with the money, but it's *their* plan. They decide what they want to do and ask God to go along with it. In other words, they do what they want but make it look like an objective decision. The third person is neither inclined to keep the money or to get rid of it. They can take it or leave it. They are truly indifferent — free of bias, ready to weigh all the alternatives objectively, ready to do what God wants them to do.

The problem isn't the money; it's our *attraction* to the money. So it is with all the things we love. How strongly are we wedded to our possessions, our career, our idea of the style of life we want to lead, our notions of how we want to spend our time and money? Can we be detached from these things? Can we walk away from them?

September 7

If It Ain't Broke, Don't Fix It

Leave things alone. Especially when the sea — people, your friends, your acquaintances — is stirred up. Life with others has its tempests, its storms of will, when it is wise to retire to a safe harbor and let the waves subside. Remedies often worsen evils.

— Baltasar Gracián, SJ

Ignatius was no fan of change for change's sake. His attitude was "if it ain't broke, don't fix it." If a past decision had been made well, his counsel was usually to let it stand even if things weren't going well at the moment. Dreams of new ventures, new relationships, new lifestyles are often fantasies distracting us from "taking advantage of what is at hand." Ignatius behaved this way as head of the Jesuits. He made many bold decisions, but he was alert to the danger of acting unnecessarily. "Very often, when he did not have full knowledge of the matter, he would postpone a decision and let some general opinions on the topic suffice for the moment," his secretary said.

Do you really need to make a decision right now? Things might be uncomfortable; you might wish that circumstances were otherwise — but that in itself isn't always a reason to make a change.

We Like the Status Quo

The research indicates that most people are inclined to stay with their current course of action if at all possible.

— Michael O'Sullivan, SJ

Sometimes we're drawn to change for its own sake, but usually not. The stronger inclination is to leave things as they are. People leave money in low-interest savings accounts when better investments are readily available and safe. People with chronic illness will stick with the current medication even if a better medication is available. We stay with failing projects and bad relationships instead of taking the risk of starting something new. Cognitive scientists call it *the status-quo bias* — a preference for the current state of affairs even when something else is clearly better.

The status-quo bias is fed by fear. We fear the unknown. We fear losing what we have. We're embarrassed to admit that we've made a mistake and that it's time cut our losses. It's easy to hide fear under the cloak of prudent skepticism: *That sounds too risky to me. How can I be sure it will work?* Life *is* risky. We can *never* be sure. Are you afraid of something? Are you the victim of the status-quo bias?

September 9

Talk to the Right People

The first sign of real prudence is finding the right person to give us advice.

— JAMES KEENAN, SJ

Chris Lowney, a former Jesuit turned investment banker, had to decide whether to take a job in Japan. It was a tough decision. He was inclined to do it, but he was worried that it would be better for his career if he stayed in New York. When Lowney asked a friend for advice, the guy was astonished and urged him not to do it: "Why would you ever do *that*?" Lowney realized that his friend's advice reflected his own values and priorities, not Lowney's.

Lowney found a friend who knew him well and gave him no advice. Instead, he asked a question: "Which choice do you think will make you happier?" It helped him clarify what he really wanted, which was to take the job in Japan. His friend was a mentor in the style of Ignatius, who insisted that spiritual coaches refrain from advice-giving. Not only should we be free from disordered attachments in order to make good decisions, but so should the people we ask to help us.

September 10

Consider Many Perspectives

We will choose more wisely and confidently by looking at dilemmas from multiple perspectives. Often, when we can't easily reach a decision about a personal matter, we keep rehashing the matter through the same exact thought processes; that's like banging our heads against a wall — it will produce a headache but little new insight.

— CHRIS LOWNEY

In the Ignatian perspective, you'll make a better choice if you look at it from different angles. Reason it out, ponder the pros and cons — look at the numbers. But also consult your feelings and hunches; bring your intuition into play. Be sure to discuss the matter with a wise counselor or two. After you've made a decision, go over it again to see if you've overlooked anything.

Ignatius suggests a couple of imaginative exercises to give new angles on a choice. Imagine that a stranger has come to you to discuss the same question you're struggling with. Listen to them as they lay out the options and talk about what they hope to accomplish. What advice would you give? Another exercise is to imagine that you're looking back on this decision at the end of your life. On your deathbed, what seems most important? These exercises can help you be objective, free from fears, and able to see what matters most.

Optimism Bias

It ain't what you don't know that gets you into trouble. It's what you know for sure that just ain't so.

— ATTRIBUTED TO MARK TWAIN

The Oscar-winning 2015 film *The Big Short* begins with these words flashed on the screen: *It ain't what you don't know that gets you into trouble. It's what you know for sure that just ain't so.* The movie is about the monumental folly that triggered the financial crisis and recession of 2008. Smart, sophisticated investors, radiating confidence and driven by greed, ignored clear danger signals and piled into dubious investments.

They were victims of *optimism bias*: one of the great impediments to good decisions. Optimism bias derives from hope, not objective analysis. It causes us to ignore what happened in the past and seize on the best-case scenario for what might happen in the future. It thinks that bad things happen to other people, not to us.

Optimism is appealing. We like stories with happy endings. It's hard to resist the cheerful fellow who brushes aside objections with the firm conviction that great things are about to happen. Resist him nevertheless — if you want to choose well.

September 12

Pessimism Bias

I never say that things can't get worse.

— BUDDY BELL, MANAGER OF THE KANSAS CITY ROYALS,
AFTER HIS TEAM'S NINETEENTH CONSECUTIVE LOSS IN 2005

The flip side of optimism bias is *pessimism bias* — the feeling that things are bad and could easily get worse. It's easy to be skeptical about just about anything — good news about the economy, your partner's ideas for home remodeling, the weather. The pessimist sounds more intelligent, more thoughtful, more experienced than the optimist: "I don't think it's going to be that easy," "I feel like we're overlooking something here," "I don't believe all those studies."

To be fair, a suspicious viewpoint often suits the world we live in. Our ancestors lived in a dangerous environment where threats could kill, so evolution favored those who overreacted to danger. There are more ways to fail than there are to succeed. We feel pain but not painlessness. A touch of evil is more noticeable than a touch of good.

But pessimism can mislead us just as surely as optimism can. Much of the time it's just a mood, an opinion, and not based on a rational assessment of the problem.

September 13

Biased Thinking

"Don't bother me with the facts; my mind is already made up" captures the essence of the belief-bias effect, also called "belief perseverance." People tend to cling to beliefs and conclusions they have reached even when these are strongly refuted by further evidence.

— Michael O'Sullivan, SJ

The 1998 rom-com *You've Got Mail* nicely illustrates how prior beliefs bias our thinking. Meg Ryan first meets Tom Hanks through an online email correspondence. She's looking for a romantic, book-loving hunk, so she interprets everything he says to bolster her idea of Mr. Right. Later, unaware that she's already met him online, Meg encounters Tom as a canny businessman whose plans threaten her business. She decides he's the epitome of Mr. Wrong and interprets everything he does to bolster this negative impression.

If new information supports what we already believe, we wave it through like a security guard passing familiar faces into a gated community. If it challenges what we believe, we ignore it or strongly doubt it. That's why Ignatius insisted that we scrupulously examine our motives and work hard to be "indifferent" — free from bias, detached from our preferences.

September 14

God Works through Attraction

Which decision allows me to truly become what God is continually creating me to be, in every moment of my life? Which decision makes me most true to myself, the deepest self, where I find God? How do I respond to God's invitation to cooperate in God's constant project of building the real me?

— TIM MULDOON

In the Ignatian view, a good decision is one that expresses our deepest desires, the "real me." It follows that it is almost always made for positive reasons and is accompanied by positive feelings. It's about doing something good, not about avoiding something bad. Admittedly, this is a rule of thumb, what psychologists call a heuristic — a mental shortcut, based on experience. Sometimes we have to make a choice to escape disaster; sometimes we won't feel very confident at all when embarking on a new venture. But most of the time a sound choice is driven by positive desires.

The most important sign of a sound choice is the presence of what Ignatius called "consolation." This is a sense of "rightness," of being in the right place, rightly connected to God and other people. If consolation is present, it's a strong indicator that you're on the right track.

September 15

The Limits of Intuition

We humans have a strong tendency to rely more on our intuition than on rational or statistical decision methods.

— MICHAEL O'SULLIVAN, SJ

Social psychologist Maria Konnikova became an expert Texas Hold'em poker player. One day, a new player joined her table in Las Vegas. He was a big man, heavily tattooed, with long hair and a gruff, vaguely menacing manner. Konnikova sized him up immediately as a stereotypical kind of bellicose male who would play very aggressively against a woman. That's a weakness that a smart opponent like her could exploit, but the guy turned out to be the exact opposite — a cautious player, highly analytical, observant, and clever.

Konnikova did something we do all the time: She went with her gut. We *know* how large tattooed men with a gruff manner are likely to behave. It's a pretty good rule of thumb, based on observation and experience. In this case, however, it was wrong. Intuition is only a rule of thumb, an indicator, an assumption, not a decisive guide to a good choice.

That's why Ignatius insisted that decisions be looked at from many angles. He valued intuition very highly, but it's only one criteria for making a good choice.

September 16

Understanding, Not Knowledge

The key to good decision making is not knowledge. It is understanding. We are swimming in the former. We are desperately lacking in the latter.

— MALCOLM GLADWELL

In his book *Blink*, Malcolm Gladwell tells story after story about poor decisions made when decision-makers could have known better. Japanese intentions were no secret before Pearl Harbor. So were the designs of the 9/11 terrorists. The problem is that the most important information was buried in a mountain of data, reports, opinions, and analysis. What was lacking was understanding of what this data meant.

Gladwell also tells many stories about "gut feelings" that miss the mark badly. His point is that the best decisions come from a blend of rational analysis and intuition guided by experience.

That's what Ignatian discernment offers. By discernment, Ignatius means both keenness of insight and skill in discriminating. It's first *seeing*, then *interpreting* what is perceived. The root of the word is the Latin word *discerno*, meaning to sever or separate. It's essentially the ability to separate what's important from what's irrelevant or misleading.

September 17

Dishonest Opinions

Our opinions were not honestly come by. We simply found ourselves in contact with a certain current of ideas and plunged into it because it seemed modern and successful.

— C. S. Lewis, *The Great Divorce*

In C. S. Lewis's fable-fantasy *The Great Divorce*, people living in hell are free to leave and go to heaven under one condition: They must admit that they had done wrong. Few of the damned can bring themselves to do this. Lewis recounts a conversation between a bishop, a resident of hell, and an old friend who is in heaven. The bishop brags about how he courageously rejected important Christian doctrines because they didn't convince his rational mind. "Honest opinions fearlessly followed — they are not sins," he declares. The bishop's friend demurs. There's nothing courageous about it, he says. You just picked up fashionable opinions and started "saying the kind of things that won applause."

It's not easy to seriously examine our worldview. It seems sound; our assumptions about life make sense to us, and they usually make sense to the people around us. Our opinions are admired. Why go the trouble of scrutinizing them?

You should make the effort because you might be wrong. If you are, and if you admit it, you might find your way.

September 18

The Good Is Plural

The good is plural. Even for the same person, there are often two or more choices that are both good. Good is kaleidoscopic. Many roads are right. The road to the beach is right and the road to the mountains is right, for God awaits us in both places. Goodness is multicolored. Only pure evil lacks color and variety.

— PETER KREEFT

Rarely does life offer a single answer to our questions. We have many opportunities, not just one or a small handful. We have second chances — and third and fourth chances. If plan A doesn't work out, turn to plan B. The good is plural. That's something to keep in mind when you're making decisions, even important ones. Especially if you're worried about making a mistake. There's no blueprint, no spec sheet, no user's manual. In the Ignatian perspective, choosing well isn't conforming to something external. It's more a matter of growing into the kind of person we're meant to be, and that's a journey with many possibilities.

September 19

Focus on the Process

Counselors need to focus on the person's decision-making processes rather than falling into the trap of paying most attention to the content of what the person is choosing. We assist others better by concentrating more on the how than on the what.

— MICHAEL O'SULLIVAN, SJ

There's a paradox in Ignatian decision-making. The actual work of discernment means getting into the weeds of the choices in front of us: assessing specifics, scrutinizing our intentions and assumptions, imagining scenarios. Details, details. But the process is more important than the specifics. It has three parts: Have the right end in mind; get free of disordered attachments; look at the question both rationally and intuitively with the inner leadings of the spirit.

You can control *how* you make a decision. You can't control how the decision turns out. In fact, if your process is sound, you'd make the same decision again even if it turned out badly the first time.

Is It from God?

When these prodigies
Do so conjointly meet, let not men say
"These are their reasons; they are natural;"
For, I believe, they are portentous things.

— WILLIAM SHAKESPEARE, *JULIUS CAESAR*

In the run-up to Caesar's assassination in Shakespeare's play, strange things start happening in Rome — animals behaving strangely, a night bird hooting and shrieking in the middle of the day, and so forth. The conspirator Casca is sure these are signs from the gods. His friend Cicero brushes him off, saying that people will interpret signs to suit their own purposes.

It's a question that comes up all the time when people with a spiritual mindset set out to make a decision. Does this feeling or leading or event mean that God favors one option? The problem is that spiritual people are predisposed to think it does. They experience things spiritually, and they are looking for signs of God's leadings.

The problem with our predispositions — religious or otherwise — is that they seem normal to us. We need to be aware of them. A sound Ignatian decision-making process demands that they be scrutinized along with everything else.

September 21

Not the Star of the Show

Often the temptation is to see ourselves as God's gift to humanity.

— J. Michael Sparough, SJ

Right after he was baptized by John, Jesus went into the desert to figure out what he was supposed to do with his life. The devil came with temptations. Jesus could turn stones into bread — have all the material things he wanted. He could stage fabulous miracles — become a famous religious leader. He could worship the devil — and take power over all the kingdoms of the world. The central temptation was to let his ego push him too far. Jesus could do wonderful things, but he'd be the center of attention. Instead, his route to glory was the road of humility and obedience.

We face the same temptation in many of our choices: good things done to excess with ourselves as the star of the show. Instead, let situations unfold in their own way without forcing things. Let coworkers share the credit. Take on modest doable tasks. Go home at a decent hour and take weekends off. Melt into the background.

September 22

Don't Make Decisions When You're Down

During a time of desolation one should never make a change.

— THE SPIRITUAL EXERCISES, 318

Patients who've had outpatient surgery or a procedure like a colonoscopy are sent home with the warning not to operate heavy equipment or make important decisions for the rest of the day. Anesthesia addles our brains; we need to wait until our heads are clear.

Ignatius gives the same advice for people who are down in the dumps: Don't decide anything important. Sleep on it and wait until we're feeling better. Sensible advice, yet it's often ignored. When we're hurting, our impulse is to act. We want to do *something* to make the bad feelings go away. Quit the job. Move away. Teach the kid a lesson. Dump the girl-friend or boyfriend (or if we're the one who got dumped, find another as quickly as possible). Sometimes a change is needed, but desolation is the worst time to figure out what it should be. Wait until the emotional storms pass, *then* decide whether anything needs to change.

September 23

Living with Uncertainty

Ignatius's life was marked by many decisions that combine fidelity to the demands of the present with openness to a future not yet revealed. He had to respect the mystery of this future until events, or some clear internal impulsion, enabled him to recognize the path that was opening up.

— Maurice Giuliani, SJ

Confidence and excitement at the beginning of a new venture are usually considered to be desirable things: a sign that all's well and on the right track. Not so fast, says the French Jesuit theologian Maurice Giuliani. Humility and a bit of confusion might be a better indicator. Giuliani points out that Moses, the prophet Isaiah, and Mary all reacted with humility and doubt when God proposed a new undertaking: *Why me? I can't do this. Lord, I am not worthy.* This was the reaction of Jesus himself at Gethsemane. This initial response paves the way for surrender to God, who is the real source of strength, followed by resolute and loving dedication to the task.

Certainly we've seen plenty of examples of the opposite trajectory. Confidence and excitement at the beginning crumble when obstacles present themselves, as they always do. This causes frustration, and soon discouragement and hopelessness. In the end, the project is abandoned.

Giuliani proposes a rule of thumb, a heuristic, not a spiritual law: Confidence is good, but often humility is better.

September 24

Heart and *Head*

Discernment and decision-making demand a balanced perspective. Put simply, it is all right to trust our feelings as long as we use our heads.

— MICHAEL O'SULLIVAN, SJ

It's easy to find lots of stories about decisions made by instinct. Business leaders set numbers aside and "trust their gut." People talk about hunches, inner voices, and "professional judgment" to describe that vague feeling of knowing something without knowing exactly how or why they know it. These are almost always stories about success — decisions that worked out well. We don't hear much about hunches that led to disaster, but this happens all the time. We just don't remember these stories; if we remember them, we're not inclined to tell our friends about them.

A good choice is one that employs both rational analysis and heartfelt instinct. This is what the Ignatian approach offers. It requires sensitive awareness of inner movements of the spirit. Ignatius's primary criterion for a good decision was the presence of "consolation," a sense of peace, a feeling of "rightness," a conviction that this option is the correct one. But the Ignatian approach is also reflective and discerning. It looks for biases. It subjects feelings to analysis. It's alert to mistakes. It's an approach to deciding that employs both the heart and the head.

Second Chances

Even our mistakes can be useful material in the next decision. In fact, it's hard to think of a decision that is absolutely bad with no redeeming qualities and possibilities.

— J. Michael Sparough, SJ

Chris Lowney's mentor told him that the best thing that happened in his business career was botching the first important decision he faced. It was a good experience because the sky didn't fall when he made a mistake. He didn't get fired. Life went on. From that point on, Chris's mentor was never afraid to make a tough decision. Lowney writes, "He learned that we can often correct mistakes, and that life frequently offers second and third chances — not always chances to undo past mistakes, sadly, but chances to do other good things."

The fate of the world doesn't hang in the balance when you face a decision. Your decision is important, but it's only one in a long succession of decisions you'll make in your life. If you make a mistake, you'll make other decisions soon. You might get a chance to correct the mistake. If not, there are three or four other good things you can do.

September 26

The "Feeling" of Feelings

In the case of those who are going from good to better, the good angel touches the soul gently, lightly, and sweetly, like a drop of water going into a sponge. The evil spirit touches it sharply, with noise and disturbance, like a drop of water falling onto a stone.

— THE SPIRITUAL EXERCISES, 335

Ignatius thought that the biggest obstacle to choosing well was "false consolation." A decision looks good, everything lines up, you and your friends feel good about it. But it turns out to be the wrong choice. You're mistaken. You've deluded yourself — or been deluded. The good feeling you had — the "consolation" — was bogus.

Ignatius's remedy for this is called *discernment of spirits*. When we're mulling over choices, we should look for signs of spiritual dissonance. Does the good feeling fit your spiritual disposition or does it seem off, like a jarring note in a pleasing melody? God's action will be gentle and delightful, like "a drop of water going into a sponge." A false consolation will be noisy and disturbing, like "a drop of water falling onto a stone." A nagging doubt, a feeling that something isn't right, a sense of discomfort — these could well be danger signals that you shouldn't brush aside.

September 27

Premortem

Projects fail at a spectacular rate. One reason is that too many people are reluctant to speak up about their reservations during the all-important planning phase. By making it safe for dissenters who are knowledgeable about the undertaking and worried about its weaknesses to speak up, you can improve a project's chances of success.

— Harvard Business Review

Ignatius thought we should conduct a postmortem after a decision goes wrong: Understand how the undertaking went awry so we can make a better decision next time. He also recommended something like a "premortem." Imagine looking back on the decision from some point in the future. How does the situation look now? What do you wish you had done differently?

A premortem is often used in business today. Before a final decision is made, the planning group does a premortem exercise: Imagine that it's six months from now. The project has been implemented — and it has failed spectacularly. Write down the reasons why. This can uncover problems and weaknesses that might otherwise be buried under a mountain of sunny optimism and wishful thinking.

The premortem is yet another angle on a decision. Failure can be your teacher.

September 28

Drawn or Driven?

A useful test to apply is this: in a particular situation, am I feeling drawn, powerfully perhaps but always gently, or am I feeling driven? Did we say yes because we felt we really, deep down, wanted to do it, or did we go along with it to please someone else or to avoid conflict?

— Margaret Silf

One of the saddest stories in *War and Peace* is Tolstoy's depiction of his protagonist's slide into a disastrous marriage. Pierre Bezukhov — young, rich, single, and naïve — didn't like or respect the conniving Hélène Kuragina. But she was beautiful, everyone in their social circle thought the match would be a splendid one, Pierre wanted to be married, and he kept running into the lovely Hélène at dinners and dances. Finally, without really wanting to, Pierre found himself engaged to her. He was pushed toward the match by the expectation of society.

Pierre did what research says that most people do when facing a tough decision: They do what they think their friends and family want them to do. Remember that God ordinarily works through attraction. If some new thing is what we really want, we'll be drawn to it, not driven to it by the expectations of other people and the pull of our disordered desires.

September 29

Take the Time You Need

Reconsider. Safety lies in looking things over twice, especially when you are not completely confident. Take time, either to concede something or to better your situation, and you will find new ways to confirm and corroborate your judgment.

— Baltasar Gracián, SJ

In David Mitchell's novel *Utopia Avenue*, the rock band at the center of the story faces a terrible dilemma when their drummer is incapacitated. Concert dates are coming up. Should they find a new drummer, cancel their dates, perform without him, or something else? The lead guitarist pipes up: "My Dutch grandfather used to say, 'If you don't know what to do, do nothing for eight days.'" He explains: "Less than eight is haste. More than eight is procrastination. Eight days is long enough for the world to shuffle the deck and deal you another hand."

Ignatian spirituality prizes reflection. If you're not sure what to do and no option looks good, the Ignatian counsel is usually to wait. Ignatius writes, "When the solutions of these difficulties are not clear, we should not hazard an answer, but first give it the study and consideration it requires."

By the way, the rock band waited, and before the eight days were up, the drummer returned.

September 30

Embrace the Downside, Too

Making good choices means accepting that even the best decisions will have drawbacks. Good decisions mean a wholehearted yes to both the positives and negatives that come with any choice.

— JAMES MARTIN, SJ

No decision has a perfect outcome. All decisions involve risks and loss. Choosing one thing means that you won't be doing another, and there's always something attractive about the other thing. The thing you choose will have drawbacks. The new job, the new relationship, the vacation, the hobby, the volunteer project will all have imperfections and unpleasant surprises, and when you choose them, you're choosing those things, too. There's always uncertainty. You can never be sure.

So relax. If no choice is perfect, you can stop worrying about making a mistake and focus on the positive benefits and possibilities of the choice you do make.

October

RELATIONSHIPS

*Love is when the center of the universe suddenly shifts
and moves toward someone else.*

— IRIS MURDOCH

October 1

Unselfish Love

I find that I am happiest and most myself when I choose to love others unselfishly; I do this freely, but it also seems to be what I am created to be and do.

— WILLIAM A. BARRY, SJ

Unselfish love is love that will sacrifice anything for the other, even the things one values the most. That's the theme of the famous O. Henry story "The Gift of the Magi." It is about a poor young couple who each sell their most treasured possession to give the other a Christmas gift. The young man sells a watch he loves to buy his wife combs for her hair, while she sells her hair to buy him a chain for his watch. The story gets at the pain that often comes with unselfish love; the husband and wife are now without the thing they value the most. But they have the other's love, more valuable than any gift.

The Jesuit essayist William Barry says that we were created to love this way. That's not immediately apparent. Selfish love comes more naturally. We're inclined to think of our needs first and to value relationships with others to the extent that they contribute to our happiness. Many people say they are in love with someone when they are really in love with the way the person makes them feel. They feel good about themselves; they like the things the other person does for them. That's conditional love, not unselfish love.

Barry says that we are really suited for love without conditions, love that gives without expectation of return, love that's entirely about someone besides ourselves. This suits us because it's a reflection of the way God loves us. In other words, unselfish love puts us in touch with the love that brought us into being.

October 2

Assume the Best

It should be presupposed that every good Christian ought to be more eager to put a good interpretation on a neighbor's statement than to condemn it. Further, if one cannot interpret it favorably, one should ask how the other means it.

— THE SPIRITUAL EXERCISES, 22

A least once today, likely more, you'll hear someone say something that strikes you as mistaken, provocative, biased, or just plain stupid. How will you respond? You might challenge the person, try to straighten them out, and waste an hour or two in fruitless argument. You might stay silent and privately condemn the person for their ignorance. Or you can do what Ignatius suggests in his "presupposition" for relationships. First, assume the best. Find a way to interpret a troubling statement positively. Second, ask what the person means.

Assume the best. Who knows — there might be something true and valuable in what they are saying. Everyone you meet knows something you don't know.

What does the person mean by it? People have reasons for what they say and do, and these are seldom outright evil reasons. Why did what they said upset you so much?

This is a pretty good way to keep relationships running smoothly. When you're troubled by something someone says, assume the best, not the worst.

October 3

The Art of Conversation

Simple, friendly, and informal conversations were the earliest and chief means that Ignatius employed in helping people. The way he started was to talk to people, men and women, young and old, about the things that really mattered to them and to him.

— John Padberg, SJ

Ignatius thought that one of the best ways of helping people was to simply talk to them honestly, openly, with genuine interest. Conversation is also a way to build bonds of brotherhood among Jesuits. He had such a high regard for it that he insisted that Jesuits learn "the art of dealing and conversing with others" as part of their training.

Ignatian conversation isn't just chitchat about the weather and the game next weekend. It's meant to convey an openness to the other person that leads to a meaningful relationship. It's a skill — something you can practice and get better at. It's intentional; you seek out opportunities for good conversation. It requires humility. A good conversationalist is a good listener who is not in love with their own opinions. Ignatian conversation is an active sharing of lives.

October 4

Self-Centered Servants

Give me the man who takes the best of everything (even at my expense) and then talks of other things, rather than the man who serves me and talks of himself, and whose very kindnesses are a continual reproach, a continual demand for pity, gratitude, and admiration.

— C. S. LEWIS

C. S. Lewis abhorred self-centeredness masquerading as selflessness. He composed this witty epitaph for the tombstone of a self-centered servant:

> Erected by her sorrowing brothers
> In memory of Martha Clay.
> Here lies one who lived for others;
> Now she has peace. And so have they.

We've all met people like Martha Clay, a servant of others who isn't really interested in other people. They are full of themselves, and blithely assume that other people are as interested in their opinions as they are. Lewis makes a subtle point; being involved with other people doesn't make you selfless. Lewis wittily argues for selfishness instead of self-centeredness. In a selfish life, he wrote, "my mind would be directed toward a thousand things, not one of which is myself."

At least be selfish. It's progress toward being genuinely selfless.

October 5

You Don't Know What's Best

When you counsel someone, you should appear to be reminding him of something he had forgotten, not of the light he was unable to see.

— Baltasar Gracián, SJ

If you want to get along with people, don't come across as a know-it-all. Chances are, you don't know what's best for someone else anyway. Even if you do, don't insist that they follow your way. Ignatius insisted that people be free to discover things for themselves. Religious superiors should not prescribe certain styles of prayer. Scholars and experts should not explain what the Bible and other texts mean. Those giving spiritual guidance should not push people in a certain direction. "Allow God to deal directly with people," he said. Don't get in the way.

October 6

No Friends, No Joy

If there were no friends in the world, there would be no joy.

— MATTEO RICCI, SJ

In the Ignatian tradition, human friendship is one of God's greatest gifts. The Society of Jesus itself emerged from a circle of close friends who gathered around Ignatius at the University of Paris. Ignatius wanted Jesuits to be good friends and to have good friends. Friendship sustains us in hard times. It mirrors the intimate relationship we have with God.

"The best way to win friends is to act like one," said the Jesuit moralist Baltasar Gracián. "Win a friend every day."

Sharing Burdens

"Come, Mr. Frodo!" he cried. "I can't carry it for you, but I can carry you."

— J. R. R. TOLKIEN, *THE RETURN OF THE KING*

At the climax of *The Lord of the Rings*, things are looking bad for the good guys. Frodo the Ring-bearer lies semi-conscious on Mount Doom, crushed by the burden of carrying the Ring and unable to continue. His loyal friend Sam can't rouse him. So Sam does what good friends do in times of trouble: He picks Frodo up and carries him to the end of the journey, saying, "I can't carry it for you, but I can carry *you*."

Sharing burdens is a big part of friendship. At some point we'll do what Sam did and help our friends carry their burdens, and they will do the same for us. It's a matter of intimacy, not problem-solving. There are no answers to many of life's problems anyway; we can only live with them — and share them with our friends.

October 8

Timing Is Everything

When helping others, we must proceed like a man who is crossing a ford. If I find a good footing — that is, some hope of helping the person — I will pass right on. But if the ford is muddied or disturbed, I will rein in and seek an occasion more favorable to what I have to say.

— IGNATIUS LOYOLA

"Timing is everything" — it's true in romance, politics, and hitting a baseball. Timing is crucial when you're trying to help someone. Ignatius's metaphor is that of a person cautiously fording a river. Proceed if the footing is good and the way is clear. Hold back if you can't see where you're going. It's easy to make mistakes.

Ignatius's letters are full of advice about timing. When you're speaking, remember that you're trying to accomplish something positive. Avoid long theoretical discussions. Avoid arguments. When weighty matters are being discussed, "Be slow to speak and say little." Listen carefully when others are giving their opinions; try to understand why they think the way they do. When the time is right, when someone is ready to hear from you, "your speech should be long, and full of charity and kindness." It's a matter of timing.

October 9

Looking Good

Authority should be gained by washing one's rags and cooking one's food without having need of anyone.

— FRANCIS XAVIER

When Francis Xavier was preparing to depart for Asia, his friend the Count de Castaneda was horrified to learn that Francis was going without a servant to wait on him. You'll lose authority in the eyes of others, the count said, if they see you washing your own clothes and cooking your own dinner. Francis replied that this is exactly the way he wanted others to see him — as the humble servant he aspired to be. He went on to say that bishops and clergy of the church would do well to follow his example. This obsession with status and appearances "is what has reduced the Church of God and prelates to the condition in which they are at this day."

Give some thought to the efforts you make to look good in the eyes of others. Are you obscuring the real you?

October 10

Don't Correct When Indignant

*Whenever we feel in ourselves stirrings of indignation, we should
hold off from rebuking the person until another time.*

— PETER FABER, SJ

Bad things happen when we speak in anger. If we fall down,
we can always get up, but once we say something, we can't
unsay it. If it was cruel and hurtful, the damage will linger.

Remember: No one does wrong on purpose. A friend
may seem to have acted foolishly, but they have reasons for
what they've done. Think of the times you've done wrong
without intending to. You forgot, and showed up for a meeting unprepared. You were irritable because you slept poorly.
You got carried away. You indulged yourself because you
didn't think anyone would notice. These are all plausible ex-
planations that deflect at least some of the blame.

Treat other people as generously as you treat yourself.

October 11

When You Screw Up

Should anyone behave badly, and be held in less esteem than before, he should thank God, who has permitted him to be humbled, so that he can be known by all for what he is. He should not wish to appear better in the eyes of others than he is in the eyes of God.

— IGNATIUS LOYOLA

Ignatius puts his finger on the reason why it's so hard to admit mistakes. We think well of ourselves, and when we screw up, we're confronted with two contradictory facts: I'm a good person, and I appear to have done this bad thing. How to explain this? It's easier to explain away the bad thing than to change our opinion of ourself: *It slipped my mind. I got too busy. An emergency came up.*

Ignatian practice tells us to admit we erred and change our opinion of ourselves. You are not the person you think you are. You do foolish, thoughtless things. You make mistakes. You fall short of the standards you set for yourself. You are not perfect. You need God's grace. You need to be forgiven, and to forgive.

October 12

You're Welcome Here

The principal cause of suffering for the leper is not an annoying, smelly, itchy skin disease but rather having to live outside the camp. So the call is to stand with them, so that the margins get erased and they are welcomed back inside. Jesus doesn't think twice: he touches the lepers before he gets around to healing them.

— GREGORY BOYLE, SJ

It seems that every teen movie has a scene featuring an outcast kid eating lunch alone in the cafeteria: a pudgy girl, a nerdy boy, a child of color from a refugee family — they're shunned and isolated. The scene packs an emotional wallop because we get it viscerally. We all know what's like to be an outcast. *You're not like us. You're not welcome here.* And if we're honest, we'll admit that we've done our share of excluding.

The Ignatian instinct is to take the side of the marginalized and excluded. Jerome Nadal, Ignatius's chief deputy, said that the mission of the Jesuits is "the care of those for whom nobody is caring." The French Jesuit Henri de Lubac said that "when we choose the poor, we are always sure, doubly sure, of having made a good choice. We have chosen like Jesus. And we have chosen Jesus."

October 13

The Trouble with Exaggerating

Never exaggerate. It isn't wise to use superlatives. They offend the truth and cast doubt on your judgment. True eminences are rare, so temper your esteem. To overvalue something is a form of lying. It can ruin your reputation for good taste and — even worse — for wisdom.

— Baltasar Gracián, SJ

Gracián's prohibition of exaggeration is itself an exaggeration. Exaggeration has its uses. It makes a point succinctly: *I didn't get any sleep last night.* It can promote social connection: *The greatest thing just happened; you won't believe it.* But Gracián isn't wrong. Exaggeration is contagious. It can easily get out of hand. We typically exaggerate to entertain our friends and to draw attention to ourselves. It feeds pride and puts us at the center of things. It's better to put others at the center of things.

October 14

Don't Give Up on People

We should be kind and compassionate with those who are sad;
speak at length with them, and show great joy and cheerfulness, to
draw them to the opposite of what they feel.

— IGNATIUS LOYOLA

Ignatius never gave up on people. If they had gone away troubled and angry, he doggedly worked to bring them back into a relationship. A letter of his survives where he instructs a Jesuit to help a man who had left the society on bad terms. Seek him out, Ignatius says — and don't say I told you to do it. Talk to him. Listen to him. If he's afraid, assure him that we're with him. "Assure him that we should be glad to help him in any way possible," he wrote.

Are there people you don't talk to anymore because they are difficult, because you had a falling out? Follow Ignatius's example and seek them out. Find out if you can do anything for them. They may be in trouble and need help. They could certainly use a friend. So could you.

October 15

Arguing Is a Waste of Time

We should not dispute stubbornly with anyone; rather we should patiently give our reasons with the purpose of declaring the truth lest our neighbor remain in error, and not that we should have the upper hand.

— Ignatius Loyola

Someone makes a dumb comment about politics. Someone scoffs at an opinion of yours. You find yourself squabbling about schedules or menus or plans for tomorrow. Ask yourself: Is there any reason to argue about this? How would a sensible person respond to provocation or garish displays of ignorance? Rarely is it worth rising to the bait. "You will only burden yourself with foolishness and annoyance," says Baltasar Gracián.

Ignatius notices that in these discussions we're often driven by a desire to have the upper hand. We want to be right. We want others to know we're right. It's best to resist this urge. Smile and change the subject.

October 16

The Trouble with Judging

We are at our least healthy when we engage in judgment. Judgment creates the distance that moves us away from each other. Judgment takes up the room you need for loving.

— GREGORY BOYLE, SJ

Judging separates us from others. It creates distance. Instead of loving, we're criticizing, finding fault. There are other problems with judging. We almost certainly don't have the whole picture. We're seeing the situation through the filter of our own biases (which are quite hard for us to detect). We're drawing a conclusion based on our guess about someone's intention, but the only thing we know for sure about someone's motives is that they make sense to the person.

It's best to resist the urge to make judgments. Take the advice of Ignatius's friend Peter Faber: "Never notice the defects of others, but be always ready to excuse them." If you must judge, judge yourself: "Be most prompt to accuse yourself of your own defects."

Don't Compete

Never compete. When you vie with your opponents, your reputation suffers. Your competitor will immediately try to find your fault and discredit you. Rivalry discovers the defects that courtesy overlooks.

— BALTASAR GRACIÁN, SJ

Freddie Freeman, the All-Star first baseman for the Los Angeles Dodgers, always has a good word for his opponents. He congratulates them for getting a hit; he encourages them when they make a tough out. "I know how hard this game is. I know how hard it is to get a hit in a major league baseball game. No matter if you just put your team up in the top of the ninth inning, I'll come over and pat you on the leg and say, 'Way to swing it.'"

People who make competitiveness a marker of their identity are playing a zero-sum game: *There's not enough to go around. My success means that you fail.* It's an ugly philosophy. It's mistaken. Life is full of blessings and opportunities. Gracián points out another problem with competitiveness that's not always obvious. People don't like to be around people who are always keeping score. Not only are they wrong about what kind of world we live in, they are bad company.

A Simple Trick

"If you can learn a simple trick, Scout, you'll get along a lot better with all kinds of folks. You never really understand a person until you consider things from his point of view... until you climb into his skin and walk around in it."

— HARPER LEE, *TO KILL A MOCKINGBIRD*

Atticus Finch's "simple trick" isn't so simple. It's hard to appreciate another person's point of view. It's harder to "climb into his skin" — to understand what it's like to be someone else. Scout manages to do it at the end of *To Kill a Mockingbird* when she grasps what it's like to be Boo Radley. Boo has been a menacing, frightening figure, a recluse who wants nothing to do with other people. Scout understands that he's a wounded man crippled by fear. She can love him for who he is. And sure enough, Boo is able to overcome his fear enough to receive Scout's love.

"If we are to love our neighbors before doing anything else, we must *see* our neighbors," said Frederick Buechner. Make the effort to see the strange lady in the neighborhood, the oddball relative, the eccentric colleague. Walk around in their skin for a while. You'll find that Atticus Finch is right: Most people are nice when you see them for who they are.

October 19

The Point of Hospitality

We are commanded to be hospitable not only for the good of the stranger but also for our own good. Nothing can elevate us more, both when we practice it and when we receive it. And nothing can bring us more pleasure, if only we let it.

— JAMES KEENAN, SJ

The gospel story of Jesus at the house of Martha and Mary is puzzling on the surface. Martha is the perfect hostess; she greets Jesus, serves him refreshment, tends to his needs — yet Jesus admonishes her. She's too busy to enjoy his company. The point is that hospitality is meant to bring us closer to others. Martha lets it become a barrier. Hospitality isn't just a duty; it's a gift, a virtue, an opportunity for us to grow in love. Jesus said that those who welcome the stranger welcome him. Hospitality models the generosity and inclusion that Jesus showed throughout his life. It opens our hearts. It's a source of great pleasure.

Isak Dinesen's short story "Babette's Feast" is about how an extravagant act of hospitality heals the sad and melancholy members of a wounded Christian congregation. Dinesen writes: "The vain illusions of this earth had dissolved before their eyes like smoke, and they had seen the universe as it really is. They had been given one hour of the millennium."

October 20

Be Generous with Your Time

Be generous with your time; that is, if you can, do today what you promise to do tomorrow.

— IGNATIUS LOYOLA

Ignatius believed in getting things done. He disliked procrastination, as his secretary noted: "If anyone were to say, 'I shall do that within two weeks or a week,' Ignatius was accustomed to say: 'How is that? Do you think you are going to live that long?'" His advice to "be generous with your time" is really about generosity, not business efficiency. It's perfectly reasonable to do tomorrow what we say we'll do tomorrow, especially if we're busy, like everyone is. Ignatius says: Do it today. Make a gift of your time. Give it away to someone else.

October 21

Know How to Say No

You can't grant everything to everybody. Saying no is as important as granting things. What matters is the way you do it. Some people's "no" is prized more highly than the "yes" of others: a gilded "no" pleases more than a curt "yes." No and yes are short words requiring long thought.

— BALTASAR GRACIÁN, SJ

You're not helping anybody by saying yes to a new commitment when you should say no. The promise is likely to weigh you down. You'll regret making it. You'll complain about it. You'll likely give it less than your best. Bad outcomes all the way around. The same dynamic applies to distractions and temptations. We know we should say no to that third or fourth drink, to the opportunity to gossip, to entertain fantasies of revenge, but we do it anyway. Pretty soon we've frittered away an afternoon, a whole day. If we're not careful, these things will consume our life.

So learn how to say no. Say it nicely to others, decisively to yourself, and spend your time on the things that matter most.

October 22

Be a Better Friend

How many times have you wondered why your friends weren't "better" friends? And how many times did being a "better friend" mean meeting your needs? How often have you wondered why your friends or family members don't support you more? How often have you worried whether you were being a good friend?

— JAMES MARTIN, SJ

Don't take your friends for granted. Spend some time and energy becoming a better friend.

You can start by saying how much you value your friends. The early Jesuits were great at this. "I am at present enjoying the company of Peter Canisius and I have no words to tell you how sweet I find it," wrote Peter Faber to another friend. "It is beyond my power not to love and cherish the very thought of you in your absence," Canisius wrote to one of his Jesuit friends. Rejoice when your friends succeed. Show them affection. If you haven't spoken in a while, arrange to have lunch. If they live far away, use the tools of modern communication to talk to them.

And when you talk, find out what they're struggling with, what they need, what you can do for them. Work to understand how *they* are.

October 23

Never Complain

Never complain. Complaints will always discredit you. Rather than compassion and consolation, they provoke passion and insolence, and encourage those who hear our complaints to behave like those we complain about. Once divulged to others, the offenses done to us seem to make others pardonable.

— BALTASAR GRACIÁN, SJ

There's something wrong with everything, so there's nothing easier than finding things to complain about. Complaining bolsters the ego, too; it makes us sound smart. It's so pleasurable that complaining can take up the greater part of the time we spend with friends and family. Complaining is contagious; one complaint leads to another, and another. It feeds arrogance and pride. It normalizes negativity and bad behavior. Soon enough, complaining will engulf us, as Gracián points out. We'll get criticism instead of compassion, sneers instead of encouragement.

"Never complain, never explain," said British prime minister Benjamin Disraeli. Don't fill your head with resentful feelings. Don't make excuses when others complain about you. If your coffee klatch turns into a pity party, change the subject or find some other people to hang out with.

October 24

Making Peace

Blessed are the peacemakers, for they shall be called children of God.

— MATTHEW 5:9

The early Jesuits were great peacemakers. They helped end many of the bloody vendettas that shook sixteenth-century Italy. They helped estranged couples to reconcile. They were often called in to mediate bitter disputes in families, businesses, and the church. Ignatius's deputy Jerome Nadal said that a "ministry of reconciliation" was part of the Jesuit vocation.

We can all make this a better world by seeing ourselves as agents of peace and reconciliation. Start by not making things worse. Don't take sides when a conflict flares up. Don't rush to offer your opinion of a disputed question. Show sympathy and understanding. Become the kind of person that others trust and you may be invited to help bring peace where there's rancor.

October 25

Find Something to Love

Ignatius taught not only by word, but also by example. The first thing to do is to concentrate one's heart and soul in loving the person you want to aid. Even if the person was a hardened sinner, he found something in him to love: his natural gifts, his belief in God, and any other good thing about him.

— JEROME NADAL, SJ

When we encounter someone who seems unlikable, it's well to remember that our judgment about them is almost certainly wrong. *We* don't like them for whatever reason. Our point of view is narrow, self-centered, distorted by biases that we're not aware of. We are applying a negative label to a person whom we don't know: *Unlovable. Lazy. Incompetent. A problem person*. It's wrong to apply these labels. It's a mistake as well. We're overlooking their good qualities.

Do what Ignatius did: Find something to love about everyone you meet. Search for it extra hard if you don't like them. The good qualities are there. You just need to find them. Compliment the person. Tell others about their good qualities. Soon you can have the basis for a real relationship.

October 26

Show Up

In ordinary ways, fidelity is practiced by the staff member who is always punctual, by the usher who reliably assumes his usual task, by the hospice worker who sits with a dying person, the parent who shows up for Little League, by the AA member who sets up for the meeting.

— James Keenan, SJ

What gets noticed, talked about, and remembered are the special things: the big check, the exceptional sacrifice, the crisis intervention. Let's have a few words of praise for doing the little things. Do what you said you would do. Call if you're going to be late. Stifle your complaints. Issue some compliments. These are the small everyday acts of fidelity that build virtue and lift the burdens of life.

"Suit up and show up" is a slogan in 12-step recovery programs. It means that recovery comes from being faithful to the things that are ordinary, routine, slightly dull. Go to meetings. Talk to people. Be kind. Pray every day. These are the small things that matter most.

Difficult Friends

An essential part of love is maintaining what you could call the difficult friendship.

— JAMES MARTIN, SJ

One of Ignatius's great challenges as head of the Jesuits was dealing with Simon Rodriguez, a close friend and one of the founders of the society. Simon had twice been assigned to important jobs and twice made a mess of them. People were angry at him. Simon didn't want any help, and he wouldn't admit there was anything wrong. There was no reason to think the situation would improve, so Ignatius made the hard decision to remove Simon from his job and recall him to Rome.

Ignatius did this while preserving his relationship with Simon. He sincerely loved his friend and told him so. "You know that I have always had a very special affection for you," he wrote. "Trust me. I will have a care for your reputation." He gave Simon the benefit of the doubt. He was direct and honest. When he finally had to make a decision, Ignatius acted decisively but kindly.

It's a lesson in how to relate to a difficult friend. Ignatius did what he had to do, painful as it was for both of them, all the while leaving no doubt in Simon's mind that Ignatius loved him. "I have always had a very special love for you," he told Simon. Simon was disappointed but he accepted Ignatius's decision. They remained friends, and the Jesuit order was stronger because Simon remained part of it. Incorporating difficult people is a sign of a true community.

October 28

People Who Can't Stand You

Know yourself: your character, intellect, judgment, and emotions. There are mirrors for the face, but the only mirror for the spirit is wise self-reflection.

— Baltasar Gracián, SJ

Every once in a while you'll run into someone who just can't stand you. They avoid you, sneer at your opinions, rebuff your efforts to be nice. You'll also occasionally meet people who think you are the greatest person they ever met. They praise everything you say and tell others you can do no wrong. It's a big mistake to take any of these people seriously.

For those who can't stand you, give them a wide berth and get on with your life. For those who think you're the best, make sure you don't believe it. Over-the-top praise is as irrational as instinctive dislike.

And ask yourself if you're one of those people for someone else. Are there people you can't stand? People who you think can do no wrong? Take care to correct that mistake.

October 29

Your Job Is to Help Others

I do not think your security of soul is relevant. If all we looked for in our vocation was to be safe from danger, we would not be associating with people. But according to our vocation, we deal with everyone.

— Ignatius Loyola

The Jesuit Diego Miró worked in the royal court of Portugal, evidently a snake pit of intrigue and temptations of the flesh. He thought it was a spiritually unhealthy place to be, so he wrote to Ignatius to ask for another assignment. Ignatius's answer was remarkable for the times: "I do not think the security of your soul is relevant." Most Christians thought that saving their soul was the most important thing. It was not unreasonable to want to get out of a place where sinners had the upper hand.

But for Ignatius, Jesuits *belonged* in that kind of place. Ignatian ministry was about "helping souls," not "saving your soul." He wouldn't admit men to the order if they were motivated by a desire to get to heaven. In fact, "helping souls" — work in the world in all its messiness — is the way to grow closer to God.

Ignatius told Miró to get back to work. And not to worry. "Christ himself will be our protection."

October 30

What Fidelity Means

Placing fidelity at the center of the moral life means that we may need to make more calls, write more letters, cook more dinners, take more strolls, linger a little longer with a friend. We may also need to disengage ourselves from the habit of counting or measuring what "the other" does or does not.

— James Keenan, SJ

"Caring about someone deeply is exhausting," says Malcolm Gladwell. It means standing with someone through good times and bad because you love them. It's about generosity, sharing, sacrifice. It means spending time with friends when you'd rather be doing something else. It means feeding the baby in the middle of the night so your spouse can sleep. To nurture and sustain relationships, we need the virtue of fidelity.

Fidelity doesn't have much to do with justice. Justice is easy. We understand rules and norms, equality before the law, due process. A child's first moral judgment is "that's not fair." Fidelity is hard. Relationships aren't about fairness. Tit for tat doesn't work with someone you love. Parents must teach children how to have relationships — to share, to be generous, to help unlikable people, to share lunch with the social outcast in the school cafeteria. These are lessons we never stop learning. Relationships are arduous.

October 31

How Are They Doing?

Your values are not what you say or print in a brochure, but how you treat people, how you run meetings, whom you hire, how you treat your child who wants to play when you come home exhausted, whether you inconvenience yourself to support your friends, and how you react in a host of other daily moments.

— CHRIS LOWNEY

In a world of constant change and long lives, the only constant is the kind of person you are. The main value is integrity. You'll have many jobs, but your "career" is becoming the person you were meant to be.

Since we're social creatures, our relationships are where we do the hard work of integrity. If you're like most people, you would be hard-pressed to think of anything that goes on in your life that doesn't involve relationships. You have a family; you are a child, sibling, spouse, parent, aunt or uncle, cousin, grandparent; you are a friend, neighbor, colleague, employee, volunteer, member of a church community, citizen. There's your answer to the question "Who am I?" Most of your life involves connections with other people. That's where you will find your joy and your pain. So regularly ask: How are they doing?

November

PRACTICAL TRUTHS

Our vocation is practical,
and all of our spiritual exercises are practical.

— Jerome Nadal, SJ

The End Comes First

Rather than examining actions and asking whether we should per-form them or not, virtue ethicists say that persons ought to set ends for the type of people they wish to become and pursue them.

— James Keenan, SJ

On the first day of his ethics seminar, the Jesuit philosopher James Keenan asks his students to write down three important ethical issues. They usually name broad social problems like climate change, abortion, racism, gender equality, global poverty. Then he has them to turn the paper over and write down three things that they woke up worrying about this morning. They write things like doing my work better, improving a relationship, taking better care of my health, figuring out how to help someone. Social problems are important, Keenan says, but the ethical issues that really press on us are personal ones: How can I become a good person? How do I live a virtuous life?

To act rightly, Ignatius said, we need to know what we're trying to accomplish. The end comes first. Know what kind of person you want to become, then set out to become that person.

November 2

People Have Reasons for What They Do

Weigh with care what you perceive as excesses or aberrations in your brother. When you and others think he is annoying or stupid or thoughtless, not only by your own but by others' votes, examine this judgment with more than usual care.

— PETER FABER, SJ

"A person does not do things without reason," said the second-century Jewish sage Rabbi Meir Baal Haness. The driver who cut you off on the expressway, the customer service person who spoke rudely to you, the friend who doesn't pick up when you call — none of these people deliberately set out to do wrong, so it's wise to withhold judgment until you know what their reasons are. Maybe they're unaware of the consequences of what they're doing. Maybe they don't know any better. Maybe they intended something very different from what you think they did. You just don't know. You may never know. So stifle your anger. Give them the benefit of the doubt.

November 3

Two Cheers for Hypocrisy

These people who can see right through you never quite do you justice, because they never give you credit for the effort to be better than you actually are, which is difficult and well meant and deserving of some little notice.

— MARILYNNE ROBINSON, *GILEAD*

Nothing gets the righteous juices flowing better than uncovering a hypocrite. Pious politicians caught lying, devout believers who cheat on their taxes, community leaders arrested for drunk driving — their shame can give us a feeling of quiet satisfaction. We think: *I'm not perfect, but at least I don't pretend to be better than I actually am.*

But wait: Would you rather that they *not* be ashamed? Would you like them to flaunt their behavior? "Hypocrisy is the homage that vice pays to virtue," the French moralist La Rochefoucauld said three hundred years ago. By pretending they are better people than they actually are, hypocrites acknowledge that virtue is worth emulating. They show the rest of us what the right standards of behavior are. Give them a break. Give yourself a break, too. You are not the kind of person that you want to be either. You're trying to do better. Withhold judgment on other people who fall short.

November 4

Hope Is Not Optimism

Hope is definitely not the same thing as optimism. It is not the conviction that something will turn out well, but the certainty that something makes sense, regardless of how it turns out.

— Václav Havel

It's easy to mistake optimism for hope. Optimism is a mood. It's a cheerful determination to be positive and upbeat at all times, including those times when circumstances are gloomy and grim. Hope, on the other hand, is conviction that the situation you are in, no matter how grim, has meaning and purpose. Hopeful people are not always optimistic. An optimistic demeanor doesn't mean that someone is genuinely hopeful. Václav Havel, who spent years as a political prisoner under the Communist regime in Czechoslovakia, explained that hope "is an orientation of the spirit, an orientation of the heart; it transcends the world that is immediately experienced and is anchored somewhere beyond its horizons."

So when you say, "Things will be OK," or "I feel good about that," in troublesome or challenging circumstances, it's a good idea to ask yourself whether you're expressing hope or merely optimism. Is it a mood? Or is it a deep conviction that all really will be well in the end?

Things Go Wrong All the Time

There is something wrong with everything.
— Tyler Cowen

Things go wrong all the time. Plans fail, troubles arise unexpectedly, each day brings unpleasant surprises. The Ignatian remedy for trouble is, first, to get rid of the idea that difficulties are an aberration. They are *normal*. We should expect them and prepare for them. Second, we should *learn* from failure. Don't "move on" when a project collapses. Understand what went wrong so you can do it better the next time. Finally, seize the opportunity to grow in virtue. "I sympathize with you in your trials," Ignatius wrote to a friend, "but I consider this a special gift. It's an occasion to practice patience, as well as faith and hope in Him."

It's also an occasion for humility. If there's something wrong with everything, there's something wrong with everything *you* do. Your understanding of anything is imperfect. There are things you don't know. Be cautious in your conclusions and hold your judgments lightly.

November 6

Don't Worry about the Outcome

Bad beats drag you down. They focus your mind on something you can't control rather than something you can, the decision. They ignore the fact that the most we can do is to make the best decision possible with the information we have. The outcome doesn't matter. If you choose wisely, you should make the same choice over and over.

— MARIA KONNIKOVA

In poker, "bad beats" are strong hands that lose to stronger hands, but Konnikova is also referring to bad beats in life when good plans don't turn out well. These are good ideas undone by unforeseen problems. A pandemic comes along to wreck your vacation plans. The new job you just started disappears when the company is unexpectedly sold. No one shows up for the concert you worked so hard on. Disappointments like these are bound to happen from time to time. We can't control the outcome of our decisions.

Ignatius's advice is to make the best decision you can and let the results take care of themselves. Don't worry about the outcome. Don't second-guess the decision if the result is disheartening. A bad outcome doesn't mean the decision was bad. At the same time, a good outcome doesn't necessarily mean the decision was good. Instead, concentrate on the process of the decision. Did you achieve "indifference" — detachment from the alternatives? Did you account for your biases — especially the tendency to look for reasons to do what you want to do? Did you have a clear idea of what you hoped to accomplish? Did you pray? These are the things you can control.

November 7

What Matters Is What You Do

A characteristic of Ignatian spirituality is the focus and insistence on action. Loyalty is expressed in service. Love is manifested in actions rather than in words. Repentance means action for change. Serious conversion to Christ means commitment of all one's resources — material and personal — and expenditure of all one's energies.

— MONIKA HELLWIG

What you do has more value than what you say. This point needs emphasis in a culture flooded with words and opinions from all corners of the internet. Too many people are satisfied with words. They think it's enough to express themselves on social media and to fill notebooks with ideas for projects they might undertake someday. The problem is worse when it comes to spiritual matters. Too often what's valued most is not action but believing the right things and thinking good thoughts.

Ignatian spirituality puts the focus on what you do. Ideas, beliefs, feelings, even prayer are not regarded as ends in themselves. The Ignatian perspective says that action is the test of conversion and spiritual enlightenment. William Barry, the great Jesuit spiritual writer, goes so far as to say that all religious beliefs are only verified in action. Barry writes, "Beliefs that do not lead to actions are not religious beliefs at all; they are thoughts about the world, not beliefs." If you believe that God works with purpose in the world, you must make some attempt to find your part in that work.

November 8

Prudence Is the Crucial Virtue

Prudence is not simply caution. Prudence is rather the virtue of a person whose feet are on the ground and who thinks both practically and realistically. Prudence belongs to the person who not only sets realistic ends, but sets out to attain them.

— JAMES KEENAN, SJ

If the proverbial genie shows up and gives you three wishes, prudence should be at the top of your list. The Anglo-Irish philosopher Edmund Burke considered prudence the queen of virtues: "Prudence is not only the first in rank of the virtues political and moral, but she is the director, the regulator, the standard of them all." Prudence doesn't like black-and-white thinking. It knows that many ideas in tension with each other can all be true. Life is full of conflicts between justice and mercy, freedom and order, boldness and restraint. Prudence looks for ways to resolve these dilemmas. Prudence knows when to make an exception to a rule. It's a master of timing; it knows when to wait and when to act. Prudence is the crucial virtue because it is the faculty of judgment, balance, and wisdom that leads us to all the other virtues.

November 9

Your Past Is Past

Conversion means to accept my past precisely as my past, that is, both mine and past, and to surrender in freedom to the new and mysterious future offered by God's love now.

— WILLIAM A. BARRY, SJ

Few people have more reason to regret the past than recovering alcoholics. Almost always they've made a mess of their lives and harmed people they love. That's why one of the most powerful parts of the 12-step recovery program is the "Twelve Promises of AA," which enumerate what people can expect if they stay sober. The second promise is perhaps the most remarkable: "We will not regret the past nor wish to shut the door on it."

No regrets: No wallowing in self-pity, no fruitless speculating about what might have been. Pay attention to the life you live now. Alcoholics often say they are glad to be alcoholics because their sober life is a better life than what they would have had otherwise.

Don't shut the door on it: At the same time, accept the past. Repair what damage you can. Move on, but take responsibility for what you have done.

November 10

The Present Is a Gift

Quite simply, the future is not here, even though we can create as many illusions about it as we'd like. The past is already over. We have to deal with things as they are in the moment.

— Jon Kabat-Zinn

There's a saying attributed to the cartoonist Bil Keane: "Yesterday's the past, tomorrow's the future, but today is a gift. That's why it's called the present." We spend an inordinate amount of time worrying about the future, which is unknowable, and regretting the past, which is unchangeable. We neglect the gift that's sitting in front of us — the present moment. It's the only moment we really have. It's where we are alive. It's the place where we meet God. Ignatian spiritual practice emphasizes the holiness of the present moment. It sharpens our spiritual senses. It trains us to reflect on our experience. It asks, "Where is God *now*?"

November 11

Waiting Enlarges the Soul

Simply by making us wait God increases our desire, which in turn enlarges the capacity of our soul, making it able to receive what is to be given to us.

— St. Augustine

We're impatient. We don't like to wait. We want to get on with things. But perhaps waiting is precisely what we need to do. Augustine says that waiting for God to do something is like a householder with a container too small to contain all the wine that needs to be carried. The person will stretch the wineskin or go off to find a bigger one. This takes time, but it's well worth it in the end. "This is how God deals with us," he says. We need to desire God more intensely to receive all he wants to give us. That means waiting. Ignatius and Augustine both say that desire is the crucial spiritual quality. Ignatius loved desire, the bigger the better. We grow closer to God as we cultivate what he called "great desires."

What do you long for? What do you want most intensely? Those are the questions God wants us to answer.

November 12

Happiness Is Not Fulfilling Desires

Vronsky meanwhile, despite the full realization of what he had de-
sired for so long, was not fully happy. He soon felt that the reali-
zation of his desire had given him only a grain of the mountain of
happiness he had expected. It showed him the eternal error people
make in imagining that happiness is the realization of desires.

— Leo Tolstoy, *Anna Karenina*

In *Anna Karenina*, Alexei Vronsky has money, power, good
health, and social status. Most importantly, he gets what he
desires most — the beautiful Anna Karenina, whom he has
seduced away from her husband and with whom he is living
in Italy. He has everything he wants, yet he is still not happy.
The problem is that he wants the wrong things: freedom to
do what he wants instead of freedom to choose the good;
a liaison with a beautiful woman instead of marriage and
family; a comfortable life instead of a meaningful one.

The other road to happiness lies in finding one's purpose
in life and pursuing it with a generous heart. This involves
the fulfillment of deeper desires than Vronsky's — the desire to bring happiness to others, the desire to know God.
Ignatius said that this is what we really want. This is what
Vronsky wants, too; sadly, his attachment to glittering, de-
ceptive, disordered desires keeps him from finding it.

November 13

You Can't Learn What You Think You Already Know

God treated him exactly as a schoolmaster treats a child — He instructed him.

— *The Autobiography of Ignatius Loyola*

We all have our own ways of doing things. We run meetings, organize our work, approach problems, and do the other duties of everyday life in particular ways that we're comfortable with. When those ways stop working, or don't work particularly well, we tend to hang on to them anyway because they are *our* ways. Trouble comes when we start to think that *our* way is the *right* way. Then people who do things differently are not just different, they're *wrong*. This attitude leads to conflict and many forms of unhappiness.

To the Ignatian mind, there's usually a *better* way to do things — more effective, more loving, frugal, more peaceful, simpler. We can learn something from every person we meet. Look for it, and be prepared to change your modus operandi when you see something better. We will never learn anything if we think we already know everything.

November 14

Pessimism Is the Dark Side of Prudence

There was in me a deeply ingrained pessimism; a pessimism, by that time, much more of intellect than of temper. I was now by no means unhappy; but I had very definitely formed the opinion that the universe was, in the main, a rather regrettable institution.

— C. S. LEWIS

In 2005, a team of psychologists and law professors published a paper purporting to explain why lawyers as a group are more unhappy than those in other professions. Some of the reasons are not surprising: stressful jobs, intense competitiveness, limited autonomy, burnout. But the number-one reason was surprising: many lawyers have negative, pessimistic personalities. The researchers theorized that the lawyers' pessimism stems from an excess of prudence.

Lawyers are selected and rewarded for their prudence. The mindset of a good lawyer is cautious, skeptical, firmly grounded in "reality." It's their job to assess the risks their clients are taking and to foresee every possible pitfall in a new venture. They look at worse-case scenarios; they plan for disaster. Many lawyers allow this prudent professional mindset to bleed into their personal lives. They look at *everything* skeptically. They respond cautiously to every new idea, reflexively identifying weakness and risks. They become unhappy pessimists, always expecting the worst.

"Have confidence in the Lord with all thy heart, and lean not upon thy own prudence," wrote Ignatius to a friend, quoting Proverbs 3:5. It's a reminder that anything can be taken too far, even virtue. If we forget to trust God, we're left to our own resources, and that's a risky place to be.

November 15

Fame Is a Danger

We are not only gregarious animals, liking to be in sight of our fellows, but we have an innate propensity to get ourselves noticed, and noticed favorably, by our kind.

— WILLIAM JAMES

In book 9 of the *Iliad*, the great warrior Achilles must decide whether to wage war in Troy and die a hero or return to Phthia to live a happy life with his loved ones and die in obscurity. It's a choice between specialness and happiness:

> If I hold out here and I lay siege to Troy,
> my journey home is gone, but my glory never dies.
> If I voyage back to the fatherland I love,
> my pride, my glory dies.

Achilles chooses death and glory. He is addicted to fame. The most important thing to him is that other people recognize his name after he's dead.

The choice would not have surprised Ignatius, who regarded the longing for praise and honor as the engine that drives human behavior. This hunger to be noticed is an obstacle to happiness. It skews our priorities and drives other people away. It's an illusion anyway. You are not special. At the center of all things is love, not you.

November 16

Experience Will Teach You

What I like about experience is that it is such an honest thing. You may take any number of wrong turnings; but keep your eyes open and you will not be allowed to go very far before the warning signs appear. You may have deceived yourself, but experience is not trying to deceive you.

— C. S. Lewis

Ignatius didn't find his way to God by reading holy texts, studying theology, or even by praying. He did it by reflecting on his personal experience. As he examined his life, he came to understand what excited him and what bored him. Ignatius had been a very worldly factotum in the royal court of Castile, but eventually he discovered that what he really wanted was a life far different from the one he had been leading, a life as a follower of Jesus. Ignatius had deceived himself with dreams of glory in a royal court. His experience taught him otherwise. All he needed to do was pay attention to it.

That's why paying attention is central to Ignatian spirituality. God is found in all things, but especially in our day-to-day experience of work, family, friendship. God is in our joys and disappointments, in the feelings we have, in our dreams and longings. Reflect on your experience. It won't deceive you.

November 17

Everyone Thinks Differently

At this meeting Pierre for the first time was struck by the endless variety of men's minds, which prevents a truth from ever appearing the same to any two persons.

— LEO TOLSTOY, WAR AND PEACE

Ignatius had a side project during the fourteen years he was superior general of the Jesuits. In his spare time he wrote *The Constitutions of the Society of Jesus*, a lengthy and detailed collection of rules covering every aspect of the society: how new Jesuits were to be admitted and trained, how leadership was to function, discipline, the relations between superiors and subordinates, what kind of work Jesuits should do and how they should do it, and every other feature of Jesuit life. But the *Constitutions* are not like other legal codes and founding documents. Almost every rule admits for exceptions. Ignatius gave superiors wide latitude to interpret the rules broadly and apply them with discretion.

Ignatius didn't insist that everyone think the same way. There are many paths to God, many ways to live a virtuous life. Ignatius didn't think he had all the answers. He thought that hearts will burn with zeal for service and love of God when people find their own unique path.

That's why he allowed exceptions to the rules and urged leaders to exercise prudence. "This is what may be said in general," he wrote to a Jesuit who wanted an answer to a problem, "but prudence will make the application in particular cases. Decide what is to be done in each case after weighing all the circumstances."

November 18

Transitions Are Normal

I've been an investment banker, hospital system board chair, author, social entrepreneur, and husband. I've lived on three continents and spent chunks of time on two more. I foresaw none of those life transitions five years before they happened; in a couple of cases, I only saw those transitions coming on the day that a boss dropped them into my lap.

— CHRIS LOWNEY

Transitions feel like an abnormal disruption to ordinary life. In fact, they are normal. You know this if you pay attention to the annual Christmas letters you get every year. They report weddings, funerals, graduations, the birth of grandchildren, job changes, illnesses, moves to another state. Sometimes it seems as if the periods of calm are abnormal disruptions to a life characterized by wrenching change.

Ignatian spirituality suits a life of transitions. It has us examine our lives regularly. It has us ask, like Ignatius, "What could this mean?" It asks if there is a better way to do things. It opens us to the possibility that God might be nudging us toward a different path than the one we are on.

November 19

Nothing Human Is Merely Human

Nothing human is merely human. No common labor is merely common. Classrooms, hospitals, and artists' studios are sacred spaces. No secular pursuit of science is merely secular. The hand of the creator can be detected by looking at galaxies through telescopes or examining cellular life in laboratories.

— RONALD MODRAS

Karl Rahner, the great German Jesuit theologian, often spoke of "everyday mysticism." By this he meant that mystical experiences are not as rare as most would believe. Ordinary people can have the intense experience of God's presence normally associated with extraordinary mystics like John of the Cross and Thérèse of Lisieux.

Ronald Modras identifies the basis of everyday mysticism: The works of human beings are not merely human. Creation is not merely an assortment of molecules, quarks, and photons. God is in all of it. He has an intimate relationship with all things human because he became part of human life through the incarnation. When we have a "mystical" experience of seeing things in a new way, of being suddenly lifted up from our normal perceptions, we are glimpsing the divine life that's really there.

If God is present in human works, then everything that deepens our humanity deepens our experience of God. Art, science, literature, music — even technology, even sports — speak of the creator. All we need to do is look for him.

November 20

The Problem Is Complacency

Our sin is usually not in what we did, not in what we could not avoid, not in what we tried not to do. Our sin is usually where you and I are comfortable, where we have found a complacency, where we rest in our delusional self-understanding of how much better we are than other people.

— James Keenan, SJ

The Jesuit philosopher James Keenan suggests that much of the wrong we do is a failure to make the effort. He contrasts Adolph Hitler and his top deputy Albert Speer. Hitler is the personification of evil. In contrast, Speer was a nice man, devoted to his family, kind to subordinates, no great believer in Nazi ideology. He was implicated in the regime's crimes, but he was careful not to know too much about them. He must have heard the rumors, but he didn't ask any questions.

Most of us are more like Speer than Hitler: We don't notice; we don't bother. Look at the people Jesus condemns: the pharisees indifferent to the burdens they put on others; the rich man who ignores hungry Lazarus at his gate; the travelers who walk past the injured man in the parable of the Good Samaritan. They are barely aware of the need right in front of them. So take heed. What are you too complacent to see?

It's Easy to Make Things Worse

If you find yourself in a hole, stop digging. When you stop digging, you are still in a hole.

— THE FIRST AND SECOND LAWS OF HOLES

The first law of holes is good advice: When you are in trouble, don't make the problem worse. Then, second, figure out how to get out of the hole. Actually it's not that simple. Despite what the second law says, consider: Are you really in a hole or does it just seem that way? Maybe you need to fight through a temporary setback. Maybe you should resume digging. Or maybe you need a new shovel or some help.

Ignatius thought that we shouldn't make major changes unless there is a good reason to do so. If the original decision to start digging was made carefully and prayerfully, he would be inclined to leave well enough alone. He was cautious about impulses to make changes. They might be coming from a bad place, from our weakness, or from malign spiritual forces seeking to derail something good. But Ignatius also felt that we should always be alert to the possibility that we should get out of the hole. In fact, nothing is more important than making good choices about how we use the gifts God has given us.

Be clear about what you hope to accomplish. Ask what you really want. But first, stop digging.

Heaven Can Wait

The task that Jesus received from God is not to save souls out of the world, but to save the world, to refocus and reintegrate all creation by drawing the human race back into its proper relationship with God — and proper relationships within the human race.

— MONIKA HELLWIG

There's a strong current of spirituality that regards the world as a bad place. "Deliver me from my enemies, O my God," prays the psalmist. "Each evening they come back, howling like dogs and prowling about the city." The Salve Regina, a traditional Catholic prayer, includes a sorrowful plea to Mary: "To thee do we send up our sighs, mourning and weeping in this valley of tears." When many people speak of salvation, they mean getting out of this miserable world. The Ignatian idea is pretty much the opposite: Salvation means getting deeply *into* the world. Christ came into the world to save it, not to save people out of it. Our mission in life is to participate in this saving work.

Ignatian spirituality is at home in the world, finding God in culture, science, politics, the arts. But it's a restless worldliness, not comfortable with things as they are. It's always looking for the places where God is working to make things better.

November 23

It's Supposed to Be Hard

Dottie Hinson: [Baseball] just got too hard.
Jimmy Dugan: It's supposed to be hard. If it wasn't hard, everyone would do it. The hard is what makes it great.

— A LEAGUE OF THEIR OWN

The consensus opinion among athletes who play many sports is that baseball is the hardest game to play well. It's hard to hit a small round object coming at you at ninety miles per hour. It's almost impossible to hit it squarely with a round bat. Most people, even stars in other sports, can't do it. Dottie Hinson's complaint as she quits the team in the movie *A League of Their Own* — "It just got too hard" — makes perfect sense to anyone who's tried to play the game. But Tom Hanks's rejoinder — "It's *supposed* to be hard" — makes sense, too. Baseball wouldn't be beautiful and thrilling if it was easy. The hard is what makes it great.

There's an Ignatian resonance to Tom Hanks's words. Much of what we need to do to live a good life is pretty hard, and satisfaction comes from doing the hard things, not avoiding them. Baseball offers another lesson: Winning involves teamwork. In other sports, a single star player can carry a team to a championship. In baseball, to win consistently, a team needs many players performing at a high level for the entire season. Life is hard, and playing the hardest game alone won't get you very far.

November 24

Throw Away the Script

You are not something you discover one day through trial and error and interior spelunking; you are something that is constantly in the process of becoming, the invention of endless revolutions. You never know who you are, because who you are is always changing.

— Elizabeth Bruenig

For most of history, people didn't have many options. The future looked very much like the past. Social roles were set; expectations were clear. What you did for work, who you married, where you would live — these questions were answered for you. Your job was to follow the script, not embark on a novel adventure.

All this changed with modernity as vast opportunities opened up. Each of us became responsible for shaping our lives as we see fit.

Ignatius played a big role in bringing about this change. He rejected the old model of religious life. He said that each of us has a unique relationship with God unmediated by priests and institutions. He proposed a systematic way to make good choices, which is the way we participate in the saving work of Christ. In the Ignatian view, we're responsible for the narratives of our lives. We don't follow a script. Through our choices to pursue the good, we become the person we are meant to be.

Wisdom Lies in the Golden Mean

I know that these holy follies have been profitably used by the saints and that they are useful to obtain self-mastery. But as one who has acquired some mastery over his self-love, I hold that the better thing is bringing oneself to the golden mean of discretion.

— IGNATIUS LOYOLA

The principle of moderation appears everywhere. Buddhists call it the Middle Way; in French politics, it's the *juste milieu*. In baseball, batters try to hit the ball on the bat's "sweet spot" in the middle of the barrel. Economists honor "the Goldilocks principle" — seeking an economy that's not too hot, not too cold, but "just right."

Ignatius invoked the golden mean in admonishing some young Jesuits who had gone overboard in their prayer practices. They were fasting, punishing their bodies, and spending too much time at it. Interestingly, Ignatius admits that these practices can be useful to some people, but for his friends they were "holy follies" born of the delusion that one can obtain God's favor by trying really, really hard.

What's lacking is discernment. What works for other people might not work for you. Reflect on the matter. Consult experienced people. You'll likely find that the answer isn't at one of the extremes but in the middle, at the golden mean.

November 26

Love Tempers Justice

The Princess never gave a thought to that proud word "justice." For all the complex laws of mankind were summed up in the one clear and simple law of love and self-sacrifice, laid down for us by Him who in His love had suffered for all mankind, though He Himself was — God. What had she to do with the justice or injustice of other people? She herself had to endure and love, and that she did.

— LEO TOLSTOY, WAR AND PEACE

Princess Marya Bolkonsky, a great character in Tolstoy's *War and Peace*, exemplifies Christ's great commandment: Love God with all your heart and soul, and love your neighbor as yourself. Princess Marya is a pious woman devoted to God, to good works, and to her elderly father, the irascible Prince Nikolai Bolkonsky. The prince criticizes his daughter incessantly. He mocks her faith; he thinks her works of mercy are useless and futile; he ridicules her personally. In one wrenching scene, Marya endures savage unjust criticism from her father, then discovers the man she thinks she loves in the arms of another woman. Anger would be entirely justified, but Marya continues to love the disappointing people in her life. She doesn't give a thought to justice. Remarkably, she thinks of their good qualities. Her impulse is to help them.

That's what love is. Love isn't merely tolerating the unlovable. It means thinking well of them.

Your Knowledge Should Benefit Others

Many great and learned men keep their learning to themselves and frustrate the main purpose of their learning — to be of benefit to others. If they were able to explain themselves, they could accomplish widespread good.

— IGNATIUS LOYOLA

Ignatius had great respect for learning but his attitude toward it was very practical: It's meant to equip us to be of use to others. He got an education himself because he wanted to help people spiritually, and the church insisted that teachers of the faith be credentialed. He wanted Jesuits to be well educated because their work demanded it. Ignatius was critical of scholars who kept learning to themselves. He disapproved of smart people who couldn't or wouldn't communicate what they knew. His attitude toward learning was guided by a couple of principles that are central to Ignatian spirituality. "Love means sharing" and the purpose of ministry is to "help souls."

Bear this in mind when you make choices about what to study. Learn something you can share with others.

November 28

Your Own Advice Is Worth Listening To

I will imagine a person whom I have never seen or known. Desiring all perfection for him or her, I will consider what I would say in order to bring such a one to act and elect for the greater glory of God.

— THE SPIRITUAL EXERCISES, 185

Psychologists have studied a curious phenomenon you may have encountered yourself: We seem to be able to give other people better advice than we give ourselves. We can assess a friend's problem sensibly and give them good advice about how to solve it. But when we face the same problem ourselves, we are baffled and confused. It's called the Solomon paradox after the Jewish king who asked for wisdom when God told him to ask for anything he wanted. Solomon turned out be a terrible leader whose mistakes caused the Kingdom of Israel to break apart. Either the wisdom he possessed disappeared (unlikely), or he found reasons to discount the good advice he was getting.

Ignatius's techniques for decision-making are intended to cut through the cognitive biases, fears, and irrational longings that blind us. One of them is to imagine that a stranger with exactly the same problem that we have comes to us for advice. We should listen to the stranger describe the problem, and then listen carefully to the advice we give. It's likely to be pretty good advice. Try this the next time you are wrestling with a tough decision. The advice you give yourself might be better than you think.

November 29

There Are No Guarantees

Just because I am trying to do God's work with every ounce of my being is no guarantee that my plans will prosper. There is no guarantee that an effective Christian disciple will not be cut down in his prime. There is no guarantee that because you love God deeply, you will not lose your job, your home, your family, your health.

— WALTER J. BURGHARDT, SJ

The story goes that a friend of the great physicist Niels Bohr noticed a horseshoe mounted on a wall in his office. He was aghast; could a brilliant scientist like Bohr really believe that horseshoes bring good luck? "Of course I don't believe that," Bohr said, "but I understand that it's lucky whether I believe it or not."

The story is probably apocryphal, but it makes a point about uncertainty. We might have a good plan, but there's no guarantee it will work. Outcomes depend on a myriad of factors out of our control. Since they depend on the actions of other people who have free will, they are out of God's control, too. If you fail, don't blame God.

On the other hand, we know where we will wind up. Love is at the center of things. If we are patient, and seek to do the right thing, love will find us.

God Doesn't Have to Be in Charge

Some things are random and other things are meant to be in our control. So God is with me when "shit happens" and God is rooting for me when I need to decide things. I'm OK with that. I don't need God to be in charge of my life. I only need God to be at the center of it.

— GREGORY BOYLE, SJ

Should we want God to be in charge of our lives? Many believers talk as if they do, but the God-in-charge idea seems to diminish the status of human beings. We're adults, making our own decisions, figuring things out for ourselves, finding our unique identity. The God-in-charge model makes us children obeying our elders or soldiers following the officers' orders.

Putting God at the *center* of our lives fits better than thinking of him as the almighty boss. "I am with you always," says Jesus at the end of Matthew's gospel. This promise comes after he gives the disciples the responsibility for continuing his work in the world. That's a lot of responsibility, and we're free to exercise it the best way we can.

What does it mean for God to be at the center of our lives? The Ignatian perspective says that we're aware of God's presence in our lives and in our world in a tangible way. We regularly connect with God personally. We try to join God's work when we see it. We try to get in touch with our deepest desires. When things do not go well, we try to understand why. We know that we're not in control of the outcome of our efforts. We do our best, trusting God who trusts us.

December

BECOMING THE PERSON YOU ARE MEANT TO BE

The real question is not "What should I do?"
but "Who should I become?"

— JAMES KEENAN, SJ

Give Thanks

At night Ignatius would go up on the roof of the house, with the sky there up above him. He would sit quietly, absolutely quietly. He would take his hat off and look up for a long time at the sky. Then he would fall to his knees, bowing profoundly to God.... And the tears would begin to flow down his cheeks like a stream but so quietly and gently that you heard not a sob or a sigh nor the least possible movement of his body.

— Diego Lainez, SJ

Ignatius thought that gratitude was *the* crucial attitude. It's important to be reverent, to be humble, to be selfless and eager to serve. But gratitude is essential. It was so important to Ignatius that he thought that ingratitude was the deadliest of sins — "the cause, beginning, and origin of all sins and evil," he wrote. A remarkable statement. We think of ingratitude as something akin to rudeness. To Ignatius it's a mortal threat to our spirit, greater perhaps than pride and lust and envy and the other seven deadly sins.

That's because gratitude is seeing reality rightly. The world is a gift, and gratitude is how we respond to gifts. Ingratitude is something like willful blindness to the truth. Gratitude leads to other virtues. It strengthens humility. It prompts us to be generous. Remembering why we are grateful is a great way to pray because it lets the grace of God touch us again and again.

December 2

Love People; Use Things

The world encourages us to love things and use people. But that's backward. Put this on your fridge and try to live by it: Love people; use things.

— ARTHUR BROOKS

One of the most famous studies of happiness followed hundreds of men who graduated from Harvard from 1939 to 1944. They were interviewed periodically for decades to see how life turned out for them. The results showed a clear pattern. The happiest men had strong family ties and close friendships. Those who neglected relationships were more likely to be suffering from depression, dementia, alcoholism, and other physical and mental health problems.

The lesson from studies like these is usually stated negatively: Don't sacrifice love and family for success. Don't become a workaholic. Don't trade love for anything. But it can be stated positively too: Use "things" to enhance your relationships. Ignatius said that the "things on the face of the earth are created for human beings." If you have some money, spend it on experiences you share with those you love. If you have energy to pursue a hobby, choose one you can do with others. If you have some time, spend it in the company of others. You'll be happier if you do.

Give It Away

The person to whom our Lord has been liberal ought not to be stingy.

— IGNATIUS LOYOLA

We like stories of selfless generosity — the friend who takes on a demanding volunteer job, the colleague who becomes a mentor for a young person, the kid who mows an elderly neighbor's lawn. We like to hear them even if we don't consider ourselves to be particularly generous. That's because the urge to give generously of ourselves is one of our basic desires. Ignatius thought so, and he also thought this desire is often buried under a great heap of fears and anxious worries about not having enough time and money for ourselves.

Unlocking this desire is one of the goals of Ignatian spiritual practice. It invites us to imagine God as the infinitely generous giver of gifts, the source of unending blessings that bathe us "just as the rays come down from the sun." This great generosity moves us to respond generously ourselves — "all my possessions and myself along with them." We don't learn to be generous. We need to release it. We already know how.

December 4

Get Used to Different

Peter: I don't get it.
Jesus: You didn't get it when I chose you either.
Peter: I'm not a tax collector. This is different.
Jesus: Get used to different.

— THE CHOSEN, SCENE IN WHICH JESUS INVITES MATTHEW,
A TAX COLLECTOR, TO JOIN HIM

Jesus's ideas were disruptive; he challenged the tribal, hierarchical rule-obsessed religious establishment. Ignatius was disruptive, too. He rejected the conventional model of religious life and removed the intermediaries standing between the individual and God. He said that God deals directly with each of us, that we need to be constantly alert for new challenges, new leadings of the spirit, better ways of doing things. Fight the human tendency to settle into routines.

Jesus's comment "Get used to different" from the streaming TV series *The Chosen* catches the spirit of Ignatian thinking. Peter had made a radical change by joining Jesus's band. He had been around Jesus long enough to know that Jesus loved blowing up conventional religious ideas. But Peter was shocked that Jesus loved a *tax collector* of all people. He was still thinking in the old way. He hadn't gotten used to different.

That's why Ignatian practice prizes the process of discernment. Life presents a constant stream of opportunities and challenges. We need to make choices all the time. Every day we ask the question: Is this action consistent with who I am and who I want to become?

December 5

Deepen Your Spiritual Practice

Every day set aside some time so that the soul will not be without its food.

— IGNATIUS LOYOLA

The church in Ignatius's time had lots of rules about how people should pray. Ignatius would have none of it. He thought that people should pray in the fashion that suits them best. However, he did have some good ideas about prayer. Here are a few from the Ignatian tradition.

Ignatian prayer is about awareness. It emphasizes noticing, seeing, and visualizing spiritual realities. Its underlying assumption is that God is active everywhere, trying to catch our attention. The essence of Ignatian prayer is becoming attuned to what is stirring spiritually within so that it becomes present to our consciousness.

That is the point of the Daily Examen, which has us examine our everyday experience for signs of God's presence. Another prayer practice is colloquy: heartfelt, free-flowing conversation with God, "speaking exactly as one friend speaks to another," as Ignatius put it.

Your spiritual practice will change over time. It's part of the pilgrimage, Ignatius's favorite metaphor for our spiritual journey. You're exploring, you're going somewhere. Tomorrow will be different from today.

Act "As If..."

When we do not feel like serving in love, it is time to act as if we do feel it. To reach out to the needy person when we feel like turning away is not dishonesty. Rather it is acting in line with what we deeply believe, even though, at this moment, the emotional drive for such acting is absent. This is mature faith: to act as if we are always feeling what we deeply believe.

— GEORGE ASCHENBRENNER, SJ

Soon after his conversion, Ignatius became oppressed by guilt. He believed that God had forgiven him, but he couldn't shake the sadness caused by the memories of his sins. He knew this was wrong, but he couldn't force himself think differently. He decided to act as if he was free and joyful. Soon he began to feel that way. He solved his emotional-spiritual problem by acting as if he didn't have it.

He used what psychologist Richard Wiseman calls "the *as if* principle." If you want to feel a certain way, act as if you already do. It sounds like a shallow self-help trick, but it's solidly based on a principle of cognitive science known as "embodied cognition" — the notion that the body influences the mind. If you act contrary to the way you're feeling, eventually your feelings will catch up. If you are feeling perversely selfish, give some money to panhandlers on the street. If you are afraid of talking to strangers, strike up a conversation with some people you don't know.

The *as if* principle *is* a kind of trick. Feeling unhappy but acting happy makes us subtly, unconsciously uncomfortable. It doesn't feel right; something has to change. So we get rid of the discomfort by bringing our unhappy feelings into line with our happy actions.

December 7

Think Big

Many of us confuse humility with self-negation. We clip our own wings, or let others clip them. We remain silent when we should speak out, and inactive when bold action is called for. Over time, like T. S. Eliot's Prufrock, we can wind up measuring out our lives with coffee-spoons.

— DEAN BRACKLEY, SJ

Applying moral precepts to different people in diverse circumstances is a tricky business. Take pride — traditionally the deadliest sin. The remedy is humility — a modest opinion of oneself, acknowledgment that we know a lot less than we think we do. Humility often means deference to others, acceptance of one's circumstances.

That's fine for people who think well of themselves and have the ability and freedom to make decisions to satisfy their desires. But it's not so fine for those who think they don't count for much and have been told to accept their unhappy circumstances. This is a large group that includes many women, poor people, minorities, people with disabilities, and others who don't fit into the mainstream. The Jesuit social activist Dean Brackley says these people need to be encouraged to think big, not small and humbly. He calls for magnanimity — a big, expansive spirit, "spontaneously generous, even prodigal, the opposite of the stingy, shrunken soul."

Might you need to hear this message? Do you take a back seat by default in deference to strong, confident people? Do you stifle your inner voice, failing to speak and act? Maybe you need to speak up, act boldly, think big.

December 8

Consider Your Habits

The way I take breakfast, the way I leave home, the way I drive to work, the way I greet people in the morning are all exercises that affect me. My morning exercises make me in part the person I will be for the rest of the day. We ought to examine our ways of acting and ask ourselves, "Are these ways making us more just, prudent, temperate, and brave?"

— James Keenan, SJ

Our habitual actions make us into a certain kind of person. A person who dances becomes a dancer. Someone who cares a lot about food becomes a foodie. A boss who incessantly corrects other people's mistakes becomes a control freak. Someone who talks all the time becomes a bore.

It's easy to make excuses for less-than-ideal behavior: *I ride herd on people because we can't make mistakes in this business. I'm away from the family all the time because the job demands it. These kids need to learn to be tougher.* In this scenario, we're a nice person who is being forced by circumstances to temporarily act meanly. But the temporary has a way of becoming permanent; a great chasm can develop between the way we see ourselves and the way other people see us.

Examine your habitual ways of acting. Are you punctual or habitually late? How do you drive? Do you eat and drink too much? Do you complain a lot? Do you put people at their ease? How you do these ordinary things is making you into the person you are.

December 9

Avoid Lies

Avoid lies, all lies, especially the lie to yourself. Keep watch on your own lie and examine it every hour, every minute.

— FYODOR DOSTOYEVSKY, *THE BROTHERS KARAMAZOV*

We call them "cognitive biases," "errors in thinking," "blind spots," "our memory playing tricks." Father Zossima, the wise elder in *The Brothers Karamazov*, calls them "lies." Twice in the novel he tells people that avoiding lies is the most important way to have a good life.

"Keep watch on your lie," he says. The lie Zossima is talking about can't be eliminated by taking a stronger dose of "truth." It's built into the structure of the way we think. We will always tend to look for reasons to do what we want to do. We will always overestimate the control we have. We will always tend to make excuses for ourselves. We will always want to look good. The best we can do is to "keep watch." Be mindful of these tendencies, and keep them from harming yourself and others.

December 10

Simplify Your Life

A simple lifestyle frees us, reminds us of our reliance on God, makes us more grateful, and leads us to desire "upward mobility" for everyone, not just for the few.

— JAMES MARTIN, SJ

Like many people renowned for their selflessness and generosity, the social activist Dorothy Day deliberately lived more simply than she needed to. She ate plain food when tastier dishes were available. Her living area was simply and cheaply furnished. Even in her old age she traveled by bus when benefactors were happy to buy her a plane ticket. This simple lifestyle was in part political — part of her prophetic identification with the poor and downtrodden. But it was also personal. Her lifestyle trained her to be the person she wanted to be.

Most of us live very comfortably surrounded by stuff that we're attached to. Do you sometimes feel that it's too much, that a simpler lifestyle would suit you better? If you feel the sting of the lifestyle question, pay attention to it. It's an invitation to freedom.

December 11

Discover What Moves You

Ignatius knew himself to be constantly subjected to different stir-rings which were often contradictory. His greatest effort was to try to discover what moved him in each situation: the impulse that leads him to good or the one that inclines him to evil.

— IGNATIAN PEDAGOGY

The first step in Ignatian "awareness" is simply being aware of our feelings. Our default mode is autopilot; we forge ahead, oblivious to the sea of feelings, random thoughts, and distractions that we're swimming in. The next step is meta-awareness — thinking about thinking. *I'm feeling this way. Why? What does it mean?*

Example: You suddenly tire of the work you're doing; you feel like getting a snack or listening to some music. On autopilot you'd follow this impulse without thinking about it. Exercising Ignatian awareness, you'd first stop and realize that you have this feeling and you need to make a choice. Then you ask why you have this feeling. You ask what it means. Have you been working too hard? Does something about the work bother you? Has this been happening often? Is something bothering you and making it hard to focus?

With this awareness, you'll be sensitive to what moves you. You'll make better choices. You'll find what you really want.

December 12

Be a Helpful Appreciator

Little by little the answer often comes to you, and you discover the way to be that helpful appreciator which invariably makes the difference.

— FRED ROGERS

Junlei Li, a Harvard professor of early childhood development, says that his whole approach to his work changed when he took to heart Fred Rogers's call to be a "helpful appreciator." Li had a pretty good idea of what should be happening in day care centers and preschools. "I knew what's not working right here and how I can fix it," he says. His results were disappointing. All that changed when he became a helpful appreciator. He looked for what was already working and built from that. Li learned to see better. His old mindset was "what's wrong here." His new filter became "what's working," and this revealed much that he wasn't able to see before.

We rarely see everything that's in front of us. We walk into problems and crisis situations with our own filters that reveal some things and hide others. A filter that highlights "what's good about this situation" has many advantages over one that emphasizes problems.

December 13

Hang Out with Wise People

To become virtuous, live among the virtuous and imitate what they do.

— MICHAEL HIMES

Aristotle believed that virtue lies midway between two vices: Generosity is between profligacy and miserliness, courage is between rashness and cowardice, and so forth. The virtue that enables us to find that precious "golden mean" is prudence — practical wisdom. You need prudence to find all the other virtues, but how do you find prudence? Aristotle's answer: Hang out with prudent people and watch what they do.

To gain practical wisdom, you need to see it in action. You can be a brilliant psychologist and still not know how to help a struggling teenager. You can be an expert in finance and not know how to help someone get control of their spending. That's why professional degree programs include internships. That's why many people say that some wise person — a teacher, a mentor, a coach — taught them more than they learned in school.

Who are your friends? Are they wise? Are you learning what they have to teach you?

December 14

Prepare for Diminishment

Unless you keel over in the prime of life, your victories will fade, your skills will decline, and life's problems will intrude. If you try to hang on to glory, or lash out when it fades, it will squander your victories and mark an unhappy end to your journey.

— ARTHUR BROOKS

Ignatius always had his eyes on the next turn of the wheel. The big turn of the wheel coming for all of us is our inevitable decline. Energy diminishes; physical ailments and disabilities pile up; it gets harder to focus. The economist and pundit Arthur Brooks calls it the "personal crucible." In this final stage of the pilgrimage, you disengage from midlife commitments and find new ways of loving and serving.

Ignatian discernment can help ease us through the tough questions we'll meet: When is it time to retire? Do I downsize? What should I keep and what should I get rid of? What do I truly enjoy? What have I been pretending I enjoy?

Another piece of Ignatian advice is useful: Prepare now for harder times. How is the final chapter of your personal narrative going to play out?

December 15

Imagine Feeling Better

One who is in desolation should strive to preserve himself or herself in patience. One should remember that after a while the consolation will return again.

— *The Spiritual Exercises*, 321

Cognitive biases are usually undesirable, but we can thank God for at least one of them. It's called "fading affect bias." Painful, negative memories fade more quickly than positive ones. You'll remember the fun times; you'll have trouble recalling the bad ones. If you remember the bad experience, you'll tend not to remember the bad feelings associated with it. Painful events feel further away in time than they actually are. (It doesn't always work this way. Many people are afflicted with vivid memories of traumatic events that cause great suffering.)

Scientists theorize that evolution favored fading affect bias because it helped human beings recover from setbacks and get on with things. Life is full of disappointments, setbacks, loss, tragedy. But the memories of these things will fade; they don't need to cripple us.

So if you're feeling bad right now, not only will you soon feel better, but you'll soon forget feeling bad. You can jumpstart the process by bringing your imagination into play. Imagine yourself months from now not feeling bad anymore — in fact struggling to remember the event that's so painful to you now. Anticipating how your future self will feel might help today's self to weather the storm.

December 16

Be Yourself

Each of us brings something to the table, and we each, through our own gifts, manifest a personal way of holiness that enlivens the community. We help build up the kingdom of God in ways that others cannot. Mother Teresa echoes this in her famous saying: "You can do something I can't do. I can do something you can't do. Together let us do something beautiful for God."

— James Martin, SJ

The message of the beloved movie *It's a Wonderful Life* is irresistible in its simplicity: Forget about "what if" and "if only." Live your life in the world as it is. It's a better place because *you* are in it. Another way to put it is "be yourself." George Bailey, the film's protagonist, shouldn't be disappointed that he didn't realize the dreams of his youth. He was a success because he lived *this* life in *this* place. He lived his own life, not someone else's.

"For me to be a saint means to be myself," said Thomas Merton. Merton distinguished between the false self and the true self. The false self is the self we present to the world. The true self is the person we are before God. This person is unique in all creation with a job only they can do. Our task is to discover who this person is and to live the life only they can live.

Do the work God has given you to do. Conduct your relationships in your unique fashion. Love God the way *you* love God, not the way someone else does.

December 17

Take Control of Media

I think those are very wrong who say that schoolboys should be encouraged to read the newspapers. Nearly all that a boy reads there in his teens will be known before he is twenty to have been false in emphasis and interpretation, if not in fact as well, and most of it will have lost all importance. Most of what he remembers he will therefore have to unlearn; and he will probably have acquired an incurable taste for vulgarity and sensationalism and the fatal habit of fluttering from paragraph to paragraph to learn how an actress has been divorced in California, a train derailed in France, and quadruplets born in New Zealand.

— C. S. Lewis

If C. S. Lewis thought that reading newspapers was a waste of time, imagine what he would think of Facebook, TikTok, Instagram, and Twitter! Social media platforms are so ubiquitous and so addictive that everyone needs to think carefully about them. Everybody complains that they're strapped for time; there are not enough hours in the day to do everything they want to do. So ask yourself: What am I *not* doing while I send tweets and scroll through social media posts?

You could be interacting with other people face-to-face. You could be working more. You could be creating something beautiful. You could do those important-but-not-urgent tasks on your to-do list that never seem to get done. If your use of social media is displacing people and important work, it's probably time for a media reset.

December 18

Don't Gossip

The common talk will fasten upon your one failing rather than your many successes. The bad are better known, and attract more gossip, than the good. Many people were practically unknown until they sinned, and all their successes aren't enough to conceal a single tiny fault. Realize that malevolence will notice all your faults and none of your virtues.

— BALTASAR GRACIÁN, SJ

The story goes that a man with a reputation as a gossip was summoned to see the rabbi. They went to the roof of a tall building, where the rabbi handed the man a pillow full of feathers and told him cut it open and let the feathers fly. The wind took the feathers and spread them hither and yon. "Now gather up all the feathers and put them back in the pillow," the rabbi said. "That's impossible," said the man. "They are spread all over the neighborhood. They are gone for good." "So it is with gossip," said the rabbi. "Once spoken, it goes everywhere, and you cannot call it back."

In a 2013 homily, Pope Francis called gossip a "crime" and "murder." Strong words for a practice that often feels relatively harmless. Baltasar Gracián explains why it's so serious. Negative reports get all the attention. They spread quickly and widely. They stick. What gets remembered about someone is the damaging gossip — the salacious rumor, the embarrassing faux pas, the character defect that the person cannot overcome.

Talk about other people only when you need to. Be mindful of your own shortcomings. Be careful; what you say can't be unsaid.

December 19

Practice Detachment

The more you know God, the more you will want to know God more. To do this, you need to maintain a measure of detachment and freedom. You want to free yourself from any excess baggage.

— James Martin, SJ

Keep things simple. Be clear about your goal. Purify your motives. Be mindful of your feelings. Practice detachment. Highlight humility. These are principles for making good choices from the Ignatian tradition. They are all important, but the first among equals is detachment, or "indifference," as Ignatius had it. Detachment is the method by which we strive to free ourselves from disordered attachments so we can look at alternatives impartially, seeking the one that achieves the greater good. Detachment is also often the goal. As we walk the journey, we want to get rid of excess baggage so we can concentrate on what matters most.

December 20

Recognize Your Deepest Desires

Lord, teach me to seek you, and reveal yourself to me as I seek; for unless you instruct me I cannot seek you, and unless you reveal yourself I cannot find you. Let me seek you in desiring you; let me desire you in seeking you. Let me find you in loving you; let me love you in finding you.

— St. Anselm of Canterbury

When you shed your fears and resentments, when you disentangle yourself from other people's ideas of what constitutes "the good life," when you get free of bogus promises and spurious dreams, what do you *really* want? Ignatius believed that when we know the answer to that question, we will know what God wants, too.

This is the Big Idea of Ignatian spirituality. We want interior knowledge of our deepest desires. It's obscured by our character defects and mistakes. We lose track of our deepest desires, so we pursue fantasies instead, pale reflections of the truth, pleasure instead of love, fame to give us self-worth, toys and trinkets instead of things that matter. We're ignorant of the "desires beneath the desires." We err not because we're in touch with our desires but because we are *not* in touch with them.

Ignatius says we should pray for what we want. This is a good thing to pray for — awareness of what we really want.

December 21

Get Off the Hedonic Treadmill

We are told to be "entrepreneurs of the self." We can't blame the boss or master or patriarch anymore, because we play those roles in our own lives, constantly whipping ourselves up to greater and greater levels of achievement — or, increasingly, falling into some psychical or nervous disorder because we feel incapable of keeping up with the pace of this unending round-the-clock game.

— TED GIOIA

Tolerance is an insidious aspect of drug addiction and alcoholism. The booze or drug gives a lot of pleasure at the beginning, but the effect wanes as the body and brain grow accustomed to it. The person needs more and more of the substance to get the same effect. Eventually, pleasure goes away completely, and the person needs the substance to dull the pain enough just to get through the day. Tolerance makes addicts.

This is what happens to people who think a happy life is a matter of having pleasurable experiences. The effect of pleasure wears off. They seek more and more pleasure, but happiness never comes. They are trapped on what psychologists call the "hedonic treadmill"; they run fast and furiously to stay in the same place.

The other path to happiness is *eudaimonia*, a Greek word meaning the pursuit of virtue and excellence. It's fulfillment derived from pursuing meaningful activities. It's other-directed and often doesn't involve much sensory pleasure. In fact, eudaimonia usually means doing deeply ordinary things like taking a walk with a friend and sharing a meal. This kind of satisfaction doesn't wear off. It's stepping off the hedonic treadmill.

December 22

Plant Your Feet Firmly in Midair

There is no guarantee that God will act in any given way with those who are trying to live the good life; one plants one's feet firmly in midair and marches on in faith, hope, and trust.

— WILLIAM A. BARRY, SJ

It seems that uncertainty is built into the nature of things. The Ignatian conviction that God can be found in all things means that no religious system is ever complete. We will never reach the end of "all things." Some things will always be hidden from us, and something will always come along to make God present in a new way. There will always be surprises.

Uncertainty doesn't mean ignorance. We can know a great deal about God; after all, he is present in all things. We can know God's love. Ignatian reflection can give us a real sense of God's presence. Ignatian discernment can shed light on the choices that best serve God's program to heal the world. None of this comes with any guarantee that things will turn out a certain way, but we don't need that. God's love is enough.

Reach Out and Take It

The grace of God means something like: Here is your life. Here is the world. Beautiful and terrible things will happen. Don't be afraid. I am with you. Nothing can ever separate us. It's for you I created the universe. I love you. There's only one catch. Like any other gift, the gift of grace can be yours only if you'll reach out and take it.

— FREDERICK BUECHNER

The Ignatian way is comfortable with tension. It plays the long game; it's a reflective spirituality that rewards patience. At the same time, there's an assertiveness about it, almost an impatience to get on with it. "Do today what you promised to do tomorrow," Ignatius said. God's grace is available right now; reach out and take it.

"What turns mere words into great purpose?" asks businessman and former Jesuit Chris Lowney. "Take it personally. Get over yourself. Go to the God of your life and talk about it 'in the way one friend speaks to another.'"

Reach out and take it.

December 24

Do It Better Next Time

The thing to do, when you have made a mistake, is not to give up what you were doing and start something altogether new, but start over again with the thing you began badly and try, for the love of God, to do it well.

— THOMAS MERTON

Sometimes the urge to do something new is worth taking seriously. But if it comes out of frustration after you have made a mistake, it's likely a temptation and a distraction. How do you know it is a mistake, anyway? You may have made a good choice that didn't work out for any number of reasons. The Ignatian perspective is usually to do it better the next time. Don't withdraw from company because you've been rebuffed or embarrassed. Don't scale back your ambitions because something didn't work. Don't make your world smaller. Do it again, better this time.

December 25

Deeds of Love

Love ought to manifest itself in deeds rather than in words.

— *The Spiritual Exercises, 230*

The Christmas season is a time of *doing* things: decorating, shopping, cooking, hosting, traveling, socializing with family and friends, and reaching out to people we haven't seen in a while. It's tiring, and some complain that the hubbub of yuletide activity is a secular stain on a solemn religious feast. What would Ignatius say? He'd probably disagree with those who separate secular Christmas from sacred Christmas. He insisted that love should be expressed in deeds rather than words. Our Christmas activities may be tiring and sometimes excessive, but they are indisputably deeds that express love.

Ignatius's saying — "love ought to manifest itself in deeds rather than in words" — is both obvious and enigmatic. It's clearly true: Talk is cheap; what you *do* matters most. But Ignatius's comment is also mysterious. Words matter, too. Loving words and loving deeds go together. Shouldn't it be both deeds *and* words, not deeds *rather* than words? Perhaps Ignatius was exaggerating a bit in order to make a point. Prayer, which is mainly words, gets a lot of attention in religious circles. Ignatius didn't want prayer to become an end in itself. There's a chronic temptation to rest contentedly in the prayer and neglect the deeds. Today, cook the special food, enjoy the travel, greet your guests. These are deeds of love.

December 26

Stick to What's Real

I have no idea what's awaiting me, or what will happen when this all ends. For the moment I know this: there are sick people and they need curing.

— ALBERT CAMUS, *THE PLAGUE*

These words are spoken by Dr. Bernard Rieux in Camus's novel *The Plague* as he ministers to the sick in a terrible plague in the Algerian city of Oran. Rieux tries to make sense of the horror around him; he wrestles with the question of the afterlife; he wonders how or even if the plague will end. Finally, he sets these unanswerable questions aside and decides to concentrate on what's in front of him: sick people whom he can help.

Much of our mental energy is taken up with unanswerable questions. There's speculative revision of the past: *I should have had a better explanation for why I was late. Why didn't I buy that stock three years ago? I can't believe I said that to her.* There are ruminations on an unknowable future: *What if I get sick? What if she's too busy to see me? What will happen to my job if my company gets sold?* Ignatian practice concentrates on the present, as Rieux does. The past is prologue and the future hasn't happened yet. Find God in your life as you are living it *right now*.

Bother to Love

When Jesus condemns people for sinful behavior, he typically does not condemn weak people who are trying to do better. More often, Jesus condemns the "strong" who could help if they wanted, but don't bother to do so.

— JAMES MARTIN, SJ

When he lived in the dorm at Fordham University, the Jesuit philosopher James Keenan heard many stories about students' fraught relationships with their parents. But if the students worked at it, they usually came to understand that their parents were trying pretty hard to do the right thing but fell short. The saddest stories Keenan heard were from students with distant, passive, emotionally detached parents. They weren't sure their parents loved them at all. The parents didn't bother to love.

A close reading of Jesus's parables suggests that people's biggest shortcoming is failing to bother. They know the right thing to do; they just don't bother to do it. There's the rich man who steps over the poor man in front of his house; the priest and the Levite who avoid the man bleeding on the Jericho road; the man who didn't invest the talent he was given; the son who didn't go into the field as he said he would. They didn't do bad things. They failed to do the good deeds that people do when they take the time to love.

The big impediment to becoming the person you are meant to be is failing to make the effort. What good deeds are you leaving undone?

December 28

Resolve to Make Changes

The fourth point is to ask pardon of God our Lord for my faults. The fifth point is to resolve, with his grace, to amend them.

— THE SPIRITUAL EXERCISES, 43

Five hundred years after Ignatius wrote *The Spiritual Exercises*, an alcoholic named Bill Wilson sat down at his kitchen table in New York City and wrote down the twelve steps of Alcoholics Anonymous. Step 6 reads: "Were entirely ready to have God remove all these defects of character." The alcoholic reaches step 6 after identifying the defects of character that need fixing. Step 6 doesn't say "*took steps* to remove all these defects of character" or even "*decided* to remove all these defects of character." It simply says "*were entirely ready*" to have God do it.

That's because we can't do these things on our own. All we can do is *resolve* to make changes, to become ready to have *God* do it. You can be ready to say goodbye to your anger problem, your critical spirit, your lust, your envy — but the power to get rid of them isn't yours. It's up to God.

It's an elegant instance of Ignatian tension. Here I am, trying not to be angry, critical, lustful, envious — resolving to be a different person, doing what I can, knowing my efforts are insufficient. The rest is up to God.

December 29

Seek the Greater Good

A familiar proverb goes "Give a man a fish and you feed him for a day; teach a man to fish and you feed him for a lifetime." This well captures what Ignatius had in mind by the more universal good.

— Barton T. Geger, SJ

In 1553, Ignatius temporarily assigned a Jesuit named Andrea Galvanello to a parish in the town of Morbegno in northern Italy. He was so successful that the townspeople begged Ignatius to make the assignment permanent. Ignatius refused and sent Galvanello elsewhere. He was happy that Galvanello was doing such good work in Morbegno, but parish work wasn't a core Jesuit ministry. He sent Galvanello somewhere else so he could do greater good.

Serving "the greater good" is the essential meaning of *magis*, a Latin word meaning "more" or "greater," which is a key Ignatian criterion for making choices. It doesn't mean working long hours, taking on extra work, or staying with a project long past the time when most people would have stopped. It doesn't mean doing the harder thing. In fact, the *magis* can mean doing the easier thing if the impact would be greater than the alternatives.

Magis means that when you're surveying your options, you favor the choice that does the greatest good. It may not be obvious what the greater good is. Reasonable people can have different opinions about it as long as they agree on the principle: It's good to do good; it's better to choose something better.

December 30

Do What You Can

If one is involved in much business, he must make up his mind to do what he can, without afflicting himself if he cannot do all that he wishes. You must not think that God requires what man cannot accomplish. There is no need to wear yourself out, but make a competent and sufficient effort, and leave the rest to Him.

— IGNATIUS LOYOLA

As pearls of Ignatian wisdom go, this is perhaps the most practical: "Do what you can." "Make a competent and sufficient effort." Have you done what you can in this situation? Have you overlooked something? Are you giving up too quickly? Or are you trying to do *more* than you can? Have you forgotten that the outcome of this venture is up to God, not you?

These are tough questions, but Ignatius reminds us that *we* can answer them. We're not to be swept up in events like a stick caught in a fast-flowing river. We're not to make these decisions thoughtlessly. We're to reflect on them, make them consciously and purposefully. We can decide to let God be God. We're not in control of everything; we control a lot less than we think we do most of the time, but we *can* control this. We can decide to let God be God and to do what we can.

December 31

"Surprise Me"

We try to be formed and held and kept by him, but instead he of-fers us freedom. And now when I try to know his will, his kindness floods me, his great love overwhelms me, and I hear him whisper, Surprise me.

— RON HANSEN, *MARIETTE IN ECSTASY*

In the end, we make our free decisions about how to take part in the great drama of repairing the world. We come to the party hoping that God will hold us close and tell us what to do, "but instead he offers us freedom." We've learned to trust God; the great miracle — hard as it might be to believe sometimes — is that God trusts *us*. God says: "I *do* hold you close. I *have* formed you. You know what's right and what's wrong. There are a thousand and one ways you can do the deeds of love. Now choose the best ones. Surprise me."

What is the greater good? What do I really want? Should I act or wait? Speak or be silent? Why am I upset? Why does this person delight me? For answers we pray and reflect on our experience and listen to the inner movements of our hearts.

And then we accept the gift of freedom and make our choices — steps on the journey toward the God who is al-ways there.

Acknowledgments

M y friend Joe Durepos was involved in this book from beginning to end. He helped develop the idea, found an excellent publisher for it, read and critiqued the manuscript. How fortunate I am to have a good friend who is a brilliant editor and one of the best literary agents in the business.

I learned most of what I know about the Ignatian way at Loyola Press, where I worked with many great writers, especially Andy Alexander, SJ; George Aschenbrenner, SJ; William Barry, SJ; Brian Doyle; Gerald Fagin, SJ; David Fleming, SJ; Tim Hipskind, SJ; Liz Kelly; Chris Lowney; James Martin, SJ; Tim Muldoon; Margaret Silf; Gary Smith, SJ; Michael Sparough, SJ; and Maureen Waldron. My thanks to them and to a host of colleagues at Loyola Press too numerous to list.

At Manresa Jesuit Retreat House in Bloomfield Hills, Michigan, my mentors were Ann Dillon; Walt Farrell, SJ; Howard Gray, SJ; and Bernie Owens, SJ.

Special thanks to four Jesuits at St. Mary Student Parish in Ann Arbor: Dennis Dillon, SJ; Jim Gartland, SJ; Ben Hawley, SJ; and Joe Wagner, SJ.

Thanks as well to many friends and family members who encouraged me. I am especially grateful to my wife, Susan, a skilled editor and perceptive reader, for her help and insight. I am grateful to the friends who read parts of the manuscript and gave me valuable advice: Ann Dillon; Henry Dyson; Bert Ghezzi; Etta MacDonagh-Dumler; Joe Wagner, SJ; and John Tagliabue.

Jason Gardner at New World Library was the perfect editor — generous with keen insight, all offered with amiable patience. My thanks to him, to Managing Editor Kristen Cashman, and to Jeff Campbell, one of the most skilled copy editors I have ever worked with.

To all of you — my thanks and gratitude.

Notes

The number before each note refers to the day of the month in which the quotation appears.

January: Awareness

Epigraph: Marilynne Robinson, *Gilead* (New York: Farrar, Straus and Giroux, 2004), 245.

1. Robert Ellsberg, *The Saints' Guide to Happiness* (New York: Doubleday, 2005), 100; Ignatius Loyola, "To the Fathers and Brothers Studying at Coimbra," in Ignatius Loyola, *Letters of St. Ignatius Loyola*, ed. and trans. William J. Young (Chicago: Loyola University Press, 1959), 240; see also http://library.georgetown.edu/woodstock/ignatius-letters/letter9.

2. Tim Muldoon, "Words and Thoughts," IgnatianSpirituality.com, https://www.ignatianspirituality.com/words-and-thoughts.

3. James Martin, SJ, *The Jesuit Guide to (Almost) Everything* (New York: HarperOne, 2010), 97.

4. *The Spiritual Exercises*, 43. All quotes from *The Spiritual Exercises* are from George E. Ganss, SJ, trans., *The Spiritual Exercises of Saint Ignatius* (Chicago: Loyola Press, 1992).

5. Peter Faber, SJ, *Spiritual Writings of Pierre Favre*, trans. Edmond C. Murphy, SJ, and Martin E. Palmer, SJ (Boston: Institute of Jesuit Sources, 1996), 157.

6. Jean-Pierre de Caussade, SJ, *Abandonment to Divine Providence* (St. Louis: Herder, 1921), 6.

7. Monika Hellwig, "Finding God in All Things: A Spirituality for Today," in George W. Traub, SJ, ed., *An Ignatian Spirituality Reader*, (Chicago: Loyola Press, 2008), 21.

8. Howard Gray, SJ, "Ignatian Spirituality," in Traub, *Ignatian Spirituality Reader*, 66.

9. William A. Barry, SJ, and Robert G. Doherty, SJ, *Contemplatives in Action: The Jesuit Way* (Mahwah, NJ: Paulist Press, 2002), 9.

10. Dennis Hamm, SJ, "Rummaging for God: Praying Backwards

through Your Day," *America*, May 14, 1994, https://www.ignatian spirituality.com/ignatian-prayer/the-examen/rummaging-for-god -praying-backward-through-your-day.

11. Martin, *Jesuit Guide to (Almost) Everything*, 141.

12. Gerard W. Hughes, SJ, *God of Surprises* (Grand Rapids, MI: William B. Eerdmans, 1985/2008), 81.

13. Martin, *Jesuit Guide to (Almost) Everything*, 87; Avery Dulles, SJ, *A Testimonial to Grace* (Kansas City: Sheed & Ward, 1946), 36.

14. Gray, "Ignatian Spirituality," 61.

15. Caussade, *Abandonment to Divine Providence*, 89.

16. Loyola, *Letters of St. Ignatius Loyola*, 7; also access at Woodstock Theological Library, Georgetown University, https://library. georgetown.edu/woodstock/ignatius-letters.

17. William A. Barry, SJ, *God's Passionate Desire* (Chicago: Loyola Press, 2008), 63.

18. Thich Nhat Hanh, *Creating True Peace* (New York: Atria Books, 2003/2015), 204.

19. Karl Rahner, SJ, quoted in Jenny Wilson, *Keeping Watch for Kingfishers: God Stories* (Durham, England: Sacristy Press, 2020), 9.

20. David L. Fleming, SJ, *What Is Ignatian Spirituality?* (Chicago: Loyola Press, 2008), 40.

21. C.S. Lewis, *Surprised by Joy* (New York: Harcourt, Brace, Jovanovich, 1966), 140.

22. Dorothy Day, quoted in David Brooks and Gail Collins, "Happy New Year, Politicians. Seriously," *New York Times*, January 4, 2014, https://opinionator.blogs.nytimes.com/2014/01/04/happy-new -year-politicians-seriously.

23. John Macmurray, *The Form of the Personal: The Gifford Lectures, 1953–54* (London: Faber and Faber, 1969), 171.

24. Caussade, *Abandonment to Divine Providence*, 5.

25. Fleming, *What Is Ignatian Spirituality?*, 52.

26. Chris Lowney, *Make Today Matter* (Chicago: Loyola Press, 2018), 79.

27. Gray, "Ignatian Spirituality," 64.

28. Lowney, *Make Today Matter*, 80.

29. Mary Oliver, *Upstream: Selected Essays* (New York: Penguin, 2016), 8.

30. Chris Lowney, *Heroic Living* (Chicago: Loyola Press, 2009), 191.

31. Pierre Teilhard de Chardin, SJ, *The Making of a Mind: Letters from a Soldier-Priest, 1914–1919* (New York: Harper, 1961), 57.

February: God

Epigraph: William Butler Yeats, *The Secret Rose* (Glasgow, Scotland: Good Press, 2019). This quote appears as an epigraph in some editions of *The Secret Rose*. It has also been attributed to the French poet Paul Eluard.

1. Karl Rahner, SJ, quoted in Robert Imbelli, "Jesuit Karl Rahner on What It Means to Love Jesus," *America*, October 9, 2020, https://www.americamagazine.org/faith/2020/10/09/jesuit-karl-rahner-what-it-means-love-jesus.

2. Graham Greene, *The Power and the Glory* (New York: Penguin, 2015), 34.

3. William J. O'Malley, SJ, *God: The Oldest Question* (Chicago: Loyola Press, 2000), 191.

4. Martin, *Jesuit Guide to (Almost) Everything*, 85.

5. Pierre Teilhard de Chardin, SJ, *The Divine Milieu* (New York: Harper Perennial Modern Classics, 1960/2001), 22; Caussade, *Abandonment to Divine Providence*, https://ccel.org/ccel/decaussade/abandonment.ii_1.i.ii.i.html.

6. Pedro de Ribadeneira, SJ, quoted in Martin, *Jesuit Guide to (Almost) Everything*, 171.

7. Hughes, *God of Surprises*, 36; Arthur C. Brooks, "A Guide to Exploring Faith as an Adult," arthurbooks.com, https://arthurbrooks.com/article/a-guide-to-exploring-faith-as-an-adult.

8. *The Spiritual Exercises*, 237.

9. *The Spiritual Exercises*, 235.

10. Gerard Manley Hopkins, "God's Grandeur," *The Poems of Gerard Manley Hopkins* (n.p.: Echo Library, 2018).

11. *The Spiritual Exercises*, 236.

12. Michael Himes, "Living Conversation," *Conversations on Jesuit Higher Education* (Fall 1995): 21–27, https://www.bc.edu/content/dam/files/offices/mission/pdf1/c9.pdf.

13. Pedro Arrupe, SJ, "Witnessing to Justice in the World," in Jerome Aixala, ed., *Justice with Faith Today: Selected Letters and Addresses — II* (Boston: Institute of Jesuit Sources, 1980), 79; see also https://jesuitportal.bc.edu/research/documents/1972_arrupewitnessingjustice.

14. Anthony de Mello, SJ, *Seek God Everywhere* (New York: Image/Doubleday, 2010), 167.

15. William A. Barry, SJ, *A Friendship Like No Other* (Chicago: Loyola Press, 2008), xiv.
16. Martin, *Jesuit Guide to (Almost) Everything*, 81.
17. William A. Barry, SJ, "What Are Spiritual Exercises?," in Traub, *Ignatian Spirituality Reader*, 123.
18. Yaa Gyasi, *Transcendent Kingdom* (New York: Alfred A. Knopf, 2020), 250.
19. Fleming, *What Is Ignatian Spirituality?*, 58.
20. Barry, *Friendship Like No Other*, 165; Mary Oliver, *Thirst: Poems* (Boston: Beacon Press, 2006), 37.
21. John O'Donohue, *Anam Cara: A Book of Celtic Wisdom* (New York: Cliff Street Books / HarperCollins, 1997), 23.
22. St. Augustine, *The Confessions of Saint Augustine*, book XI, chapter IX; available online at Christian Classics Ethereal Library, https://www.ccel.org/ccel/augustine/confess.xii.ix.html.
23. William A. Barry, SJ, "Prayer as Conscious Relationship," in Traub, *Ignatian Spirituality Reader*, 102.
24. Walter J. Burghardt, SJ, "Contemplation: A Long Loving Look at the Real," in Traub, *Ignatian Spirituality Reader*, 91.
25. Lisa Kelly, quoted in Jim Manney, *An Ignatian Book of Days* (Chicago: Loyola Press, 2014), 40.
26. William A. Barry, SJ, "Discernment of Spirits as an Act of Faith," in Traub, *Ignatian Spirituality Reader*, 169.
27. Gray, "Ignatian Spirituality," 63.
28. Ronald Modras, *Ignatian Humanism: A Dynamic Spirituality for the 21st Century* (Chicago: Loyola Press, 2004), 43.

March: Love

Epigraph: William Blake, "The Little Black Boy," *Songs of Innocence* (1789); see https://www.poetryfoundation.org/poems/43671/the-little-black-boy.
1. *The Spiritual Exercises*, 231.
2. *The Spiritual Exercises*, 231.
3. C. S. Lewis, *Mere Christianity* (New York: HarperCollins, 1952/2001), 96.
4. George Aschenbrenner, SJ, *Stretched for Greater Glory: What to Expect from the Spiritual Exercises* (Chicago: Loyola Press, 2004), 62.

5. Brian Doyle, quoted in William A. Barry, SJ, *An Invitation to Love: A Personal Retreat on the Great Commandment* (Chicago: Loyola Press, 2018), 190.
6. Fleming, *What Is Ignatian Spirituality?*, 9.
7. *The Spiritual Exercises*, 56.
8. Faber, *Spiritual Writings of Pierre Favre*, 332.
9. Greene, *Power and the Glory*, 131.
10. Chris Lowney, *Heroic Leadership: Best Practices from a 450-Year-Old Company That Changed the World* (Chicago: Loyola Press, 2005), 170.
11. Barry, *An Invitation to Love*, 79.
12. David Brooks, "The Difference Between Happiness and Joy," *New York Times*, May 7, 2019, https://www.nytimes.com/2019/05/07/opinion/happiness-joy-emotion.html.
13. Faber, *Spiritual Writings of Pierre Favre*, 379.
14. Amy Welborn, *The Words We Pray: Discovering the Richness of Traditional Catholic Prayers* (Chicago: Loyola Press, 2005), 141; see also https://www.ignatianspirituality.com/ignatian-prayer/prayers-by-st-ignatius-and-others/suscipe-the-radical-prayer.
15. Fyodor Dostoyevsky, *The Brothers Karamazov*, trans. Richard Pevear and Larissa Volokhonsky (New York: Farrar, Straus and Giroux, 2002), 58; see also Mary Ann McGivern, "Love in Action," *National Catholic Reporter*, October 2, 2015.
16. Faber, *Spiritual Writings of Pierre Favre*, 307.
17. Ignatius Loyola, *A Pilgrim's Testament: The Autobiography of Ignatius Loyola*, ed. Barton T. Geger, trans. Parmananda R. Divarkar (Boston: Institute of Jesuit Sources, 2020), 33.
18. Jerome Nadal, SJ, quoted in John W. O'Malley, *The First Jesuits* (Cambridge, MA: Harvard University Press, 1993), 151.
19. Barry, *Invitation to Love*, 114.
20. Lowney, *Heroic Leadership*, 180.
21. Faber, *Spiritual Writings of Pierre Favre*, 306.
22. Dorothy Day, *All the Way to Heaven: The Selected Letters of Dorothy Day*, ed. Robert Ellsberg (New York: Image Books, 2010), 236.
23. William A. Barry, SJ, "Jesuit Spirituality for the Whole of Life," *Studies in the Spirituality of Jesuits* 35, no. 1 (March 13, 2003), https://ejournals.bc.edu/index.php/jesuit/issue/view/496.
24. Jerome Nadal, SJ, quoted in Eileen Burke-Sullivan and Kevin F. Burke, *The Ignatian Tradition* (Collegeville, MN: Liturgical Press, 2009), 31.

25. Barry, *God's Passionate Desire*, 14.
26. Nadal, quoted in O'Malley, *First Jesuits*, 82.
27. Jerome Nadal, SJ, quoted in Joseph Henchey, *Fr. Jerome Nadal, SJ: The Theologian of Ignatian Spirituality* (2000); ebook, http://s638693668.onlinehome.us/wp-content/uploads/2016/11/nadal.pdf.
28. Fleming, *What Is Ignatian Spirituality?*, 14.
29. David Lonsdale, "Discernment of Spirits," in Traub, *Ignatian Spirituality Reader*, 171.
30. This prayer is commonly attributed to Pedro Arrupe, SJ, but it was actually written in 1981 by Joseph Whelan, SJ (1932–1994), former provincial of the Maryland province and American assistant to the superior general. See Barton T. Geger, SJ, "Ten Things That St. Ignatius Never Said or Did," *Studies in the Spirituality of Jesuits* 50, no. 1 (2018), https://ejournals.bc.edu/index.php/jesuit/article/view/10443.
31. Dorothy Day, *Catholic Worker*, June 1946, quoted in Michael Boover, *15 Days of Prayer with Dorothy Day* (Hyde Park, NY: New City Press, 2013), 123.

April: Freedom

Epigraph: Ron Hansen, *Mariette in Ecstasy* (New York: HarperCollins, 1991/2009), 179.
1. Martin, *Jesuit Guide to (Almost) Everything*, 392.
2. Thomas Merton, *The Seven Storey Mountain* (New York: Harcourt, 1948/1998), 362.
3. De Mello, *Seek God Everywhere*, 43.
4. Lowney, *Heroic Living*, 127.
5. Gerald Fagin, SJ, *Putting on the Heart of Christ: How the Spiritual Exercises Invite Us to a Virtuous Life* (Chicago: Loyola Press, 2010), 48.
6. J. Michael Sparough, SJ, Jim Manney, and Tim Hipskind, SJ, *What's Your Decision?: How to Make Choices with Confidence and Clarity* (Chicago: Loyola Press, 2010), 3.
7. *The Spiritual Exercises*, 23.
8. John Kavanaugh, SJ, *The Word Encountered: Meditations on the Sunday Scriptures* (Maryknoll, NY: Orbis Books, 1996); see also "Living by Appearances," *The Word Embodied*, February 14, 2021, https://liturgy.slu.edu/6OrdB021421/theword_kavanaugh.html.

9. *The Constitutions of the Society of Jesus and Their Complementary Norms* (Boston: Institute of Jesuit Sources, 1996), sec. 51, https://jesuitas.lat/uploads/the-constitutions-of-the-society-of-jesus-and-their-complementary-norms/Constitutions%20and%20Norms%20SJ%20ingls.pdf.

10. John Kavanaugh, SJ, quoted in Joe Hoover, SJ, "What the Jesuit John Kavanaugh Understood about Our Consumer Society," *America*, April 6, 2021, https://www.americamagazine.org/arts-culture/2021/04/06/jesuit-john-kavanaugh-christ-capitalism-240389.

11. Joseph Wagner, SJ, unpublished homily at St. Mary Student Parish, Ann Arbor, Michigan, n.d.

12. Ignatius Loyola, "To Father Nicolás Bobadilla," in Loyola, *Letters of St. Ignatius Loyola*, 76; see also https://library.georgetown.edu/woodstock/ignatius-letters/letter6.

13. Manu Samhita, *The Laws of Manu*, trans. George Bühler (Charleston, SC: BiblioBazaar, 2008), 6; see also http://oaks.nvg.org/manu-samhita.html#6.

14. Joseph Tetlow, SJ, *Choosing Christ in the World: Directing the Spiritual Exercises of St Ignatius Loyola* (Boston: Institute of Jesuit Sources, 2015), 201.

15. Faber, *Spiritual Writings of Pierre Favre*, 305.

16. *The Spiritual Exercises*, 155.

17. Margaret Silf, *Inner Compass: An Invitation to Ignatian Spirituality* (Chicago: Loyola Press, 1998), 104.

18. Martin, *Jesuit Guide to (Almost) Everything*, 187.

19. Loyola, *Pilgrim's Testament*, 34.

20. Silf, *Inner Compass*, 133.

21. *The Spiritual Exercises*, 2.

22. Exodus 33:18–23.

23. Barry, *God's Passionate Desire*, 70.

24. *Constitutions of the Society of Jesus*, sec. 67.

25. William A. Barry, SJ, *Here's My Heart, Here's My Hand: Living Fully in Friendship with God* (Chicago: Loyola Press, 2009), 208.

26. F. Scott Fitzgerald, *This Side of Paradise* (New York: Penguin, 1996), 143.

27. Jonathan Franzen, *Crossroads* (New York: Farrar, Straus and Giroux, 2021), 547.

28. O'Malley, *God: The Oldest Question*, 194.

29. Lisa Kelly, "Disordered Attachments," in *This Ignatian Life* (blog), November 2, 2009, https://web.archive.org/web/20091203175704 /http://ignatianlife.org/disordered-attachments/.

30. David Foster Wallace, "This Is Water," commencement speech at Kenyon College (2005), https://fs.blog/david-foster-wallace-this-is -water.

May: Work

Epigraph: Faber, *Spiritual Writings of Pierre Favre*, 309.

1. Midrash of Kohelet Rabbah, 3:14, https://www.sefaria.org/Kohelet _Rabbah.

2. Fleming, *What Is Ignatian Spirituality?*, 4.

3. Dorothy Day, quoted in Patrick Jordan, *Dorothy Day: Love in Action* (Collegeville: Liturgical Press, 2015), 79.

4. Ignatius Loyola, *Letters and Instructions of St. Ignatius Loyola, Volume 1: 1524–1547*, ed. A. Goodier, trans. D. F. O'Leary (New York: Cosimo, 2007), 37.

5. Faber, *Spiritual Writings of Pierre Favre*, 373.

6. Mark Salzman, *Lying Awake* (New York: Vintage, 2000), 173.

7. Loyola, "To the Fathers and Brothers Studying at Coimbra," 124.

8. Ignatius Loyola, "Letter to John Stephen Manrique De Lara," in Loyola, *Letters of St. Ignatius Loyola*, 265.

9. Lowney, *Heroic Living*, 142.

10. Jerome Nadal, SJ, quoted in John W. O'Malley, SJ, and Timothy W. O'Brien, SJ, "The Twentieth-Century Construction of Ignatian Spirituality: A Sketch," *Studies in the Spirituality of Jesuits* 52, no. 3 (November 23, 2020), https://ejournals.bc.edu/index.php/jesuit /article/view/12953.

11. Jean Danielou, SJ, quoted in George Lane, SJ, *Christian Spirituality: A Historical Sketch* (Chicago: Loyola Press, 1984/2004), 48.

12. Ignatius Loyola, "Letter to Father John Alvarez," in Loyola, *Letters of St. Ignatius Loyola*, 192.

13. Gray, "Ignatian Spirituality," 73.

14. Walter Ciszek, SJ, *He Leadeth Me: An Extraordinary Testament of Faith* (New York: Image, 1973/2014), 103.

15. Ignatius Loyola, "Letter to Jerome Vines," in Loyola, *Letters of St. Ignatius Loyola*, 404.

16. Daniel Kahneman, "Focusing Illusion," in "2011: What Scientific Concept Would Improve Everybody's Cognitive Toolkit?," *Edge*, https://edge.org/response-detail/11984.

17. William A. Barry, SJ, *Changed Heart, Changed World* (Chicago: Loyola Press, 2011), 45.

18. Martin, *Jesuit Guide to (Almost) Everything*, 361.

19. William C. Spohn, SJ, "The Chosen Path," *America*, July 21, 2003, https://www.americamagazine.org/issue/440/article/chosen-path.

20. Loyola, *Letters of St. Ignatius Loyola*, 441.

21. Peter Schineller, SJ, *Jesuit Reader*, unpublished manuscript, n.d.

22. Nadal, quoted in O'Malley, *First Jesuits*, 61.

23. This saying is widely attributed to Nelson Mandela, but it is uncertain where he first wrote or said it.

24. Ann Garrido, "More Than a Desk Job: The Spirituality of Administration," *America*, July 6, 2009, https://www.americamagazine.org/issue/702/article/more-desk-job.

25. Lowney, *Heroic Living*, 118.

26. Aleksandr Solzhenitsyn, *One Day in the Life of Ivan Denisovich* (New York: Farrar, Straus and Giroux, 2005), 17.

27. Gerard Manley Hopkins, SJ, *The Sermons and Devotional Writings of Gerard Manley Hopkins* (Oxford: Oxford University Press, 1967), 240.

28. Philip Caraman, SJ, *Ignatius Loyola: A Biography of the Founder of the Jesuits* (New York: HarperCollins, 1990), 150.

29. Fleming, *What Is Ignatian Spirituality?*, 40.

30. Nadal, quoted in Henchey, *Fr. Jerome Nadal*.

31. Dorothy Day, "Love Is the Measure," *The Catholic Worker* (June 1946), 2. http://www.catholicworker.org/dorothyday/articles/425.pdf.

June: Desire

Epigraph: *The Spiritual Exercises*, 65.

1. Margaret Silf, *On Making Choices* (Oxford: Lion Hudson, 2013), 54.

2. Martin, *Jesuit Guide to (Almost) Everything*, 60.

3. Aschenbrenner, *Stretched for Greater Glory*, 7.

4. *The Spiritual Exercises*, 65.

5. Lewis, *Surprised by Joy*, 14.

6. Martin, *Jesuit Guide to (Almost) Everything*, 204.

7. St. Augustine, *Confessions of Saint Augustine*, book I, chapter I.

8. William A. Barry, SJ, *Letting God Come Close: An Approach to the Ignatian Spiritual Exercises* (Chicago: Loyola Press, 2001), 35.

9. Edward O. Wilson, *Consilience: The Unity of Knowledge* (New York: Alfred A Knopf, 1998/2014), 294.

10. Andy Warhol, quoted in *Painted Words of Andy Warhol* (n.p.: UB Tech, 2018), https://www.scribd.com/book/392239359/Painted-Words-of-Andy-Warhol-300-Andy-Warhol-Quotes.

11. Mark E. Thibodeaux, SJ, *God's Voice Within: The Ignatian Way to Discover God's Will* (Chicago: Loyola Press, 2010), 167.

12. Saul Bellow, *Henderson the Rain King* (New York: Penguin, 1958/1999), 24.

13. John Kavanaugh, *The Word Embodied: Meditations on the Sunday Scriptures* (Maryknoll, NY: Orbis Books, 1998); see also "The Higher Wisdom," *The Word Embodied*, July 26, 2020, https://liturgy.slu.edu/17OrdA072620/theword_kavanaugh.html.

14. Edward Kinerk, SJ, "Eliciting Great Desires: Their Place in the Spirituality of the Society of Jesus," *Studies in the Spirituality of Jesuits* 16, no. 5 (November 1, 1984), https://ejournals.bc.edu/index.php/jesuit/article/view/3730.

15. Loyola, "To the Fathers and Brothers Studying at Coimbra," 122.

16. Jerome Nadal, SJ, quoted in John W. Padberg, SJ, "Jeronimo Nadal, S.J.: The Chronicle: The Beginning of His Vocation," *Studies in the Spirituality of Jesuits* 24, no. 3 (May 1, 1992), https://jesuitonlinelibrary.bc.edu/?a=d&d=sis19920501-01.2.12&e=-------en-20--1--txt-txIN-------.

17. Baltasar Gracián, SJ, *The Art of Worldly Wisdom: A Pocket Oracle*, trans. Christopher Maurer (New York: Doubleday, 1992), 20.

18. Lonsdale, "Discernment of Spirits," 173.

19. Kinerk, "Eliciting Great Desires."

20. Barry, *God's Passionate Desire*, 7.

21. Martin, *Jesuit Guide to (Almost) Everything*, 62.

22. Silf, *Inner Compass*, 115.

23. Tim Muldoon, "The Triangulation of Desire," IgnatianSpirituality.com, https://www.ignatianspirituality.com/the-triangulation-of-desire.

24. Quote from "July 11: A Turning Point," *Daily Reflections: A Book of Reflections by A. A. Members for A. A. Members* (New York: Alcoholics Anonymous World Services, 1990/2014).

25. Thomas Merton, *Thoughts in Solitude* (New York: Farrar, Straus and Giroux, 1958/1999), 79.

26. Gray, "Ignatian Spirituality," 75.

27. Fleming, *What Is Ignatian Spirituality?*, 15.

28. Mark E. Thibodeaux, SJ, quoted in Sean Salai, "Discerning Good and Bad Spirits: Wisdom from a Jesuit Spiritual Writer," *America*, January 11, 2017, https://www.americamagazine.org/faith/2017/01/11/discerning-good-and-bad-spirits-wisdom-jesuit-spiritual-writer.

29. Caussade, *Abandonment to Divine Providence*, 5.

30. "I should have bought more crap" cartoon in *The New Yorker*, November 18, 2002.

July: Humility

Epigraph: Flannery O'Connor, *A Prayer Journal* (New York: Farrar, Straus and Giroux. 2013), 3.

1. Doyle, quoted in Barry, *Invitation to Love*, 190.

2. C. S. Lewis, *The Screwtape Letters* (New York: HarperCollins, 1942/2001), 70.

3. This is my retelling of a classic Jewish joke.

4. Brian E. Daley, SJ, "To Be More like Christ," *Studies in the Spirituality of Jesuits* 27, no. 1 (January 1, 1995), https://jesuitonlinelibrary.bc.edu/?a=d&d=sis19950101-01&e=-------en-20--1--txt-txIN-------.

5. Tim Muldoon, "Why Young Adults Need Ignatian Spirituality," *America*, February 26, 2001, https://www.americamagazine.org/issue/339/article/why-young-adults-need-ignatian-spirituality.

6. St. Augustine, quoted in Daley, "To Be More like Christ," 10.

7. Rick Warren, *The Purpose Driven Life: What on Earth Am I Here For?* (Grand Rapids, MI: Zondervan, 2002/2012), 21.

8. Lewis, *Mere Christianity*, 128.

9. Faber, *Spiritual Writings of Pierre Favre*, 303.

10. Dean Brackley, SJ, "Expanding the Shrunken Soul: False Humility,

Ressentiment, and Magnanimity," *Studies in the Spirituality of Jesuits* 34, no. 4 (2002), https://ejournals.bc.edu/index.php/jesuit/article/view/3991.

11. De Mello, *Seek God Everywhere*, 46.

12. Greene, *Power and the Glory*, 196.

13. 1 Corinthians 13:12.

14. Ignatius Loyola, "Letter to Sister Teresa Rejadell," in Loyola, *Letters of St. Ignatius Loyola*, 20.

15. Kevin O'Brien, SJ, *The Ignatian Adventure: Experiencing the Spiritual Exercises of St. Ignatius in Daily Life* (Chicago: Loyola Press 2011), 182.

16. Loyola, *Letters of St. Ignatius Loyola*, 20.

17. Ignatius Loyola, "To the Fathers Attending Council of Trent," in Loyola, *Letters of St. Ignatius Loyola*, 94; see also https://library.georgetown.edu/woodstock/ignatius-letters/letter8.

18. Ignatius Loyola, "To Bartolomeo Romano," in Loyola, *Letters of St. Ignatius Loyola*, 363; see also https://library.georgetown.edu/woodstock/ignatius-letters/letter37.

19. Brackley, "Expanding the Shrunken Soul."

20. Georges Bernanos, *The Diary of a Country Priest* (Cambridge, MA: Da Capo Press, 1937/2002), 130.

21. Barry and Doherty, *Contemplatives in Action*, 36.

22. Gregory Boyle, SJ, "The Power of Boundless Compassion: An Evening with Fr. Greg Boyle," YouTube, posted March 5, 2014, youtu.be/IYLV9Kr_uw8.

23. Bill Wilson, *Twelve Steps and Twelve Traditions* (New York: Alcoholics Anonymous World Services, 1953), 55.

24. Wallace, "This Is Water."

25. Micah 6:8.

26. Ciszek, *He Leadeth Me*, 58.

27. *Constitutions of the Society of Jesus*, sec. 66.

28. Rafael Merry del Val y Zulueta, "Litany of Humility," en.wikipedia.org/wiki/Litany_of_humility.

29. Ignatius Loyola, "To the Fathers and Brothers at Padua," in Loyola, *Letters of St. Ignatius Loyola*, 148; see also https://library.georgetown.edu/woodstock/ignatius-letters/letter10.

30. Thérèse of Lisieux, quoted in Vernon Johnson, *Spiritual Childhood:*

The Spirituality of St. Thérèse of Lisieux (San Francisco: Ignatius Press, 1953/2001), 67.

31. Thomas Merton, *New Seeds of Contemplation* (New York: New Directions, 1961/2007), 101.

August: Compassion and Trust

Epigraph: Dalai Lama, quoted in *Wildmind Meditation* (blog), May 16, 2007, https://www.wildmind.org/blogs/quote-of-the-month/dalai -lama-compassion-quote; John Henry Newman, *Spiritual Writings*, ed. John Ford (Maryknoll, NY: Orbis Books, 2012), 98.

1. Each of the 114 chapters of the Quran, with one exception, begins with this verse.

2. Fleming, *What Is Ignatian Spirituality?*, 85.

3. Faber, *Spiritual Writings of Pierre Favre*, 260.

4. William A. Barry, SJ, *Seek My Face: Prayer as Personal Relationship in Scripture* (Chicago: Loyola Press, 1989/2009), 83.

5. Gregory Boyle, SJ, "Compassion and Kinship: Fr. Gregory Boyle at TEDxConejo 2012," YouTube, posted June 20, 2012, https://www .youtube.com/watch?v=ipRokWt1Fkc.

6. Gerhard Kalkbrenner, quoted in Faber, *Spiritual Writings of Pierre Favre*, 385.

7. Michael Ivens, SJ, *Understanding the Spiritual Exercises* (Leominster, England: Gracewing, 2016), 151.

8. Fagin, *Putting on the Heart of Christ*, 164.

9. Pirkei Avot, 1:13, https://www.sefaria.org/Pirkei_Avot.1.13?ven =Mishnah_Yomit_by_Dr._Joshua_Kulp&vhe=Torat_Emet_357 &lang=bi.

10. Matthew 7:3.

11. Mark 10:17, 21–22.

12. Frederick Buechner, *Listening to Your Life: Daily Meditations with Frederick Buechner*, ed. George Connor (New York: HarperCollins, 1992), 239.

13. Isaiah 49:13.

14. Barry, *Seek My Face*, 125.

15. William Shakespeare, *King Lear*, act 3, scene 4.

16. Kavanaugh, *Word Encountered*; see also "Faith Doing Justice," *The Word Encountered*, September 18, 2018, https://liturgy .sluhostedsites.org/24OrdB091618/theword_kavanaugh.html.

17. Matthew 25:34–36.

18. Modras, *Ignatian Humanism*, 43.

19. Loyola, *Letters of St. Ignatius Loyola*, 405.

20. Alban Goodier, SJ, *The School of Love: And Other Essays* (n.p.: Roman Catholic Books, 1919), 79.

21. Gracián, *Art of Worldly Wisdom*, 45.

22. Confucius, *The Analects*, 22; see also https://ctext.org/analects /wei-zheng.

23. Ignatius Loyola, quoted in Joseph De Guibert, SJ, *The Jesuits: Their Spiritual Doctrine and Practice* (Boston: Institute of Jesuit Sources, 1964), 100.

24. Tim Muldoon, *The Ignatian Workout: Daily Exercises for a Healthy Faith* (Chicago: Loyola Press, 2004), 114.

25. Barry, "Discernment of Spirits," 162.

26. Fleming, *What Is Ignatian Spirituality?*, 34.

27. Hamm, "Rummaging for God."

28. Kavanaugh, *Word Embodied*; see also "God in the Quiet and in the Chaos," *The Word Embodied*, August 13, 2017, https://liturgy .sluhostedsites.org/19OrdA081317/theword_embodied.html.

29. Jim Campbell, "Pedro Arrupe, SJ," accessed July 7, 2022, https:// www.ignatianspirituality.com/ignatian-voices/20th-century -ignatian-voices/pedro-arrupe-sj/.

30. Thomas Merton, *Peace in the Post-Christian Era*, ed. Patricia Burton (Maryknoll, NY: Orbis Books, 2004), xii.

31. James Martin, SJ, *My Life with the Saints* (Chicago: Loyola Press, 2006), 369.

September: Choosing Well

Epigraph: Gracián, *Art of Worldly Wisdom*, 29.

1. Gracián, *Art of Worldly Wisdom*, 30.

2. Sparough, Manney, and Hipskind, *What's Your Decision?*, 153.

3. Martin, *Jesuit Guide to (Almost) Everything*, 306.

4. Thibodeaux, *God's Voice Within*, 147.

5. William Shakespeare, *Hamlet*, act 2, scene 2.

6. Fagin, *Putting on the Heart of Christ*, 42.

7. Gracián, *Art of Worldly Wisdom*, 77.

8. Michael O'Sullivan, SJ, "Trust Your Feelings, but Use Your Head: Discernment and the Psychology of Decision Making," *Studies in the Spirituality of Jesuits* 22, no. 4 (September 1, 1990), https://archive.org/details/trustyourfeeling2240sul.

9. James Keenan, SJ, "Virtue Ethics," in *Christian Ethics: An Introduction*, ed. Bernard Hoose (New York: Continuum, 1998), 87; online at https://www.academia.edu/9872001/Christian_ethics.

10. Lowney, *Heroic Living*, 138.

11. This saying is often attributed to Mark Twain, but who said this and the original source are unknown.

12. Buddy Bell, quoted in Joe Posnanski, "The Royal Streak," Joe Blogs, August 25, 2021, https://joeposnanski.substack.com/p/the-royal-streak?s=r.

13. O'Sullivan, "Trust Your Feelings, but Use Your Head."

14. Muldoon, *Ignatian Workout*, 22.

15. O'Sullivan, "Trust Your Feelings, but Use Your Head."

16. Malcolm Gladwell, *Blink: The Power of Thinking Without Thinking* (New York: Little, Brown and Company, 2005), 201.

17. C. S. Lewis, *The Great Divorce* (New York: Collier Books, 1984), 40.

18. Peter Kreeft, "Discernment," https://www.peterkreeft.com/topics/discernment.htm.

19. O'Sullivan, "Trust Your Feelings, but Use Your Head."

20. William Shakespeare, *Julius Caesar*, act 1, scene 3.

21. Sparough, Manney, and Hipskind, *What's Your Decision?*, 95.

22. *The Spiritual Exercises*, 318.

23. Maurice Giuliani, SJ, "Saint Ignatius Embracing the Future," *The Way* 58, no. 1 (January 2019), https://www.theway.org.uk/websubs/581.pdf.

24. O'Sullivan, "Trust Your Feelings, but Use Your Head."

25. Sparough, Manney, and Hipskind, *What's Your Decision?*, 14.

26. *The Spiritual Exercises*, 335.

27. Gary Klein, "Performing a Project Premortem," *Harvard Business Review*, September 2007, https://hbr.org/2007/09/performing-a-project-premortem.

28. Silf, *Inner Compass*, 86.
29. Gracián, *Art of Worldly Wisdom*, 74.
30. Martin, *Jesuit Guide to (Almost) Everything*, 337.

October: Relationships

Epigraph: This saying is attributed to Iris Murdoch, but its source is uncertain.

1. Barry, *Invitation to Love*, 186.
2. *The Spiritual Exercises*, 22.
3. John Padberg, SJ, quoted in Schineller, *Jesuit Reader*.
4. Lewis, *Surprised by Joy*, 130.
5. Gracián, *Art of Worldly Wisdom*, 4.
6. Matteo Ricci, SJ, quoted in Modras, *Ignatian Humanism*, 107.
7. J. R. R. Tolkien, *The Return of the King* (New York: Del Rey / Ballantine Books, 1955/2012), "Mount Doom," Book VI, Chapter 3.
8. Loyola, "Letter to Sister Teresa Rejadell," 23.
9. Francis Xavier, quoted in Alfonso Rodríguez, *Practice of Perfection and Christian Virtue , vol. 2* (Chicago: Loyola University Press, 1929), 298.
10. Faber, *Spiritual Writings of Pierre Favre*, 385.
11. Ignatius Loyola, "To the Scholastics at Alcalá," in Loyola, *Letters of St. Ignatius Loyola*, 440; see also https://library.georgetown.edu/woodstock/ignatius-letters/letter5.
12. Gregory Boyle, SJ, *Barking to the Choir: The Power of Radical Kinship* (New York: Simon & Schuster, 2017), 166.
13. Gracián, *Art of Worldly Wisdom*, 23.
14. Ignatius Loyola, "To Fathers Broët and Salmerón," in Loyola, *Letters of St. Ignatius Loyola*, 52; see also https://library.georgetown.edu/woodstock/ignatius-letters/letter1.
15. Loyola, "To the Scholastics at Alcalá," 440.
16. Boyle, *Barking to the Choir*, 54.
17. Gracián, *Art of Worldly Wisdom*, 63.
18. Harper Lee, *To Kill a Mockingbird* (New York: HarperCollins, 2006), 33.

19. James F. Keenan, SJ, *Virtues for Ordinary Christians* (New York: Sheed & Ward, 1996), 110.

20. Loyola, "To Fathers Broët and Salmerón," 52.

21. Gracián, *Art of Worldly Wisdom*, 40.

22. Martin, *Jesuit Guide to (Almost) Everything*, 243.

23. Gracián, *Art of Worldly Wisdom*, 72.

24. Matthew 5:9.

25. Nadal, quoted in Burke-Sullivan and Burke, *Ignatian Tradition*, 31.

26. Keenan, *Virtues for Ordinary Christians*, 62.

27. Martin, *Jesuit Guide to (Almost) Everything*, 248.

28. Gracián, *Art of Worldly Wisdom*, 50.

29. Ignatius Loyola, "To Father Diego Miró," in Loyola, *Letters of St. Ignatius Loyola*, 284; see also https://library.georgetown.edu/woodstock/ignatius-letters/letter24.

30. Keenan, *Virtues for Ordinary Christians*, 62.

31. Lowney, *Heroic Living*, 82.

November: Practical Truths

Epigraph: Nadal, quoted in Henchey, *Fr. Jerome Nadal*.

1. Daniel J. Harrington, SJ, and James F. Keenan SJ, *Paul and Virtue Ethics* (Lanham, MD: Rowman & Littlefield, 2010), 4.

2. Faber, *Spiritual Writings of Pierre Favre*, 332.

3. Robinson, *Gilead*, 98.

4. Václav Havel, *Disturbing the Peace: A Conversation with Karel Hvizdala* (New York: Alfred A. Knopf, 1990), 181.

5. Tyler Cowen, "Tyler Cowen's Three Laws," *Marginal Revolution* (blog), April 15, 2015, https://marginalrevolution.com/marginalrevolution/2015/04/tyler-cowens-three-laws.html.

6. Maria Konnikova, *The Biggest Bluff: How I Learned to Pay Attention, Master Myself, and Win* (New York: Penguin Press, 2020), 135.

7. Hellwig, "Finding God in All Things," 35.

8. Harrington and Keenan, *Paul and Virtue Ethics*, 5.

9. Barry, *Here's My Heart*, 49.

10. Jon Kabat-Zinn, quoted in Barry Boyce, "The Pioneer: Jon Kabat-Zinn on Working toward a Mindful Society," Lion's Roar, March 1, 2010, https://www.lionsroar.com/mindful-living-the-pioneer-toward-a-mindful-society.

11. St. Augustine, quoted in Philip Schaff, ed., *Nicene and Post-Nicene Fathers*, series 1, vol. 2, *Homilies on the Gospel of John* (Peabody, MA: Hendrickson Publishers, 1886/1996); see also https://www.ccel.org/ccel/s/schaff/npnf107/cache/npnf107.pdf.

12. Leo Tolstoy, *Anna Karenina*, trans. Richard Pevear and Larissa Volokhonsky (New York: Penguin, 2002), 465.

13. Loyola, *Pilgrim's Testament*, 27.

14. Lewis, *Surprised by Joy*, 60.

15. William James, *Psychology: The Briefer Course* (New York: H. Holt, 1923), 179.

16. Lewis, *Surprised by Joy*, 171.

17. Leo Tolstoy, *War and Peace*, trans. Ann Dunnigan (New York: Signet Classic, 2007), 528.

18. Lowney, *Make Today Matter*, 96.

19. Modras, *Ignatian Humanism*, 32.

20. James Keenan, SJ, *Moral Wisdom: Lessons and Texts from the Catholic Tradition* (Lanham, MD: Rowman & Littlefield, 2010), 57.

21. Traditional adage.

22. Hellwig, "Finding God in All Things," 57.

23. *A League of Their Own*, directed by Penny Marshall, written by Lowell Ganz and Babaloo Mandel (Los Angeles: Columbia Pictures, 1992).

24. Elizabeth Bruenig, "I Became a Mother at 25, and I'm Not Sorry I Didn't Wait," *New York Times*, May 7, 2021, https://www.nytimes.com/2021/05/07/opinion/motherhood-baby-bust-early-parenthood.html.

25. Loyola, "To the Fathers and Brothers Studying at Coimbra," 128.

26. Tolstoy, *War and Peace*, 584.

27. Ignatius Loyola, "Letter to Father James Lainez," in Loyola, *Letters of St. Ignatius Loyola*, 134.

28. *The Spiritual Exercises*, 185.

29. Walter J. Burghardt, SJ, "No Guarantees," IgnatianSpirituality.com, https://www.ignatianspirituality.com/no-guarantees.

30. Boyle, *Barking to the Choir*, 22.

December: Becoming the Person
You Are Meant to Be

Epigraph: Keenan, "Virtue Ethics," 84.

1. Diego Lainez, SJ, quoted in Martin, *Jesuit Guide to (Almost) Everything*, 16.

2. Arthur Brooks, "Are We Trading Our Happiness for Modern Comforts?," *The Atlantic*, October 22, 2020, https://www.the atlantic.com/family/archive/2020/10/why-life-has-gotten-more -comfortable-less-happy/616807.

3. Ignatius Loyola, passage 12, "Prayerful Thoughts: Passages 1–25," Woodstock Theological Library, Georgetown University, https:// library.georgetown.edu/woodstock/ignatius-letters/passages-1-25.

4. *The Chosen*, episode 7, "Invitations," directed by Dallas Jenkins, aired November 26, 2019 (Provo, UT: Angel Studios).

5. Ignatius Loyola, passage 35, "Prayerful Thoughts: Passages 26–50," Woodstock Theological Library, Georgetown University, https:// library.georgetown.edu/woodstock/ignatius-letters/passages-26-50.

6. George A. Aschenbrenner, SJ, "The Spiritual Blahs" *Ignatian Imprints*, November, 2006, https://web.archive.org/web/20100218 124915/http://www.ignatianimprints.org:80/fall06/blahs.shtml.

7. Brackley, "Expanding the Shrunken Soul."

8. Keenan, "Virtue Ethics," 89.

9. Dostoyevsky, *Brothers Karamazov*, 58.

10. Martin, *Jesuit Guide to (Almost) Everything*, 203.

11. *Ignatian Pedagogy: A Practical Approach* (Jesuit Institute, 1993), http://jesuitinstitute.org/Pages/IgnatianPedagogy.htm.

12. Fred Rogers, "1998 Address to the National Association for the Education of Young Children," quoted in Fred Rogers Center newsletter, December 2020, https://www.fredrogerscenter.org/wp -content/uploads/2020/12/FRC-Newsletter-December-2020.pdf.

13. Himes, "Living Conversation."

14. Arthur Brooks, "Why So Many People Are Unhappy in Retirement," https://arthurbrooks.com/article/why-so-many-people-are -unhappy-in-retirement.

15. *The Spiritual Exercises*, 321.

16. Martin, *My Life with the Saints*, 382.

17. Lewis, *Surprised by Joy*, 153.
18. Gracián, *Art of Worldly Wisdom*, 96.
19. Martin, *Jesuit Guide to (Almost) Everything*, 392.
20. St. Anselm of Canterbury, *Proslogion 1*, https://www.vatican.va /spirit/documents/spirit_20000630_anselmo_en.html.
21. Ted Gioia, "Multitasking Isn't Progress — It's What Wild Animals Do for Survival," The Honest Broker, January 24, 2022, https:// tedgioia.substack.com/p/multitasking-isnt-progressits-what?s=r.
22. Barry, "Discernment of Spirits," 164.
23. Buechner, *Listening to Your Life*, 289.
24. Thomas Merton, *The Sign of Jonas* (New York: Harcourt Brace Jovanovich, 1979), 242.
25. *The Spiritual Exercises*, 230.
26. Albert Camus, *The Plague*, trans. Stuart Gilbert (New York: Vintage Books / Random House, 1948/1991), 127.
27. Martin, *Jesuit Guide to (Almost) Everything*, 89.
28. *The Spiritual Exercises*, 43.
29. Barton T. Geger, SJ, "What *Magis* Really Means and Why It Matters," *Jesuit Higher Education: A Journal* 1, no. 2 (2012), https:// www.xavier.edu/jesuitresource/resources-by-theme/documents /WhatMagisReallyMeansPublishedCopy.pdf.
30. Loyola, "Letter to Jerome Vines," 45.
31. Hansen, *Mariette in Ecstasy*, 179.

People Who Are Quoted

Saul Alinsky (1909–1972) was an American community activist and political theorist. His best-known book is *Rules for Radicals: A Pragmatic Primer*.

Anselm of Canterbury (1033/4–1109) was an Italian monk, theologian, and philosopher regarded as the founder of the scholastic school of philosophy.

Pedro Arrupe, SJ (1907–1991) was a Spanish Basque Jesuit who served as superior general of the society from 1965 to 1983.

George Aschenbrenner, SJ (1932–2021), was a spiritual director and author known especially for renewing interest in the Daily Examen. He is author of *Quickening the Fire in Our Midst* and *Stretched for Greater Glory*.

St. Augustine (354–430 CE) was a theologian and philosopher viewed as one of the most important church fathers of the Latin Church in the patristic period.

William A. Barry, SJ (1930–2020), was the author of many books on Ignatian spirituality, including *A Friendship Like No Other* and *An Invitation to Love*.

Bill Belichick has been head coach of the New England Patriots since 2000. His teams have won six Super Bowl titles.

Buddy Bell was the manager of the Kansas City Royals from 2005 to 2007. He is vice president and senior advisor to the general manager for the Cincinnati Reds.

Robert Bellarmine, SJ (1542–1621), was an Italian Jesuit and cardinal of the Catholic Church. He was one of the most important figures in the Counter-Reformation.

Saul Bellow (1915–2005) was a novelist. He received the Nobel Prize in Literature in 1976.

Georges Bernanos (1888–1948) was a French novelist best-known for *The Diary of a Country Priest*.

William Blake (1757–1827) was an English poet and painter whose mystical vision and highly expressive work were widely appreciated only after his death.

Niels Bohr (1885–1962) was a Danish physicist who was a key figure in the development of quantum theory. He received the Nobel Prize in Physics in 1922.

Gregory Boyle, SJ, is the founder and director of Homeboy Industries, the world's largest gang-intervention and rehabilitation program. He is author of *Tattoos on the Heart* and *Barking to the Choir: The Power of Radical Kinship*.

Dean Brackley, SJ (1946–2011), was a theologian and social activist known especially for his work in El Salvador.

Arthur Brooks is a social scientist, musician, and columnist for *The Atlantic*.

David Brooks is a columnist and cultural commentator who writes for the *New York Times* and other publications.

Elizabeth Bruenig is an opinion writer for *The Atlantic*.

Frederick Buechner is a novelist, poet, and theologian. He is an ordained Presbyterian minister and the author of more than thirty published books.

Walter J. Burghardt, SJ (1914–2008), was an American Jesuit theologian best known for his many books on preaching.

Albert Camus (1913–1960) was a French novelist and philosopher. His best-known novels are *The Stranger*, *The Plague*, and *The Myth of Sisyphus*.

Philip Caraman, SJ (1911–1998), was a British Jesuit, novelist, and biographer.

Jean-Pierre de Caussade, SJ (1675–1751), was the author of *Abandonment to Divine Providence*.

Walter Ciszek, SJ (1904–1984), was an American Jesuit who spent twenty-four years in confinement in the Soviet Union for conducting clandestine missionary work. Five of those years were spent in the infamous Lubyanka prison in Moscow.

Confucius (551–479 BCE) was a Chinese philosopher whose teachings remain influential across China and East Asia to this day.

Tyler Cowen is an economist, columnist, and blogger at Marginal Revolution.

Brian E. Daley, SJ, is emeritus professor of theology at the University of Notre Dame.

Jean Danielou, SJ (1905–1974), was a French Jesuit theologian and prelate.

Dorothy Day (1897–1980) was a Catholic social activist and founder of the Catholic Worker movement. Her autobiography is *The Long Loneliness*.

Isak Dinesen (1885–1962, aka Karen Blixen) was a Danish author known for her short stories and her memoir *Out of Africa*.

Benjamin Disraeli (1804–1881) was a British politician who twice served as prime minister.

Robert G. Doherty, SJ (1929–2017), taught pastoral and spiritual theology for many years at the Weston Jesuit School of Theology in Boston. He developed some of the first training programs for spiritual directors.

Fyodor Dostoyevsky (1821–1881) was a Russian novelist.

His most acclaimed novels include *Crime and Punishment*, *The Idiot*, *Demons*, and *The Brothers Karamazov*.

Brian Doyle (1956–2017) was a novelist, magazine editor, and essayist. His novels include *Mink River* and *The Plover*.

Avery Dulles, SJ (1918–2008), was an American Jesuit, theologian, and cardinal of the Catholic Church. He was a professor of theology at Fordham University for many years.

Robert Ellsberg is the publisher of Orbis Books and the author of *The Saints' Guide to Happiness*.

Ralph Waldo Emerson (1803–1882) was an American essayist and philosopher who was a leader of the transcendentalist school of ethics.

Peter Faber, SJ (1506–1546), was a founder of the Society of Jesus. He was canonized in 2013.

Gerald Fagin, SJ (1938–2012), taught theology for many years at Loyola University in New Orleans.

F. Scott Fitzgerald (1896–1940) was an American novelist, essayist, short story writer, and screenwriter.

David L. Fleming, SJ (1934–2011), was the author of *What Is Ignatian Spirituality?* and *Draw Me Into Your Friendship*, a contemporary translation of *The Spiritual Exercises*.

Viktor Frankl (1905–1997) was an Austrian psychiatrist, philosopher, and Holocaust survivor best-known for his book *Man's Search for Meaning*.

Jonathan Franzen is a novelist and essayist whose novels include *The Corrections*, *Freedom*, and *Crossroads*.

Freddie Freeman is a first baseman for the Los Angeles Dodgers. He is a five-time MLB All-Star and was National League MVP in 2020.

Ann Garrido is associate professor of homiletics at Aquinas Institute of Theology in St. Louis.

Barton T. Geger, SJ, is general editor of the quarterly monograph series *Studies in the Spirituality of Jesuits.*

Ted Gioia is a jazz musician, jazz critic, and music historian.

René Girard (1923–2015) was a French philosopher, literary critic, and historian known for his theories about ethical systems of desire.

Maurice Giuliani, SJ (1916–2003), was the principal editor of the standard French edition of Ignatius's writings. He was the founding editor of *Christus*, the French Jesuit journal of spirituality.

Malcolm Gladwell is a Canadian writer and podcaster. His books include *The Tipping Point*, *Outliers*, and *Blink*.

Alban Goodier, SJ (1869–1939), was a British Jesuit who wrote many popular works of spirituality.

Baltasar Gracián, SJ (1601–1658), was a Spanish Jesuit, moralist, and philosopher.

Howard Gray, SJ (1930–2018), was a spiritual director and retreat leader. He wrote more than sixty articles and essays on Ignatian spirituality, ministry, and the apostolic mission of Jesuit high schools and universities.

Graham Greene (1904–1991) was an English writer and journalist regarded by many as one of the leading English novelists of the twentieth century. His novels include *The Power and the Glory*, *The Heart of the Matter*, and *The End of the Affair*.

Andy Grove (1936–2016) was CEO of Intel. He is regarded as one of the key figures in the growth of the tech industry in Silicon Valley.

Yaa Gyasi is a Ghanian American novelist and author of *Homegoing* and *Transcendent Kingdom*.

Jonathan Haidt is an American social psychologist known for his work on the foundations of moral reasoning.

Dennis Hamm, SJ, is professor emeritus of theology at Creighton University.

Ron Hansen is a novelist, essayist, and screenwriter. He is known for his novels about the Old West, as well as for *Mariette in Ecstasy* and other works exploring faith.

Václav Havel (1936–2011) was a Czech statesman, playwright, and former dissident who served as the president of the Czech Republic from 1993 to 2003.

Monika Hellwig (1929–2005) was a German-born British academic, author, and educator. She was a professor of theology at Georgetown University.

O. Henry (1862–1910; aka William Sydney Porter) was an American short story writer.

Michael Himes is a priest of the Roman Catholic Diocese of Brooklyn and a theologian at Boston College.

Gerard Manley Hopkins, SJ (1844–1889), was an English poet and Jesuit priest, whose posthumous fame placed him among leading Victorian poets.

Gerard W. Hughes, SJ (1924–2014), was a Scottish Jesuit theologian and philosopher. His books include *God of Surprises*.

Michael Ivens, SJ (1933–2005), was a British Jesuit spiritual director and scholar of *The Spiritual Exercises*.

William James (1842–1910) was an American philosopher and psychologist. *The Varieties of Religious Experience* is his best-known book.

Jon Kabat-Zinn is a biologist known for his work to integrate Buddhist mindfulness techniques with scientific findings.

Daniel Kahneman is an Israeli American psychologist, economist, and Nobel laureate. He is best known for *Thinking, Fast and Slow*, which summarizes much of his research.

Gerhard Kalkbrenner (1494–1566) was a friend and colleague of Peter Faber, SJ.

John F. Kavanaugh, SJ (1941–2012), was professor of philosophy at Saint Louis University. His best-known book is *Following Christ in a Consumer Society*.

Bil Keane (1922–2011) was a cartoonist known for the newspaper comic *The Family Circus*.

James Keenan, SJ, is a moral theologian, bioethicist, writer, and the Canisius Professor of Theology at Boston College.

Lisa Kelly is an Ignatian associate who has worked in Ignatian ministries in the United States and Latin America.

Edward Kinerk, SJ, was president of Rockhurst University in Kansas City, Missouri, from 1997 to 2019. He currently works at Sacred Heart Jesuit Retreat House in Sedalia, Colorado.

Maria Konnikova is a psychologist, television producer, and writer. She is author of *The Biggest Bluff: How I Learned to Pay Attention, Master Myself, and Win*.

Peter Kreeft is a professor of philosophy at Boston College.

Diego Lainez, SJ (1512–1565), was a Spanish Jesuit and theologian and the second superior general of the Society of Jesus.

Dalai Lama is a spiritual leader of Tibetan Buddhism and a widely-admired speaker and author.

Harper Lee (1926–2016) was an American novelist best known for her 1960 novel *To Kill a Mockingbird*.

C.S. Lewis (1898–1963) was a British writer known for his fiction, including *The Chronicles of Narnia* and *The Screwtape Letters*, and nonfiction Christian apologetics, including *Mere Christianity* and *Surprised by Joy*.

Junlei Li is lecturer in early childhood education at Harvard University.

David Lonsdale teaches Christian spirituality at Heythrop College, University of London. He is author of *Eyes to See, Ears to Hear: An Introduction to Ignatian Spirituality*.

Chris Lowney is a writer, public speaker, and leadership consultant. A former Jesuit, he was a managing director of JP Morgan. His books include *Heroic Leadership* and *Make Today Matter*.

Ignatius Loyola (1491–1556) is founder of the Society of Jesus and author of *The Spiritual Exercises*.

Niccolo Machiavelli (1469–1527) was an Italian diplomat, philosopher, and historian best-known for *The Prince*. He has often been called the father of modern political philosophy and political science.

John Macmurray (1891–1976) was a Scottish philosopher. The main themes of his thinking were the primacy in human life of action over theory and the essentially relational nature of human beings.

Maimonides (1138–1204), also known by the acronym Rambam, was a medieval Jewish philosopher and scientist whose writings on law and ethics are a cornerstone of Jewish scholarship.

Nelson Mandela (1918–2013) was a South African anti-apartheid revolutionary and political leader who served as the first president of South Africa from 1994 to 1999.

James Martin, SJ, is an editor at *America* magazine. His books include *The Jesuit Guide to (Almost) Everything* and *My Life with the Saints.*

Rabbi Meir Baal Haness (circa second-century CE), known as Rabbi Meir the Miracle Worker, was a second-century Jewish sage renowned for his humility and love of peace.

Anthony de Mello, SJ (1931–1987), was an Indian Jesuit, psychotherapist, and author. He is known for introducing Eastern mindfulness-based practices to the West.

Rafael Merry del Val y Zulueta (1865–1930) was a cardinal and spiritual writer.

Thomas Merton (1915–1968) was a Trappist monk, writer, theologian, mystic, poet, and social activist.

David Mitchell is an English novelist and screenwriter. His novels include *Cloud Atlas, The Thousand Autumns of Jacob de Zoet,* and *Utopia Avenue.*

Ronald Modras (1937–2018) was a professor of theology at Saint Louis University and the author of *Ignatian Humanism.*

Tim Muldoon is a theologian at Boston College. His books include *The Ignatian Workout* and *Living against the Grain.*

Iris Murdoch (1919–1999) was a British novelist and philosopher.

Jerome Nadal, SJ (1507–1580), was a Spanish Jesuit and a close collaborator of Ignatius in governing the early Jesuits. He is known as the "Ignatian theologian" for having developed the theology behind Ignatian spirituality.

John Henry Newman (1801–1890) was an English theologian and poet. He was canonized as a saint of the Catholic Church in 2019.

Isaac Newton (1642–1727) was an English mathematician

and physicist who is regarded as one of the key figures in the Enlightenment.

John Newton (1725–1807) was an English Anglican priest, writer, and hymnist. He turned from a career in the slave trade to become a prominent abolitionist.

Kevin O'Brien, SJ, is a theologian who has held leadership positions in many Jesuit universities.

Flannery O'Connor (1925–1964) was an American novelist, short story writer, and essayist.

John O'Donohue (1956–2008) was an Irish poet, author, and priest. He is known for popularizing Celtic spirituality.

Mary Oliver (1935–2019) was an American poet, winner of the National Book Award and Pulitzer Prize, who is known for her nature-inspired poetry.

William J. O'Malley, SJ, is an author and actor known for his portrayal of Father Dyer in *The Exorcist*, for which he was also a technical advisor. He is the author of thirty-seven books, including *Choosing to Be Catholic*, *Why Be Catholic?*, and *God: The Oldest Question*.

Michael O'Sullivan, SJ, is an Irish Jesuit and director of the Spirituality Institute for Research and Education.

John Padberg, SJ (1926–2021), was a professor of history at Saint Louis University and director of the Institute of Jesuit Sources.

Karl Rahner, SJ (1904–1984), was a German Jesuit priest and theologian. His books include *Foundations of Christian Faith*.

Pedro de Ribadeneira, SJ (1527–1611), was a Spanish Jesuit who held important posts in the order while Ignatius Loyola was superior general. He wrote the first biography of Ignatius.

Matteo Ricci, SJ (1552–1610), was an Italian Jesuit priest and one of the founding figures of the Jesuit China missions.

Marilynne Robinson is a novelist and essayist who is best known for her novels *Housekeeping* and *Gilead*.

Francois de la Rochefoucauld (1613–1680) was a French writer and moralist known for his maxims.

Norman Rockwell (1894–1978) was an American painter and illustrator famous for his iconic images of American life.

Fred Rogers (1928–2003) was the creator, showrunner, and host of the preschool television series *Mister Rogers' Neighborhood*, which ran from 1968 to 2001.

Nick Saban has been the football coach at the University of Alabama since 2007. His teams have won seven national titles.

Mark Salzman is a writer known for his novel *Lying Awake* and his memoir *Iron & Silk*.

Peter Schineller, SJ, is a retreat director at Jogues Retreat Center in Cornwall, New York.

Margaret Silf is a British spiritual director, retreat leader, and author.

Swami Sivananda (1887–1963) was a Hindu spiritual teacher and author. He was a proponent of the school of Hindu philosophy known as Vedanta.

Aleksandr Solzhenitsyn (1918–2008) was a Russian novelist, philosopher, historian, short story writer, and political prisoner. Solzhenitsyn was an outspoken critic of communism and helped to raise awareness of political repression in the Soviet Union.

J. Michael Sparough, SJ, is a retreat leader and spiritual director based in Chicago.

William C. Spohn, SJ (1944–2005), was a theologian who taught for many years at Santa Clara University.

Pierre Teilhard de Chardin, SJ (1881–1955), was a paleontologist, theologian, philosopher, and teacher. His books include *The Divine Milieu* and *The Phenomenon of Man*.

Mother Teresa (1910-1997; aka Mary Teresa Bojaxhiu) was famed for her work among the poor of India. She founded the Missionaries of Charity and is honored as a saint in the Catholic Church.

Joseph Tetlow, SJ, is the director of Montserrat Jesuit Retreat House in Lake Dallas, Texas. He previously served for eight years in Rome as head of the Secretariat for Ignatian Spirituality.

Thérèse of Lisieux (1873–1897) was a French Carmelite nun widely admired for her simple and practical approach to the spiritual life.

Mark E. Thibodeaux, SJ, is a Jesuit spiritual director and author of books on prayer and discernment.

Thich Nhat Hanh (1926–2022) was a Vietnamese Buddhist monk, peace activist, author, and poet.

Leo Tolstoy (1828–1910) was a Russian novelist and Nobel laureate. He wrote *Anna Karenina* and *War and Peace* and many short stories and essays.

Joseph Wagner, SJ, is a campus minister at St. Mary Student Parish in Ann Arbor, Michigan. He taught mathematics for many years at Xavier University in Cincinnati.

David Foster Wallace (1962–2008) was a novelist, short story writer, and essayist widely known for his 1996 novel *Infinite Jest*.

Andy Warhol (1928–1987) was an artist, film director, and producer who was a leading figure in pop art.

Rick Warren is a Southern Baptist evangelical Christian pastor and author.

Amy Welborn is an editor and author who blogs at "Charlotte Was Both." Her books include *The Words We Pray: Discovering the Richness of Traditional Catholic Prayers*.

Bill Wilson (1895–1971) was the founder of Alcoholics Anonymous.

Edward O. Wilson (1929–2021) was an American biologist, naturalist, and writer. He has been called "the father of sociobiology."

Francis Xavier (1506–1552) was a founder of the Society of Jesus. He is well known for his missionary work in India and Japan.

William Butler Yeats (1865–1939) was an Irish poet and a leading figure in the Irish Literary Revival. He was awarded the Nobel Prize in Literature in 1923.

About the Author

Jim Manney is a graduate of Saint Peter's University in Jersey City, New Jersey. He has worked as a newspaper reporter, a corporate communicator, a technical writer, a magazine editor, and a book editor for several Catholic publishers. He was a senior editor at Loyola Press from 1998 until his retirement in 2014.

He is the author of *A Simple, Life-Changing Prayer*; *God Finds Us*; *What's Your Decision?*; *What Do You Really Want?*; and *Ignatian Spirituality A to Z*. He also compiled and edited *Charged with Grandeur: The Book of Ignatian Inspiration* and *An Ignatian Book of Days*.

He is the founding editor of the popular website Ignatian Spirituality.com and the blog *dotMagis*, where he has contributed hundreds of blog posts. He has published videos on the Daily Examen and other Ignatian topics, and has taught courses and workshops on Ignatian spirituality.

Jim and his wife, Susan, have four adult children and live in Ann Arbor, Michigan.

www.jimmanneybooks.com

NEW WORLD LIBRARY is dedicated to publishing books and other media that inspire and challenge us to improve the quality of our lives and the world.

We are a socially and environmentally aware company. We recognize that we have an ethical responsibility to our readers, our authors, our staff members, and our planet.

We serve our readers by creating the finest publications possible on personal growth, creativity, spirituality, wellness, and other areas of emerging importance. We serve our authors by working with them to produce and promote quality books that reach a wide audience. We serve New World Library employees with generous benefits, significant profit sharing, and constant encouragement to pursue their most expansive dreams.

Whenever possible, we print our books with soy-based ink on 100 percent postconsumer-waste recycled paper. We power our Northern California office with solar energy, and we respectfully acknowledge that it is located on the ancestral lands of the Coast Miwok Indians. We also contribute to nonprofit organizations working to make the world a better place for us all.

Our products are available wherever books are sold.

customerservice@NewWorldLibrary.com
Phone: 415-884-2100 or 800-972-6657
Orders: Ext. 110
Fax: 415-884-2199
NewWorldLibrary.com

Scan below to access our newsletter
and learn more about our books and authors.